VOLUME EDITOR

S. WALLER is an Associate Professor of Philosophy at Montana State University Bozeman. Her areas of research are philosophy of neurology, philosophy of cognitive ethology (especially dolphins, wolves, and coyotes), and philosophy of mind, specifically the parts of the mind we disavow.

SERIES EDITOR

FRITZ ALLHOFF is an Assistant Professor in the Philosophy Department at Western Michigan University, as well as a Senior Research Fellow at the Australian National University's Centre for Applied Philosophy and Public Ethics. In addition to editing the *Philosophy for Everyone* series, Allhoff is the volume editor or co-editor for several titles, including *Wine & Philosophy* (Wiley-Blackwell, 2007), *Whiskey & Philosophy* (with Marcus P. Adams, Wiley, 2009), and *Food & Philosophy* (with Dave Monroe, Wiley-Blackwell, 2007).

PHILOSOPHY FOR EVERYONE

Series editor: Fritz Allhoff

Not so much a subject matter, philosophy is a way of thinking. Thinking not just about the Big Questions, but about little ones too. This series invites everyone to ponder things they care about, big or small, significant, serious ... or just curious.

Edited by S. Waller

SERIAL KILLERS
PHILOSOPHY FOR EVERYONE

Being and Killing

Foreword by John M. Doris

A John Wiley & Sons, Ltd., Publication

Registered Office
John Wiley & Sons Ltd, The Atrium, Southern Gate, Chichester, West Sussex, PO19 8SQ, United Kingdom

Editorial Offices
350 Main Street, Malden, MA 02148-5020, USA
9600 Garsington Road, Oxford, OX4 2DQ, UK
The Atrium, Southern Gate, Chichester, West Sussex, PO19 8SQ, UK

For details of our global editorial offices, for customer services, and for information about how to apply for permission to reuse the copyright material in this book please see our website at www.wiley.com/wiley-blackwell.

The right of S. Waller to be identified as the author of the editorial material in this work has been asserted in accordance with the UK Copyright, Designs and Patents Act 1988.

Wiley also publishes its books in a variety of electronic formats. Some content that appears in print may not be available in electronic books.

Designations used by companies to distinguish their products are often claimed as trademarks. All brand names and product names used in this book are trade names, service marks, trademarks or registered trademarks of their respective owners. The publisher is not associated with any product or vendor mentioned in this book. This publication is designed to provide accurate and authoritative information in regard to the subject matter covered. It is sold on the understanding that the publisher is not engaged in rendering professional services. If professional advice or other expert assistance is required, the services of a competent professional should be sought.

Library of Congress Cataloging-in-Publication Data

Serial killers – philosophy for everyone: being and killing / edited by S. Waller.
   p.   cm. — (Philosophy for everyone)
   Includes bibliographical references.
   ISBN 978-1-4051-9963-6 (pbk.: alk. paper)   1. Serial murderers—Psychology. 2. Psychology, Pathological.   I. Waller, S.   II. Title: Serial killers – philosophy for everyone.
   HV6515.S475 2010
   364.152′32—dc22

                                                            2010004731

A catalogue record for this book is available from the British Library.

Set in 10/12.5pt Plantin by SPi Publisher Services, Pondicherry, India
Printed in Singapore

2   2011

CONTENTS

FOREWORD

Why a philosophy book about serial killers? For all that, why think about serial killers at all? Haven't we got enough spiders in our heads without filling up on stuff like that?

I know I do. I'm a recovering serial killer addict. I've read more than I can remember – or care to – about such aberrations, both factual and fictional. But I'm older now, and possibly a little wiser; I've gotten clean, and shaken my infatuation with moral obscenity. Maybe this is the natural course of things; towards the end of a long and admirable life, much of it dedicated to the prevention of cruelty to children, my father watched little but comedies. When you've done all you can, who needs reminding about places so far beyond the reach of goodness?

In graduate school, when I first heard about Milwaukee's Jeffrey Dahmer, I got a bit frayed. Dahmer lived in a dumpy apartment building much like mine, anonymous and unhopeful. I stared at the pictures of his front door: so far as I could tell, it was made of the same wood-like substance that fronted the entrance to my flat. What causes the man in Ann Arbor to fill his rooms with overdue seminar papers, and the man in Milwaukee to fill his with dismembered body parts?

My thoughts began to foul. In the office of the Rock-n-Roll club where I worked as a "doorperson," I posted a signup sheet for the *Jeffrey Dahmer Fan Club and Recipe Exchange*. I pestered any tolerably coherent customer I was able to corner: "Did you hear about that Dahmer guy?" Not entirely my fault; the workplace was not conducive to optimal psychological sanitation. Under the inevitable "Women – can't live with 'em, can't live without 'em," scrawled on the men's room wall, someone had written, in a careful hand, "But you can cut their bodies into little pieces and leave them in the woods."

Why the nervous laughter? Not merely voyeurism. Even as we drown in an ocean of digitized imagery that both stretches and deadens the imagination, I'm betting the bulk of us don't have voyeuristic interests quite *that* prurient. Then maybe it's because we're more like serial killers than we care to admit; maybe we're somehow more producer than consumer. Do we see our own fragile countenances in Ted Bundy's unholy smirk?

It is tempting to suspect a certain complicity. The victims of serial murder are often persons who have been repeatedly ill-treated before their final victimization: Dahmer's victims were gay men of color, while Gary Ridgeway, the Green River Killer, targeted prostitutes. (The tragic indifference of the Milwaukee police in the Dahmer case provides emphasis here.) And so far as I can tell, no serial killer has targeted Goldman Sachs executives or derivatives traders. White males are the bulk of serial killers, and white males may well be the bulk of serial fans, so perhaps there's a kind of collusion.

But when one learns that white males are also the bulk of serial *victims*, matters seem more complex. Maybe there would be fewer serial killers in a more just society, but injustice can't explain the peculiar fascination. There are lots of lethal injustices, and lots of complicities: industrial food, tobacco, automobiles, and criminally inadequate health insurance kill far more Americans than serial killers (who are, after all, a sort of statistical anomaly). But these more prosaic inequities don't make for the same kind of story; names like Bundy, Gacy, and Dahmer are likely to be remembered long after we've forgotten which Wall Street megalomaniac spent how much on his office wastebasket.

If forced to guess, I'd say the fascination owes more to difference than similarity. Maybe serial killers are most like science fiction characters, uninvited travelers from some distant moral galaxy. One might begin to appreciate this ethical expanse with a characteristically philosophical bit of rhetorical therapy: it's not odd to admire someone because they never raise their voice to children or animals, but it *is* odd to admire someone because they've never been a serial killer. A person might, even with the best of intentions, lose their temper with a willful child or unruly dog, but that same person will not become a serial killer, no matter how trying the plague of brat or beast descending on their home. Not even close.

I remember a friend asking, during one of my Dahmer ruminations, "What could things *look* like to him?" Sort of like a "how the dragonfly sees the world" picture in an elementary science book, all jagged and geometric? I can't imagine. And there's something legitimately philosophical here, where imagination fails. It emerges with a familiar philosophical expedient: if you want to figure out what something does, find out what happens when that something goes bad; if a tamping rod through the frontal lobes has unfortunate effects on someone's civility, as it did for Phineas Gage, maybe the frontal lobes have something to do with civility. Likewise, one way to illuminate what is valuable about human persons is to think seriously about departures from full humanity.

This might happen in a variety of ways – if anything is fragile, humanity is. But serial killers have departed the fold in ways that seem quite distinct from more ordinary calamities. They are not dead – not literally, anyway. Nor are they incapacitated in the familiar senses associated with catastrophes like brain injury and disease. In fact, while the serial-killer-as-genius archetype exaggerates reality, it may well be that serial killers – at least those categorized as "ordered" as opposed to "disordered" – often enjoy cognitive capacities not so different from the rest of us.

Yet serial killers are different – and not just a little. The differences need contemplating, even at the risk of cerebral spiders. Consider the moral vastness that separates them from us and, most importantly, consider how those distances may be preserved. The great majority of us reading this volume are not (I expect and hope) likely to visit the outlands that are the subject of this volume. But there are kindred states of more ordinary proximity – government functionaries are much more prolifically homicidal than serial killers – and these regions also desperately need avoiding. Perhaps staring into the moral distance will help us to better do so.

JOHN M. DORIS

ACKNOWLEDGMENTS

I am greatly indebted to many people for their help in bringing this volume together into a cohesive whole. Without them, it simply would not have happened:

Fritz Allhoff, series editor for *Philosophy for Everyone*, for answering an infinite number of questions with infinite patience and a good sense of humor.

Jeff Dean, Wiley-Blackwell Power that Be, for making great suggestions throughout the process.

Tiffany Mok, Wiley-Blackwell Power that Be, for remembering all the things I forgot.

Scott Lowe, for creating brilliant author guidelines, for brainstorming with me, and for being enthusiastic about popular philosophy.

Susan Coleman, for getting me hooked on Dexter, which started the whole thing, and for knowing talented police officers willing to comment on this topic, as well as for having comprehensive knowledge of the crime fiction world, for listening to me rant, and putting up with my fits and glazed eyes.

Diane Amarillas and Karen Kos, for giving me, and the readers, their exciting insights on murderers and murder investigations.

Darlene Craft, for finding fabulous research on philosophy and serial killers that I would have missed.

Elizabeth Brown, for knowing all about the true crime literature. Those nights you frightened yourself out of your mind reading about serial killers finally paid off – at least, for me.

All the contributing authors, who wrote great essays in spite of my constant demands and poor leadership, who were polite to me in spite of getting emails meant for other people; more emails that bizarrely included my flight itineraries; and even more emails with contradictory information and confusing instructions on the essay requirements. I want to thank all of you for writing such wonderful musings, and especially, for not killing me.

Wendy Zirngibl, for being my second set of eyes and catching many grammatical and content errors, typos, instances of sexist language, and all else that I missed.

Henry Fargot and the Little Known School Press, for helping me with basic formatting and such. Henry deserves the title of co-editor. If anyone reading this hasn't seen *A Nuisance of Cats* and *A Deluge of Dogs*, please have a look at the webpage: www.littleknownschoolpress.com.

My wonderful, supportive colleagues at Case Western Reserve University and Montana State University, Bozeman.

The Cats (Maki, Dieter, Spit, and Anya) for providing day-to-day inspiration and information from practicing serial killers.

You, readers, for your love of wisdom and enthusiasm for the macabre. Thank you!

S. Waller
Bozeman, MT

INTRODUCTION

Meditations on Murder, or What is so Philosophical about Serial Killers?

The problem of crime is the problem of human existence.

Colin Wilson[1]

Death has pursued philosophers across history, just as they have pursued it. Socrates (469–399 BCE) reassured his followers that doing philosophy *is* practicing death, and so the diligent philosopher will face death easily. Heidegger (1889–1976) described us as projecting ourselves forward toward death, and gave us the chilling reminder that we all die alone; one's death is one's own. *Existentialism* is an entire school of philosophical thought motivated by the eventual death of all human beings. Questions of death haunt ethical discussions focused on medical care, human rights, and legal punishments. We are all interested in death, for it threatens all of us. But death, for philosophers, has usually been approached as something that happens to us, not as something that killers do. We reflect on the act of dying far more than we reflect on killing – and there is little philosophy that meditates on murder as an activity that might be repeated, or even practiced with care.

One prior work on the topic, *The Philosophy of Murder* by John Paget, is an 1851 discourse on the methods of murder. The work focuses on "progress" in the arena of killing, specifically, the increasing popularity of poisoning, as poison was difficult to detect. As poisoning became a more popular means to an end, the "more blatant modes" of killing – crowbars, butchery by knife, or "sudden blows with a ragged stick" – fell from favor, losing disciples and becoming passé. Paget also notes that there are murderers who are not ever labeled as such:

> ... the thousand and one ogreisms of your petty domestic czar, will wither the greener blessings of the lives of those who sit round his own fireside into hard and dry leaves – nay, shorted those barren lives many years; and yet to him assault and battery may be an abhorrent and impossible thing. The difference, however, it is very apparent, is only in appearances – in the manner of the theft and of the cruelty.[2]

Clearly, there are many ways to kill! But even this work approaches murder primarily from the point of view of potential victims, and what must be done to stop, and to punish, the killing. There is a gap in the literature of murder; few have examined the killers themselves from a philosophical point of view. Until now.

Here, then, is a philosophy book on practicing death from the perspective – not of dying – but of inflicting death on others. These essays contemplate those who hasten the death of others in a systematic, premeditated fashion: serial killers. This introduction will first tell you a few important facts about serial killers, and then about the essays in the volume.

How Common Are Serial Killings?

It is difficult to know exactly what percentage of murders committed in the United States each year are serial murders. The FBI does not break down murder statistics according to serial or mass murder. Even if they did, a single murder one year might, in the end, be part of a much longer string of killings over a number of years. Experts agree, however, that whatever the percentage (one expert puts the number at 1 percent), serial murder accounts for a very small number of the total number of murders each year in the United States.[3] If the 1 percent figure is correct, an American, in any given year, is 150 times more likely to die of the flu and its complications than at the hands of a serial killer.[4]

If real serial killers are, in the world of kinds of murderers, statistically very small, the same cannot be said for fictional serial killers. If you search for "serial killer" on major American newspaper sites, you will get many more hits for novels, plays, television shows, and movies that deal with serial killers than articles on actual serial killers. Serial killers hold a fascination in the popular imagination far disproportionate to their actual social significance. You would think we were in the midst of a serial killing epidemic, but, as we have seen, the statistics strongly suggest that this is not the case. All of this points to the fact that we are much more apt to have our view of serial killers framed by fictional popular culture than by criminological research or FBI definitions and categories. Eric W. Hickey, a criminal psychologist, notes that between 1920 and 1959, a total of 12 films were made about serial killers. In the next 30 years, 55 films of this genre were produced, and in the 1990s alone, over 150 serial-killer-themed films were offered to movie-going audiences.[5]

The conspicuous increase in films with a serial murder theme in the 1990s may have to do with the fact that although the crime we call serial murder has been reported throughout the centuries, the term "serial killer" did not exist until the early 1980s. Prior to this time, a serial killer would have been called a "mass murderer," which, as we will see shortly, is now defined differently from "serial murder" by the Federal Bureau of Investigation and other law enforcement agencies. With the identification of "serial killer" as its own class of murderer, it has been possible to concentrate research on what makes a serial killer tick. We thus find much written about the "profile" of a serial killer, as if they all share a common set of traits.

What is a Serial Killer?

With all the competing versions of what a serial killer is, from novels and films to FBI profiles and criminologist typologies, what do we really know and believe about serial murderers? The serial killer is, at least in our collective common sense, qualitatively different from other kinds of killers. We do not, for instance, assume that someone who kills a family member in a fit of impassioned rage is of the same profile as one driven to kill in serial fashion. Nor would we typically characterize a soldier in battle as a serial killer despite the fact that some of the constituent parts of a definition of serial killer would appear to fit with the actions of the soldier (such as killing multiple times over an extended period).

So, what is a serial killer? That is, how do we define the term? How do we know when a killer is acting serially, as opposed to acting as a "spree killer" or mass murderer? In the 1980s the FBI established a typology of murder. A slightly revised typology appears in the FBI's *Crime Classification Manual*, 2nd edn. (2006). It lists six kinds of murder with the following definitions:

single murder:	"one victim and one homicidal event"
double murder:	"two victims who are killed at one time in one location"
triple murder:	"three victims who are killed at one time in one location"
mass murder:	"one person operating in one location at one period of time, which could be minutes, hours or even days"
spree murder:	"a single event with two or more locations and no emotional cooling-off period between murders"
serial murder prior to 2005:	"three or more separate events in three or more separate locations with an emotional cooling-off period between homicides"
serial murder 2005–present:	same definition as previously but the number of events and separate locations has been reduced from three to two

This categorization system, though it accounts for the number murdered, the location(s), and the timeframe(s) involved, tells us little about the motivations of the serial killer or their psychological profile. Nor do these definitions account for our own emotional response to the acts of a serial killer. The same *Crime Classification Manual* provides us some help with digging deeper into the psyche of the serial killer:

> The serial murder is hypothesized to be premeditated, involving offense-related fantasy and detailed planning. When the time is right for him [*sic!*] and he has cooled off from his last homicide, the serial killer selects his next victim, and proceeds with his plan. The cooling-off period can last for days, weeks, or months and is the key feature that distinguishes the serial killer from other multiple killers.[6]

Now we know that serial killers are calculating, detail-oriented, and precise. But what else are they?

The problem with understanding the thoughts and actions of the serial killer is that there are, in addition to the typologies and descriptions we've just seen, numerous other ways that criminologists and law enforcement have categorized the people who commit serial murder. It is not that the typologies are inherently bad, but that they focus on particular aspects of serial murder to the exclusion of others. It depends on what you want to find as to which categorization scheme is "best." For instance, one well-known typology, developed by criminology scholars Ronald Holmes and James DeBurger, breaks serial killers into four types (for another typology, see chapter 14):

- *Visionary type:* This type is "impelled to murder because he has heard voices or has seen visions which demand that he kill a certain person or a category of persons."[7] Whether they are addressed by gods or by demons, these killers are mentally removed from reality and driven by psychotic hallucinations.
- *Mission-oriented type:* This type of killer is far more grounded in reality. Rather than being pressed by hallucinatory commands, these killers have "a self-imposed duty to rid the world of an unworthy group of people. The victims may be prostitutes, young women, Catholics, or any other group he defines as unworthy to live with decent people.... He lives in the real world and interacts with it on a daily basis. Typically when this type of killer is arrested, his neighbors cannot believe that he is the person responsible for the deaths of so many people."[8]
- *Hedonistic type:* "There are some people who can kill simply for the thrill of it. These people kill not because of a goal in their life to rid the community of undesirables; neither do they kill because they hear voices or see visions. They kill because they enjoy it. They kill because the thrill becomes an end in itself. The lust murderer can be viewed as a subcategory of the hedonistic type because of the sexual enjoyment experienced in the homicidal act. Anthropophagy, dismemberment, necrophilia or other forms of sexual aberration are prevalent in this form of serial killing."[9] Holmes and DeBurger believe this type of serial killer is psychopathic.
- *Power/control-oriented type:* This type "receives gratification from the complete control of the victim.... By exerting complete control over the life of his victim, the murderer experiences pleasure and excitement, not from the sexual excitation or the rape, but from his belief that he does indeed have the power to do whatever he wishes to do to another human being who is completely helpless and within his total control. This type of serial murderer is not psychotic ... and is aware of the rules and regulations that he is expected to abide by. He chooses, however, to ignore them. He lives by his own code and

typically fits the patterns of a psychopathic or sociopathic type of personality. His behavior indicates a character disorder, not a break from reality."[10]

According to Holmes and DeBurger, "each type is labeled in keeping with the kinds and motives that seem to predominate in the killer's homicidal actions. Within each of these types, it is apparent that the motives function to provide the serial killer with a personal rationale or justification for the homicidal violence."[11]

This typology may move us closer to a more precise sense of what serial killers are – their motives, their mindsets, their socially aberrant needs. But even those who have spent a lifetime studying these killers admit that the typologies only go so far in clarifying the phenomenon of the serial murderer. There are always those who seem to slip between or across categories, or who otherwise seem to betray the clarity that typologies suggest. As soon as things get complicated – because they are hard to define, difficult to explain, and not easily settled by the numbers alone – we start to ask *why?* And it is here that facts end and philosophy begins. A guide to the philosophy in this volume is next.

I Think Therefore I Kill: The Philosophical Musings of Serial Killers

The opening essays feature the words of the serial killers themselves, and these words invite us to do a little philosophy.

The first essay, "Man is the Most Dangerous Animal of All," by Andrew Winters, brings us a philosophical gaze into the writings of the Zodiac Killer. Never captured, this killer terrorized California as the 1960s came to a close, taunting both police and public through cryptic letters written to the *San Francisco Chronicle* amidst his killing spree. In this Sartrean essay, Winters casts a *phenomenological* eye on the words of the Zodiac, showing us how we change when we are aware that someone (especially a killer) is gazing at us. We have a new experience of ourselves when we look through the eyes of another. Zodiac helped us understand ourselves as victims, as pieces on a gameboard that he controls, and when we think of him, still out there, still watching, we again experience ourselves, with a chill.

The second essay, "A Philosophy of Serial Killing: Sade, Nietzsche, and Brady at the Gates of Janus," is brought to us by well-known expert on serial killers, David Schmid. He focuses on the writings of "Moors Murders" perpetrator Ian Brady. Brady's 2001 book, *The Gates of Janus: Serial Killing and Its Analysis*, discusses the motivations and justifications for his murders using Sade and Nietzsche, and critiques the actions of other serial killers against the high standards of Nietzsche's "superman." Schmid offers us a reading of Ian Brady that reveals intriguing secrets of this contemporary killer, ranging from his *moral relativism* to his likeness to the *Sadean Hero*. These heroes take pleasure in their own punishment, and so have the mental ability to always overcome the most horrific circumstances and triumph – just as Nietzsche's superman would. In this capacity, they are literally undefeatable, for if we punish them, they delight in our cruelty as they would in their own. Schmid shows exactly how much philosophy can enlighten us about the thoughts and serial killers, and lets us walk through the *Gates of Janus* into the darker side of human nature.

The third exciting essay, Mark Alfano's "The Situation of the Jury," features a discussion of how human beings are prone to change their moral judgments when placed in different situations. Working from actual, recent correspondence with "Sunset Strip Killer" Douglas Clark, Alfano shows us how we might be swayed by the manipulative, the mal-intentioned, and the bloodthirsty; we don't realize just how much we obey authorities, or scapegoat questionable characters in the midst of a messy or smelly environment. The essay showcases the philosophical view called *situationism*: we are very influenced by context, and so the context in which we find ourselves impacts our view as to Clark's guilt or innocence regarding the eight murders of women in the early 1980s. The situationist dilemma – that we make different decisions when we consider facts against different backgrounds – leaves us unsettled at the end of the essay, and ready for more.

Can You Blame Them? Ethics, Evil, and Serial Killing

This unit opens with a fine and quite comprehensive history of serial killers from the ancient world to the present, "Serial Killers as Practical Moral Skeptics: A Historical Survey with Interviews." Crime writer

Amanda Howard looks at their methods of killing, preferred victims, and means of escaping justice, and notes that many serial killers had a privileged station in life. Howard theorizes that serial killers are motivated by the possibility of acting out hostile urges with relative impunity – that is, power corrupts. History shows that many people with the power to fulfill their fantasies have no moral motivation to do good things, or avoid harming others: they do it simply because they can. In this essay, we think about whether serial killers have no answer to the question "Why be good?"

In a masterful essay "Are Psychopathic Serial Killers Evil? Are they Blameworthy for What They Do?," philosopher Manuel Vargas argues that serial killers are profoundly evil and yet not responsible for their actions. Evil people, for Vargas, are those who enjoy or desire harm for harm's sake and not for any other reason. This essay travels through several philosophical adventures, including the human inability to research morality with the sciences (this is why philosophy is so important), and what a psychopath really is. Vargas helps us explore these concepts by looking at rules that are merely conventional (widely accepted, but more easily broken), like "a football team has 11 players on the field at a time" and more serious moral rules, like "babies are not to be harmed for fun." Vargas suggests that psychopaths suffer from a sort of rule-blindness, so they can't tell which rules can be broken for fun and which must be respected at all times. We cannot hold the blind responsible for what they cannot see. Their actions are still evil, but we can't blame them for doing what they do!

Matthew Brophy offers a stunning counterpoint in "Sympathy for the Devil: Can a Serial Killer Ever Be Good?," in which he makes a case that serial killers *can* be good, and chooses Showtime's Dexter as his example-on-trial. He presents evidence of Dexter's goodness to a jury of you, the readers, with four arguments. First, utilitarians will approve of Dexter's actions because they produce the greatest good for the greatest number of people. Second, Kantians too would declare Dexter good, because his actions are *universalizable*, that is, we wish that everyone would do what Dexter does. Third, we find that Dexter strives to be moderate, that he practices his talents and that he reflects on his actions regularly. Dexter lives the examined life, and he flourishes: virtue theorists must agree that Dexter is good. Fourth, social contract theorists judge Dexter as beneficial to society – as helping to create a society we would all agree to live in. The defense rests. Has Brophy made his case? You are the jury. Dexter awaits your decision!

Dangerous Infatuations: The Public Fascination with Serial Killers

Eric Dietrich and Tara Fox Hall explain "The Allure of the Serial Killer" (and other monsters) by appealing to several facets of human nature. First, we have a need to understand unusual behaviors and explain events in our world. When something out of the ordinary happens, we stop and stare (or we want to, but obey social rules that tell us to stop staring.) Second, we often desire to *co-activate* positive and negative feelings – this is how we enjoy both horror novels and roller coasters – so we can enjoy being afraid. Third, we are able to situate ourselves within a *protective frame* through which we can safely view dangerous people and frightening activities. Safe on the living room couch, we settle in for a marathon of Hannibal Lecter. But this protective frame also shields us from our own moral feelings, like empathy for the victim. They argue that humans naturally follow rules, and conforming to social boundaries brings us many fine things in life, from restaurants to poetry slams. But blending in with the crowd can be tiresome and leave us feeling the need to assert ourselves as individuals, as separate from homogenous society. Serial killers break society's rules and we revel in their individuality. We watch them from inside a protective frame, enjoy our fear, and learn about their deeds in order to understand and explain their unusual, and alluring, behaviors. You may not want to know this much about yourself, but you won't be able to turn away.

Susan Amper tempts Dexter fans with a new philosophy of killers and heroes in "Dexter's Dark World: The Serial Killer as Superhero." She shows us that we relate to Dexter as a good guy because we are allowed to see an intimate portrayal of his daily thoughts and inner struggles. We love Dexter because we too often feel at odds with ourselves, and we too worry about how different we may be from other people. According to Amper, Dexter suffers some of Sartre's angst regarding his freedom, and represents some of Freud's concepts of the id, as Dexter wrestles with his insatiable inner drives. We love Dexter because we too struggle with our freedom and our inner drives. Finally, Amper defends Dexter's actions by comparing them to utilitarian and Kantian standards, showing that we have good reason to love Dexter – a philosophical defense of Dexter's actions as highly moral, perhaps even heroic.

A Eulogy for Emotion: The Lack of Empathy and the Urge to Kill

What's love got to do with it? This section looks at whether serial killers feel emotion or not, and how their emotions (present, stunted, distorted, or non-existent) impact their urges to kill.

Is it true that girls are more emotional? Well-known serial killer experts Elizabeth and Harold Schechter feature a fearsome foray into feminism in their essay "Killing with Kindness: Nature, Nurture and the Female Serial Killer." Evidence suggests that dangerous ladies (like Jane Toppan and Aileen Wuornos) have their own deadly methods. They are, well, more nurturing than those of their male counterparts. Women kill those close to them, and through motherly methods, such as feeding them ... poison. Thus, female serial killers both violate and conform to the stereotype of woman as caretaker. The Schechters take a frightfully close look at the dark side of female caretaking, and remind us that damsels are definitely dangerous, and that not all serial killers are young white males.

So, is it true that boys don't cry? Chris Keegan's essay, "It Puts the Lotion in the Basket: The Language of Psychopathy" chills us with words that turn a person into a thing. The speaker of these words, *Silence of the Lambs* villain James "Buffalo Bill" Gumb, describes his victim not as a living, breathing human, but as a thing that puts lotion on its skin – a thing that does what it's told. There is not a trace of human emotion here. Why do we shiver? Why are we so repulsed? Keegan explains our urge to recoil through Habermas's *communicative rationality*, which is the human ability to take the point of view of someone else, or to stand in another person's shoes. Without this basic empathetic response, we have nothing out of which to build a moral code, and so we wish to flee. Morality lets us function in a society, with other people: if we cannot relate to other people, then we have no method for understanding good and evil. Keegan argues that serial killers just don't understand what there is to cry about!

We so often think of serial killers as "cold-blooded" that we take for granted that they kill because they don't feel for others. In "Are Serial Killers Cold-Blooded Killers?" Andrew Terjesen suggests the empathy-based hypothesis is confused and desperately in need of a philosophical tune-up. Walking us through several classical philosophical techniques, he shows us that the concept of *empathy* is all but empty. First, he reveals that the word "empathy" has many, many meanings, so determining who has it and who doesn't is very difficult. Second, many serial killers, real-life

(Dahmer) and fictional (Dexter), seem to form emotional attachments to other people, and might even be driven to kill by these emotions. Third, saying that "killers kill because they don't feel for others" does not really explain their murderous urges – if they have no feelings, then why kill rather than get a sandwich or go bowling? Fourth, there are cases in which killers kill because they are empathetic with the pain of their victims, like the ladies of *Arsenic and Old Lace*. Instead of being unfeeling killers, perhaps serial killers kill because they have trouble controlling their impulses. Hmm – have you ever had an urge to kill your boss?

Creepy Cognition: Talking and Thinking about Serial Killers

William E. Deal brings us new research in cognitive science implying that "The Serial Killer was (Cognitively) Framed." That is, we judge them as more or less morally responsible according to how much – and what kind of – information we have about them. Deal reviews what we know about the biographies of fictional serial killer Dexter and real-life serial killer John Wayne Gacy, and gives evidence suggesting that we see killers as morally responsible only when we are given the right information about their personal feelings and their life choices. In other words, we judge killing to be morally wrong only when it is framed in an impersonal way for us. We know enough about Dexter's personal life to refrain from judging his murder habit too harshly. If understood in a less intimate cognitive frame, Dexter might seem monstrous; if we knew more about Gacy's inner thoughts, he might seem a hapless victim, or even a friendly guy. Deal makes us shiver when he tells us the moral of the story: our moral judgments are easily manipulated by how the story is told.

Are serial killers in touch with their animal nature? In "Wolves and Widows: Naming, Metaphor, and the Language of Serial Murder," Wendy Zirngibl looks at how we name, identify, discuss, and think about serial killers based on their physical or other characteristics, such as their crimes and their methods. She shows us that the nicknames we give them (for example, "Black Widow") reveal how we associate these killers with certain qualities. What do we mean when we call someone a black widow? Why do we, as a society, do this? What work does naming – or nicknaming – do for us? Zirngibl argues that we tend to associate bestial traits with serial killers through these labels, and also unreflectively and destructively hold animals like wolves to human moral standards.

In "An Arresting Conversation: Police Philosophize about the Armed and Dangerous," I find out how two former California law enforcement officials talk about serial killers, and learn the ABCs of finding and capturing murderers and serial killers. The officers describe several murder cases, and a surprise emerges in the middle of the interview when one officer reveals that her grandfather was a serial killer! The discussion winds through a variety of philosophical topics, including theory-making and theories of psychological pathology, killing vs. letting die, evidence for differentiating killers and non-killers, our popular delusions about serial killers, and more.

Psycho-ology: Killer Mindsets and Meditations on Murder

Criminal justice theorist Richard M. Gray offers a powerful psychological account of the behavior of serial murderers in "Psychopathy and Will to Power: Ted Bundy and Dennis Rader." Gray reviews the inner mental workings of several killers and offers a Nietzschean defense of their morality. He explains that although psychopathic offenders are driven by fantasy, serial killers remain apparently sane, rational, and able to function in the world. How do they do it? The essay highlights many of the unusual mental capacities of psychopaths: uncommon mental focus, an ability to bypass empathetic responses to their victims, unusual verbal skills, an aptitude to learn some types of things along with an inability to learn other things, and more. This rare cognitive skill set allows psychopaths to act in a way that is fundamentally "beyond" good and evil, at least in their minds.

In "The Thread of Death," Jerry Piven continues the psychological approach to the murderous mindset, arguing that serial killers and terrorists share an inner thread of dread and terror. Their shared deep personal hatred compels them to kill, but how much does this separate them from "normal," less violent humans who may inflict themselves on others in virulent but banal ways, or ardently kill en masse when socially sanctioned? Piven suggests that this inner violence is both shared and denied by those of us who control our urges to kill. We too turn to violence when we feel helpless and vulnerable, or when we need to mask our sexual problems and feel virtuous; most of us are not sociopaths, but the inner abjection and wounds that make us susceptible to inflicting atrocities edge us uncannily closer to those we seek to understand. Herein lies human nature. Ultimately, terrorism and serial killing persist because of the denial of "normal" people. We want to identify ourselves with the strong and the safe rather than with the weak and defenseless, and so we avoid examining the mind of the serial murderer directly. Our own self-flattery, our distaste for admitting that we are vulnerable in the face of an attacker, is what allows the serial killer to continue to flourish.

A Solemn Afterword: A Message from the Victim's Network

Mary Miller gives us a brief overview of the founding of Friends and Families of Missing Persons and Violent Crime Victims Network. This organization helps those who are waiting, wondering, and worrying when a loved one disappears. This short piece is both empowering and inspirational.

A Timeline of Serial Killers

Amanda Howard provides a view most gory: a detailed summary of who killed how many – the where, when, and how of it. The data tell a murderous tale, albeit somewhat tempered as we also learn the fate of the serial killer, once (if) apprehended.

☠

I learned a lot editing this volume. I learned that there is a scholarly journal called *Homicide Studies* and that there are Ed Gein comic books. I learned that there is a website at which one can buy auctioned serial killer goods and products, as well as a killer wall calendar: www.serialkillercalendar.com,[12] and that there is a measuring scale for depravity at www.depravityscale.com.[13] I learned that the Internet Movie Database has an entry for Ed Gein,[14] not because he was a great actor, but because so many movies have been based on him. I learned that serial killers are no longer necessarily young white males with high IQs, because now women and non-caucasians have taken up the activity.

What can I say from what I have learned? If thoughts could kill, this collection would be deadly. A new body of thought has been created, sliced up nicely by these talented authors and their philosophical scalpels. They've covered it all: what serial killers are thinking, how they do philosophy, what philosophers think of them. Terror. Ethics. Depravity ratings. Human nature. Psychological profiles. Dexter. Bundy. Gacy … I'm sure that you will learn something in these pages, whether you are a philosopher, a crime buff, both, or neither. These essays will make you think, and you will likely get that creepy feeling that someone is watching you as you read ... and that in itself is food for thought.

Enjoy, with a nice Chianti!

NOTES

1 Colin Wilson, *Written in Blood I: Detectives and Detection* (New York: Warner Books, 1991), p. 303.
2 John Paget, "The Philosophy of Murder," *Tait's Edinburgh Magazine* 22, 8 (1851): 171–6.
3 See, for instance, the discussion on violent crime statistics in James Alan Fox and Jack Levin, *The Will to Kill: Making Sense of Senseless Murder* (Boston: Allyn and Bacon, 2001), p. 102; Eric W. Hickey, *Serial Murderers and Their Victims*, 4th edn. (Belmot: Thompson Wadsworth, 2006), pp. 6–8; or Elliott Leyton, *Hunting Humans: The Rise of the Modern Multiple Murderer* (New York: Carroll and Graf, 2001), pp. 58–9.
4 According to the Centers for Disease Control and Prevention (CDC), some 30,000 Americans died from flu and its complications in 2006. See the CDC report *Deaths: Final Data for 2006*, available online at www.cdc.gov/nchs/data/nvsr/nvsr57/nvsr57_14.pdf (accessed September 25, 2009).
5 Hickey, *Serial Murderers and Their Victims*, p. 3.
6 John E. Douglas et al. (eds.) *Crime Classification Manual: A Standard System for Investigating and Classifying Violent Crimes*, 2nd edn. (San Francisco: Jossey-Bass, 2006), pp. 96–7.
7 This typology was originally formulated by Ronald M. Holmes and James E. DeBurger, *Serial Murder* (Newbury Park: Sage, 1988). The version quoted here is from Ronald M. Holmes and James E. DeBurger, "Profiles in Terror: The Serial Murderer" in Ronald M. Holmes and Stephen T. Holmes (eds.) *Contemporary Perspectives on Serial Murder*, 2nd edn. (Thousand Oaks: Sage, 1998), pp. 10–14.
8 Holmes and DeBurger, "Profiles in Terror," p. 11.
9 Ibid., p. 12.
10 Ibid., p. 13.
11 Ibid., pp. 13–14.
12 Accessed September 25, 2009.
13 Accessed September 25, 2009.
14 The Internet Movie Database, *Biography for Ed Gein*, online at www.imdb.com/name/nm1273684/bio (accessed September 25, 2009).

PART I

I THINK THEREFORE I KILL

The Philosophical Musings
of Serial Killers

CHAPTER I

MAN IS THE MOST DANGEROUS ANIMAL OF ALL

A Philosophical Gaze into the Writings of the Zodiac Killer

Battle not with monsters, lest ye become a monster, and if you gaze into the abyss, the abyss gazes also into you.

Friedrich Nietzsche[1]

Who is the Zodiac Killer?

Killers are not always caught. For those who remember December 1968, you might recall getting ready for a holiday party, looking forward to the end of a semester, or thinking about what you would accomplish in the year that would bring us Woodstock and a moon landing. For those who lived in Northern California during that time, you most likely did not think that December would be the beginning of an 11-month haunting. For in that month, a killer, who would later be called *Zodiac*, was preparing himself to begin collecting slaves for the afterlife. Those of us who do not remember December 1968, or who did not live in Northern California at that time, are probably familiar with the image of Zodiac wearing a black-hooded executioner outfit adorned with the marksman symbol that has become his logo. So, although Zodiac has not been caught, most of us have already met him.

Zodiac's murders and letters have become the subject of multiple films, books, song lyrics, and websites. For example, the Zodiac Killer's slayings have served as foundations to many films since the 1970s, including *Dirty Harry*. Of the many books written about Zodiac, Robert Graysmith's *Zodiac* has been one of the most impressive accounts of Zodiac's horrific deeds. Graysmith was a cartoonist for the *San Francisco Chronicle* at the time Zodiac first struck, thereby giving him access to Zodiac's letters as they arrived. The Zodiac Killer has also found his way into the underground music scene with bands such as Macabre, Balzac, and Machine Head using Zodiac's letters and killings as inspiration for such lyrics as "The best part of it is that when I die I will be reborn in paradise / And those I have killed will become my slaves."[2] The discussion boards on www.zodiackiller.com[3] further indicate Zodiac's popularity.

What is it then about a person who claims to have killed 37 people (only seven have been confirmed) that makes him so intriguing? Are we, at our core, all murderers who find comfort in the demise of our fellow species? I don't believe this is the case, but I do believe that there is something interesting about us humans insofar as we are drawn to the macabre. This is made evident by the ways in which many murderers such as Bundy, Dahmer, and Gacy have reached near-celebrity status. They have even become the topic of philosophical discussion, as this very volume illustrates. Perhaps we are attracted by things which exhibit the power to unfetter themselves from societal norms. If anything will give us a clue as to why we are drawn to such abominable acts as those conducted by murderers, it will be the letters, paintings, and impressions left by them.

Zodiac is no exception here. His letters to the press show his desire to be recognized, and his taunts to the police further demonstrate his cockiness. By looking at a small sample of Zodiac's writings and his ciphers (of which three of the four have not been translated), we can gain entry into the world of a murderer, and perhaps gain further access to the reasons why we are drawn to such a killer.

Peek-A-Boo: You Are Doomed!

At first glance, such an investigation would seem answerable by the works of psychology. It seems plausible that by looking into the psychological background of each of the individuals who are drawn to the macabre, and whatever overlapping features we find, those will likely be the key features of the *macabre-interest*. But this doesn't seem to account for the overwhelming interest in the macabre. Horror films make their way to

ANDREW M. WINTERS

the screen each Halloween, entire genres of music dedicate themselves to images of the grotesque, and the horror novel has yet to see its end. So a psychological account of our "interest" seems hardly sufficient. In other words, a psychological account can tell us something about the individuals who are drawn to the macabre, but it doesn't give us a complete picture as to why the macabre has such a strong following.

So if psychology is inadequate for the task of identifying the underlying tenets of macabre fanaticism, then what method will suffice? I propose that we adapt a *phenomenological* method for better understanding the impact macabre artifacts have upon us to then better understand why we are drawn to such objects. To briefly summarize, phenomenology is the philosophical study of phenomena – that is, appearances, or how things seem to us. Phenomenologists study how things look, feel, sound, smell, and taste; they explore how the world appears to us. Phenomenology concerns itself with experiences as they're being experienced by the person experiencing them – from the *first person perspective*. A phenomenological analysis of emotions, for example, involves an account of how emotions are experienced by a person as she experiences them.

Take, for instance, the emotion of fear, which is appropriate for the subject of this essay. When a person experiences fear she may experience a sense of fleeting, as if the world disappears except for the cause of the fear. She may find herself only experiencing her body as an object for a threat to be directed at. For this reason she feels stripped of any ability to make decisions insofar as she only sees herself as an object exposed to the threat imposed by the other.

Think of a time when you truly experienced fear. Perhaps you were a child who heard a strange noise at your window, or maybe you were a parent who lost your child in a mall. For the child, the only thing that existed was the noise at the window and the feeling that whatever was causing the noise wanted to harm you. One of your parents may have come into your room and tried to comfort you. But the way that your parent might have comforted you was by turning on the light and showing you what was causing the noise. Maybe it was rain or a branch hitting the window, and you came to understand that neither rain nor a branch has the intent of harming you. So you began to feel safe. But up until the moment of understanding that it was only rain or a branch causing the noise, you did not experience yourself as a person in your home. Instead, your home seemed to have disappeared and you could only think about the noise at the window and whether or not the cause of the noise would harm you.

For the parent who has lost a child in a shopping mall, the place where you lost the child seemed to disappear. You could only focus on the idea that your child was in danger, and you desperately tried to think of ways to rescue your child. Throughout this process, the stores within the mall no longer appeared as places to enjoy the day. The stores, instead, seemed to transform into dark hideaways for strangers to harbor children. Each patron became a stranger capable of stealing children, and more importantly was capable of having taken your child. The mall and its patrons remain as threats to you until you see that your child is safe. If you don't see your child again, then the world will have forever changed for you.

The phenomenological approach is in stark contrast to what contemporary philosophers take to be an *analytic* approach. When applying the analytic method to an emotion such as fear, the emotion is analyzed from the *third person perspective* by attempting to understand the objective features of fear that others would be able to observe. The emotion fear would first be understood as a concept to which a definition is ascribed. By formulating a definition of fear, the philosopher is then able to provide a framework for understanding what fear is in light of the events that evoke fear. The aim of providing an analysis of the concept of fear is to then understand how fear functions in the world beyond our experiences. Analytic philosophers might go on to identify the emotional state of fear with chemical reactions occurring within the brain, and so they might discuss a *neurophysiological* account, discussing the chemical processes that transpire when a person experiences fear.

By approaching fear using these methods, we are able to do many things, such as provide medications for overly fearful people, and shape reactions to fear into responses that can intelligently protect us if we are in danger. These approaches, however, fall short of providing a complete picture of what it is like to experience fear from the perspective of the person experiencing fear. By obtaining a complete picture of what it is like to experience fear we can better understand our attraction to macabre figures such as the Zodiac Killer.

The phenomenological approach, however, is not a novel approach to experiences. Jean-Paul Sartre (1905–80) provides a similar analysis. In his book *Being and Nothingness* Sartre considers what it is like to experience being looked at by another person. For Sartre, the way that we see ourselves is commonly determined by the way that others interpret us. For example, if we are warmly welcomed by friends in a café, we see ourselves as a person who is not a threat and, perhaps, is even enjoyable. On the other hand, if we enter a café and people scream "Oh my God!"

ANDREW M. WINTERS

while pointing at us in horror, we would not feel comfortable and may even begin to question what is wrong with us – thereby scrutinizing ourselves as a potential threat, or at least as someone who is not welcomed.

Sartre, however, points out that eyes alone do not determine how we experience a look from another person. The look may be experienced even when eyes are not present. For example, if we take an evening walk and a light appears in the window of a house, we no longer feel alone in the night. Instead, we may come to feel that the appearance of the light is similar to the opening of someone's eye. This is analogous to experiencing the waking of a person – at one moment the person was asleep and unaware of our actions, and suddenly she becomes awake and aware of our presence. When the person was asleep we experience her as an object of our perception, and we experience ourselves as someone who perceives the person as someone who is asleep. But we are turned into the object of her perception when she awakens; even if she has not yet opened her eyes, we know that she could turn and see us and we experience ourselves as an object – as something potentially watched. In a similar fashion, when the light is turned on in the window of the house that we pass by, we experience ourselves as someone who is seen because we *can* be seen, even if no one looks out at us. Sounds are also capable of producing the experience of being seen. When sitting in a park, the snap of a twig from behind us may give us the feeling that a person is there. Since a person is someone capable of seeing us, we then experience ourselves as something that is seen.

These occurrences of experiencing ourselves as a thing which is seen allow us to experience ourselves as others perceive us. Not only do these incidents allow us to realize that we are visual objects, but we are also presented with the opportunity to realize that we are bodies. A body is an object that is physical insofar as it occupies space, and along with being physical comes the opportunity to be physically altered. Among the ways in which a body, such as ours, may be physically altered includes the possibility of being physically harmed. From this discovery it follows that to experience ourselves as things which are seen is to experience ourselves as things which are vulnerable to another person.

To be vulnerable is to have our options limited by the person, or the idea of a person, that causes the experience of being seen. This is not to say that we are no longer free to make any choice, but instead, the choices that we are able to make are restricted by whatever produces the experience of being seen. If we are sitting in a park and we hear the snap of a twig from behind us, we are no longer free to do anything we wish.

Unseen, we might do wickedly private things, make socially unacceptable gestures, express vulgarities and more, with no self-awareness or self-condemnation. However, just because a noise has occurred, it does not necessarily mean that a person is there to see us, or that we are threatened. The sound could have been produced by a bird gathering a twig. We do not know if it was a bird or a person who broke the twig. Because we do not know, Sartre suggests we still experience ourselves as someone who is seen because there remains the lingering possibility that a person did produce the sound.

Other people and the idea of other people aren't the only factors in determining which choices are available to us; many of them are determined by what Sartre calls our *facticity*. Facticity is the way the world is and the way that we actually are in the world that determines how our choices will appear to us. Some other components of our facticity are the language, culture, and environment within which we are born. For example, a person who is born into a modern culture that has English as its dominant language will find that her available choices are radically different than a person who is born in a tribal culture with a different language.

So what does being seen and facticity have to do with the Zodiac Killer? First, Zodiac was an actual threat. He is confirmed to have killed seven people and has claimed responsibility for the deaths of 30 others. For those people living in the Vallejo area during the late 1960s, a sound behind you not only meant that there was possibly a person behind you. There was the added possibility that there was a person behind you and that person was the Zodiac Killer. Second, Zodiac has not been caught and remains unidentified. So there is the more important possibility that even those who you do see and are seen by are potentially the Zodiac Killer. So, like the sounds in the park and the light in the window, Zodiac remains unseen, yet he has given clues to how he sees us. Through his letters we have come to realize that we are in danger and that while Zodiac remains free, it is a permanent feature of the world that we are in danger. By analogy, it seems that Zodiac's letters are like the crackling of a bush from behind us – revealing to us that we are bodies which are susceptible to the dangers that he introduces into the world. We are seen by him, and through his letters we understand that we are seen no longer as persons living in the world, but are transformed into objects for him to collect. It is this transformation that determines which choices are available to us.

There seems to be a greater issue at hand. Zodiac seems to believe that he is in control of a game. The rules of his game stem from a belief that humans are inadequate for this world, but are worthy of serving him in another one. This essay is by no means an attempt to justify Zodiac's game, but is an effort to provide a phenomenological account of the ways in which Zodiac's letters and killings change our experience of the world and ourselves by attempting to understand the way that Zodiac sees us.

This is the Zodiac Speaking

The murders, horrific as they may be, are not what make Zodiac unique. It is his letters. Not since Jack the Ripper (about 1888) has a murderer communicated so flippantly with the authorities. Among the 18 letters known to be from Zodiac (there may have been more), there were four ciphers. All four of the ciphers are composed of symbols found in Greek, English, Morse code, weather, astrology, and navy semaphore, and the one translated cipher contains a disturbing and perverse message. Unfortunately, the case was closed in 2002 by Lt. John Hennessey of the San Francisco Police Department and three ciphers remain untranslated. It is possible that these three contain Zodiac's identity.

Those who have been alive during Zodiac's entire reign have been transformed into many things: objects which are protected by the law, participants in a twisted game, and mere cattle who must wander the fields hoping that today is not the day of slaughter. Zodiac has given himself the role of a rancher deciding who will survive. We must accept our vulnerability. To do otherwise is to deny ourselves knowledge of who we really are.

Summer slaughter

The first letter was sent to the *San Francisco Chronicle* on August 1, 1969 – more than eight months after the first killings. In the letter, Zodiac gives descriptions of the bodies and ammunition used in the murders that only the police and the killer would know. Along with the letter was a cipher in which Zodiac provides his motives for the murders.

The letter aims to separate Zodiac from anyone who might claim responsibility for the deaths of David Faraday and Betty Lou Jensen (both killed on December 20, 1968) and Darlene Ferrin (killed on July 4, 1969). Zodiac demands in the letter for the cipher to be printed on the front page of the *San Francisco Chronicle*. If his demands were not met, he would go on a killing spree that would only end with the deaths of 12 people. The letter to the *San Francisco Chronicle*, however, was not the only one. The *San Francisco Examiner* and the *Vallejo Times-Herald* both received letters and ciphers. All three letters were nearly identical in content, but the ciphers were different. The ciphers delivered to the newspapers were not three separate messages, but were individual parts of the same message. Zodiac used a different number of stamps on each of the envelopes to determine the sequence of the ciphers. After 20 hours, Donald and Betty Harden (a couple in Salinas) solved the ciphers. This is the message that emerged from the strange symbols:

I LIKE KILLING PEOPLE BECAUSE IT IS SO MUCH FUN IT IS MORE FUN THAN KILL-ING WILD GAME IN THE FORREST [*sic*] BECAUSE MAN IS THE MOST DANDEROUE [*sic*] ANIMAL OF ALL TO KILL SOMETHING GIVE [*sic*] ME THE MOST THRILLING EXPERIENCE IT IS EVEN BETTER THAN GETTING YOUR ROCKS OFF WITH A GIRL THE BEST PART OF IT IS THAT WHEN I DIE I WILL BE REBORN IN PARADICE [*sic*] AND THEI [*sic*] HAVE KILLED WILL BECOME MY SLAVES I WILL NOT GIVE YOU MY NAME BECAUSE YOU WILL TRY TO SLOI [*sic*] DOWN OR STOP MY COLLECTING OF SLAVES FOR MY AFTERLIFE EBEORIETEMETHHPITI [*sic*]

The last letters are thought to be an anagram for Zodiac's real name. When being exposed for the first time to this letter, we come to realize that Zodiac is on a task that will not end until it is complete. His mission being the collecting of slaves for the afterlife changes our experience of the world. We no longer see ourselves as being primary decision makers who have the ability to determine our individual fates. Instead, we are confronted with the possibility that our own fate is determined by another person who wishes to pursue us – we are the hunted. We are also viewed as slaves for the afterlife. No longer do we purely experience ourselves as free beings capable of living the life of someone who is not hunted, but instead we must accept the possibility that we are seen through a sniper's scope. Along with the shift in the experience of ourselves, our impression of the world has also changed. The world is no longer simply a place for us to reside and create within, but has also become a place in which a hunter lurks waiting to take our lives.

In addition to the change in our experience of the world, Zodiac has also changed our interpretation of the afterlife. In general, the idea of an afterlife leads people to conduct strange rituals in this life to ensure that the afterlife will surpass this one. Most people believe that this life is temporary, and for those who believe in an afterlife of some sort, the afterlife is permanent and unchanging. The Zodiac seems to be no different in this regard. Most people, however, do not believe that the afterlife is an arena in which they serve another human. Zodiac's letter changes the idea of a peaceful eternity to one that is fraught with the demands of a killer.

More interestingly, Zodiac does not explain why he believes humans to be the most dangerous animal of all. Zodiac seems to justify the hunting of humans on the grounds that humans are dangerous. But why would dangerous animals be servants? Does Zodiac serve a god who rewards Zodiac for removing dangerous animals from the earth by giving him slaves? But why does Zodiac only kill humans who most of us would not consider to be very dangerous? Perhaps we are not convinced by Zodiac's letter that we are the most dangerous animal, but he does lead us to reflect on what constitutes a dangerous animal and question whether or not we are the most dangerous one.

Moreover, this seems to be a game for which Zodiac creates rules and determines who will die. Is awareness of his game enough for us to experience ourselves as pieces for him to collect? Although Zodiac's letter on its own is not enough for us to experience ourselves as pawns for sacrifice, Zodiac's demands indicate that if we are to win then we need to realize the way in which Zodiac sees us. The appearance of Zodiac's first letter, however, does change how the authorities perceive the common citizen. No longer do the authorities experience themselves as protecting citizens from everyday miscreants, but realize they have a role in preventing harm by acknowledging Zodiac's game as such.

Before the results of the cipher were printed in the papers, Zodiac sent a second letter on August 7, 1969. It was the first time that he referred to himself as Zodiac by beginning the letter with the common dictum "This is the Zodiac speaking." But why *Zodiac*? It was later discovered a large component of the symbols used by Zodiac were part of a thirteenth-century alphabet called the *Zodiac Alphabet*, thereby serving as further evidence that Zodiac delved into occult subject matter.

Buttons

Zodiac is not only mysterious in his method of communicating with the police and press. His demands became stranger than merely making demands for his letters to be printed in the papers. He began demanding that people wear buttons bearing the marksman symbol. No one wore the buttons and Zodiac wrote a letter on July 26, 1970 describing his frustration and intentions:

This is the Zodiac speaking Being that you will not wear some nice ⊕ buttons, how about wearing some nasty ⊕ buttons. Or any type of ⊕ buttons that you can think up. If you do not wear any type of ⊕ buttons I shall (on top of everything else) torture all 13 of my slaves that I have wateing [*sic*] for me in Paradice [*sic*]. Some I shall tie over ant hills and watch them scream and twitch and squirm. Other shall have pine splinters driven under their nails and then burned. Others shall be placed in cages and fed salt beef until they are gorged then I shall listen to their pleass [*sic*] for water and I shall laugh at them. Others will …

The list goes on for five pages. It is the second longest of the Zodiac letters and contains no cipher. In this letter Zodiac claims to have collected at least 13 slaves so far, although only seven murders had been directly linked to him. If he is correct in stating that he has killed 13 people so far, then this letter demonstrates the inadequacy of the law officials to closely watch Zodiac's actions. If Zodiac is lying about the number of people that he has killed, then he at least causes the authorities to second-guess their efforts. Either way, this seemingly simple statement causes distress among those who are attempting to capture Zodiac.

This letter goes further by revealing to us our facticity as the audience for Zodiac's letters. Zodiac reveals to us that we must confront the choice to wear buttons or not. To choose not to choose is still to opt not to wear buttons. To do so, according to Zodiac, is to doom those who have already died to a torturous fate. How should this realization make us feel? By deciding not to wear buttons we inadvertently become killers. But this doesn't seem right. To be a killer seems to require some sort of intention behind the killing. But if we become aware of an action that does contribute to someone's death, shouldn't we be held somewhat culpable for the person's death? If not, then it would seem that we need to redefine what it means to be a killer. If so, then Zodiac presents us with the choice of being a killer or not. To not confront this choice is to deny the way the world is insofar as Zodiac presents it.

The last known letter

On April 24, 1978 the *San Francisco Chronicle* received what would be the last letter from Zodiac. He writes that although there was a 54-month gap from his last letter, he never left. What Zodiac does in this letter is suggest that he is now in complete control, and that the world is his game for us to play out. He writes:

ANDREW M. WINTERS

Dear Editor

This is the Zodiac speaking I am back with you. Tell herb [*sic*] caen [*sic*]
I am here, I have always been here. That city pig toschi [*sic*] is good but I am
smarter and beter [*sic*] he will get tired then leave me alone. I am waiting
for a good movie about me. who [*sic*] will play me. I am now in control of
all things.

Yours truly:
⊕ – guess
SFPD – O

The score card at the bottom of the letter disconcertingly suggests two
things. First, police records of the number of deaths tied directly to
Zodiac are inadequate. Second, the San Francisco Police Department
has made no significant advancements in apprehending Zodiac.

Throughout the timeline of these three letters, Zodiac reveals how he
sees us and the world. We are no longer individual persons capable of
determining our own fate, but are slaves for collecting. But we are also
capable of contributing to the deaths of others even when we don't act.
Is this what Zodiac means by "man is the most dangerous animal of
all"? More importantly, although Zodiac does present opportunities to
lessen the frequency and severity of his killings, there really is no escape
from his game. For this reason, as the third letter above suggests, Zodiac
has won.

Zodiac, however, is more than another serial killer in the world. Very
few serial killers have taken the initiative to explain their motives, and
to moreover explain the rules that they abide by. In doing so, Zodiac
offers us insight into the world as he perceives it. But he also offers
insight into what the world is like so that we may become aware of what
type of creatures we are and what choices are available to creatures such
as ourselves.

Conclusion

To sum up the discussion, this essay has applied a phenomenological
approach to Zodiac's letters. Although both psychology and analytic philosophy offer valuable insights as to the nature and motives behind
Zodiac's letters, they are both incapable of accounting for the experience

had by individuals reading his letters. The phenomenological approach accounts for the experiences a person has when she realizes that she is hunted and is a potential contributor to the deaths of others. It also provides an account of the experiences of realizing that the world has shifted into a place where serial killers like Zodiac exist, and that the afterlife might not be so serene.

Overall, this approach has been an attempt to understand the impact that macabre artifacts such as Zodiac's letters have upon us to better understand why we are drawn to such objects. By understanding the way that Zodiac's letters are able to alter the experiences of the world and ourselves, we can begin to see ourselves in a similar light to how he sees us. Through this lens, we can see ourselves as vulnerable objects. To see ourselves in this way provides an additional interpretation for understanding ourselves – even if it is an unpleasant one. By analogy, then, other macabre artifacts provide us with an opportunity to see ourselves the way that others might see us. To see ourselves as such is to begin to understand ourselves as we truly are.

NOTES

1 Friedrich Nietzsche, *Beyond Good and Evil: Prelude to a Philosophy of the Future*, trans. Walter Kaufmann (New York: Vintage, 1989), aphorism 146.
2 Macabre, "Zodiac," *Sinister Slaughter*, Nuclear Blast Records, 1993.
3 Accessed September 25, 2009.

CHAPTER 2

A PHILOSOPHY OF SERIAL KILLING
Sade, Nietzsche, and Brady at the Gates of Janus

Serial killer Ian Brady's 2001 book *The Gates of Janus: Serial Killing and Its Analysis* uses the writings of the Marquis de Sade and Friedrich Nietzsche to set standards for living – and killing. Brady's arrest, trial, conviction, and subsequent long imprisonment provided ample fodder for media stories about his preferred reading, and allowed him to be portrayed as simply drawn to domination, the subjugation of others, and *will to power* in the style of Hitler. This essay will show that Brady's writings capture a more in-depth understanding of these philosophical works, creating a full-blown philosophy of serial murder.

Brady's Life and Crimes

Ian Brady was born Ian Duncan Stewart in Scotland in 1938. After a childhood marked by family instability and frequent episodes of juvenile delinquency and petty crime, Brady moved to Manchester, England in 1954 to live with his mother and stepfather, whose name he adopted. Between 1963 and 1965 Brady and his lover Myra Hindley killed at least five children and may be responsible for a number of other murders. The killings became known as the "Moors Murders" because they buried most of their victims on Saddleworth Moor in Northern England. Partly due to the young age of the victims, and partly because of Hindley's active participation in the extraordinarily cruel crimes, the Moors Murders are probably Britain's most notorious criminal case after the Jack the Ripper murders, and Brady and Hindley are undoubtedly the most reviled people in British criminal history.

With the death penalty in Great Britain having been abolished just a few weeks before their conviction in 1966, Brady and Hindley were both sentenced to life imprisonment. Hindley died in prison in 2002 as a result of a heart attack, but as of this writing, Brady is still in jail, as he has been for the past 43 years, making him the current longest serving prisoner in England and Wales. Since 1985, when he was declared criminally insane, Brady has been housed in secure mental hospitals. Since 1999, he has been trying to commit suicide by starving himself to death, but he has been repeatedly force fed in order to keep him alive. The case still makes regular headlines in the British media.

Philosophy and the Moors Murders

Given the nature of the crimes of which he and his lover were convicted, one can easily understand why Brady and the Moors Murders case continue to provoke such outrage. In this essay, however, rather than restate the details of those crimes as so many journalistic and true crime accounts of the case have done over the years, I want to focus on an aspect of Brady's crimes that has been virtually unstudied in any serious or systematic manner, namely, their philosophical context. I will first discuss how and why accounts of the case at the time were preoccupied not only with the crimes themselves, but also with Brady's educational level, and in particular with his reading of Sade and Nietzsche. I will then focus on how popular accounts of the Moors Murders have tended to characterize both the Sadean and Nietzschean philosophical systems and the influence of those systems on Brady's thinking and actions, before discussing the inaccuracies of such accounts. Finally, through a reading of *The Gates of Janus*, I will search for evidence of Sade and Nietzsche's actual influence on Brady's understanding of serial murder, and then conclude by explaining the implications of that understanding for a more general account of the relationship between serial murder and philosophy.

Brady's Library

Not surprisingly, Brady's trial, and the media coverage of that trial, focused on the crimes of which Brady and Hindley were accused, but the level of Brady's education, his reading habits, and the influence of his reading on his crimes also fascinated both lawyers and commentators. Numerous items from Brady's personal library (including volumes on Nazism, torture, and Sade's *Justine*) were introduced as evidence during the trial, apparently because Brady had instructed his friend David Smith (whom Brady and Hindley tried to implicate as their accomplice) to dispose of these books before his arrest. In practice, however, the presence of the books in the courtroom gave the attorneys the opportunity to sneer at Brady's choice of reading, as when one lawyer dismissed Brady's collection as nothing more than "dirty books." Interestingly, Brady's response to this dismissal was to claim "There are better collections than that in lords' manors all over the country."[1]

Brady's response highlights the class assumptions that influenced much media coverage of the case. What the lawyers and the press objected to in Brady's reading was not only the subject matter but also that Brady (who had been born in a working-class slum in Glasgow) had the audacity to present himself as an educated and cultured person. Sometimes the class dimensions of this aspect of the case are explicit, as when one commentator refers to Brady as "a remarkable specimen of a lumpen-proletarian intellectual,"[2] but mostly the class-inflected resentment of Brady's pretended learning is more implicit.

There was much more at stake here than just the effort to demean a single individual. Part of the reason the Moors Murders case received such widespread coverage was because it was quickly identified by many as being symptomatic of larger changes taking place in British culture in the 1960s. The Moors Murders were seen as "a crime of our age" in the sense that they indicated that society was becoming "dangerously permissive and already permeated with the atmosphere of violence."[3] This is why Brady's library received so much attention. According to cultural commentator Pamela Hansford Johnson, who published a book about the Moors Murders case in 1967, "There is a direct correlation with sadistic pornography in this case. I am sure that Brady and Hindley were affected by what they read."[4]

A Little Knowledge is a Dangerous Thing

The influence of his reading on Brady's thinking and actions is a major element of the true-crime accounts of the case that began to appear after Brady's conviction in 1966, such as *Beyond Belief: A Chronicle of Murder and Its Detection* by Emlyn Williams. Williams charts the evolution of Brady's interests through the growth of his library, starting with books on Nazism, evolving into volumes on torture, and culminating in Brady's reading of Sade, which, according to Williams, hit Brady "like the tolling of a bell, every sentence a resonant stroke."[5]

Although at other points in his argument Williams minimizes the influence of Brady's reading and emphasizes instead the role that biology played in his crimes, arguing that "From the day of his birth, the spell had been woven,"[6] in this passage Williams clearly implies that the experience of reading Sade set Brady on the path to murder. What disturbs commentators about this apparent relation between text and action in Brady's murders is that it suggests that Brady had developed philosophical justifications for his crimes; quite apart from the crimes themselves, it was these justifications that made the case so controversial and so troubling. One response to the anxiety caused by the philosophical context of Brady's crimes, as we have already seen, was to minimize its importance by either mocking Brady or emphasizing the way in which he personifies the saying "a little knowledge is a dangerous thing." A related tactic was to mischaracterize and oversimplify the ideas of the two philosophers most often mentioned as influences on Brady: Nietzsche and Sade.

In the case of Nietzsche, whenever he is mentioned in popular accounts of the Moors Murders case, it is in relation to two concepts – the *übermensch* and the *will to power* – both of which play an important and complex role in Nietzsche's philosophy. For Nietzsche, the übermensch (usually translated as "superman" or "overman") is a goal for humanity to set itself. It involves the overcoming of ordinary human limitations and the achievement of a superior state of being. The will to power (in German, *der Wille zur Macht*) is related to the concept of the übermensch in the sense that Nietzsche believes the will to power to be the main driving force in humanity, that sense of ambition and striving that will enable humankind to reach the highest possible position in life. I will say more later in the essay about these two concepts, but for the moment I want to stress that, in coverage of the Brady case, both of these concepts are presented in a very oversimplified way. To the extent that either of these

DAVID SCHMID

concepts are explained at all, they are presented only as the inspiration for Hitler and Nazism (World War II was only 20 years in the past at the time of Brady's arrest) and therefore as synonymous with domination; in other words, there is no mention of the fact that the übermensch concept is about overcoming one's own limitations rather than subjugating others, and the will to power is never associated with self-assertion, but only with the control of others.

Sade, if anything, fares even worse than Nietzsche in popular discussions of the Moors Murders. Rather than engaging with his ideas in any substantive (or even cursory) manner, Sade is simply dismissed as the mad libertine, the "inventor" of sadism who does not deserve to be taken seriously at all. It is easy to imagine the reasons why the ideas of Nietzsche and Sade are treated so dismissively (not the least of which is that this dismissal helps the media present Brady as an insane monster), but before moving on to the question of Brady's *actual* engagement with these philosophers as evidenced in *The Gates Of Janus*, I want to discuss a question the answer to which is assumed rather than demonstrated by the blanket dismissals: if one were looking for a philosophical justification for (serial) murder, could one find such a thing in the work of Nietzsche and Sade?

Nietzsche

If we turn to the works of Nietzsche first, we will find much there that would appeal to someone like Brady, although there are also details that remind us of the caricature of Nietzsche that we find in coverage of a case like the Moors Murders. In *Thus Spoke Zarathustra*, for example, Nietzsche speaks of how the will to power leads to a desire "to create the world before which you can kneel,"[7] which suggests that there is more to the will to power than simple domination; there is also the overcoming of one's own limitations. There can be no doubt, however, that the will to power is an absolutely fundamental concept in Nietzsche's philosophy. In *Beyond Good and Evil*, for example, Nietzsche stresses the centrality of the will to power in the practice of philosophy, describing philosophy as "this tyrannical drive itself, the most spiritual will to power, to the 'creation of the world'."[8] With this centrality in mind, it makes perfect sense that Nietzsche often defines the philosopher as someone characterized by aggressive activity, and later in *Beyond Good and Evil* Nietzsche says of philosophers that their "knowing is creating, their creating is a legislation, their will to truth is – will to power."[9]

For Nietzsche, philosophy is a creative, world-making activity, and this creativity comes from the philosopher's ability to recognize the necessity of thinking outside of the terms set by standard, conventional notions of what defines good and bad behavior. This is what Nietzsche means when he speaks in *Twilight of the Idols* of the need for philosophers to place themselves "beyond good and evil."[10] In *Thus Spoke Zarathustra* the title character notes that people in different parts of the world have different understandings of what constitutes good and bad behavior: "Much that was good to one people was scorn and infamy to another.... Much I found called evil here, and decked out with purple honors there,"[11] and this belief that there are no universal, absolute, concrete rights and wrongs, but only standards that vary from culture to culture and from individual to individual, has often been described as moral relativism, and it is in this respect that Nietzsche's philosophy most closely resembles that of Sade.

Sade

With Sade, however, we encounter a celebration of crime much more detailed, systematic, and explicit than anything to be found in Nietzsche; indeed, it is Sade who provides the philosophical framework within which the murderer can be considered a hero. The significance of Sade is such that he is far more than an individual who wrote comprehensively, indeed, obsessively about violence and sexual debauchery. Rather, Sade is a massive, almost overwhelming cultural fact whose presence and influence on our thinking about murder must be assumed even where it cannot be clearly identified. Moreover, when we consider the work of Sade, we assume not only his impact on the way those who haven't murdered think about murder, but also his impact on the way that murderers think about themselves: who they are, why they do what they do, and so on. This is not to say that these murderers have read and consciously incorporated Sade's ideas into their self-definition to the extent that Brady may have done, but rather to say that Sade's ideas are inevitably part of the models murderers have available to them to make sense of their behavior.

In their book about sexual murder, *The Lust to Kill*, Deborah Cameron and Elizabeth Frazer describe how the emergence of the category of "sex killing" at the turn of the century "provided a self-conscious role or identity for individuals to take up and define their acts by."[12] Whether we are discussing the general public's view of serial murder or serial murderers' view of themselves, the influence of Sade is clearly visible, as we can see by showing how closely the characteristics of the quintessential Sadean hero mesh with those of the popular image of the serial murderer.

One of the keys to understanding the psychology and behavior of the Sadean hero is to appreciate the importance of his egoism. Maurice Blanchot has described Sade's "basic philosophy" as being one of "self-interest, of absolute egoism: Each of us must do exactly as he pleases, each of us is bound by one law alone, that of his own pleasure."[13] The life of each and every one of Sade's heroes demonstrates strict adherence to this principle. This adherence is facilitated by the usually exalted social position of the Sadean hero. Sade's heroes are generally rich and powerful, and this enables them to indulge their vices both with impunity and on a grand scale.

Sadean heroes always evaluate conventional morality through the prism of self-interest. If conventional morality suits the purposes of Sadean heroes (which it rarely does), they are prepared to follow it. If not, they ignore it without a second thought. And yet, to imply that Sadean heroes ever proceed without thought is inaccurate. For, apart from their egoism, the other principal distinguishing characteristic of Sadean heroes is their addiction to self-justification. At the slightest provocation, they will pause in the midst of their debauches and undertake the most exhaustive (and repetitive) explanation of why they are entirely justified in their chosen course of action by speaking of the relativity of moral concepts. The following example from "Eugénie de Franval" is typical of the dozens of examples of this tendency that exist throughout Sade's *oeuvre*: "there's nothing real in the world, nothing that deserves praise or blame, nothing that is worthy of being rewarded or punished, nothing unjust here that may not be lawful a thousand miles away; in short, there's no real evil or unchanging good."[14] Sadean libertines who are attempting to persuade their neophytes that the life of debauchery they are embarking on is perfectly justified frequently use this type of moral relativism.

The Sadean Hero and the Serial Killer

The Sadean hero shares many characteristics with the popular image of the serial murderer, an image that defines most coverage of the Moors Murders case. The serial murderer, for example, frequently demonstrates the kind of egoism that characterizes the Sadean hero. For serial killers, the satisfaction of their own desires always has absolute priority over any other considerations. They are never swayed from their murders by the idea that what they are doing is morally repugnant. Indeed, an awareness of this repugnance is frequently one of the sources of pleasure that serial killers derive from their murders.

Both the Sadean hero and the serial killer are looking for ways to impress their desires upon the world. Unlike Sadean heroes, however, this desire among serial killers may frequently be explained by such killers' almost total lack of social power or influence. Acutely aware of their status as nonentities, the murderous methods of serial killers become their way of asserting both their identity and their ability to exert some kind of control over their environment. In his book *Hunting Humans: The Rise of the Modern Multiple Murderer*, Elliott Leyton has described multiple murderers as intensely class conscious:

> Among serial murderers, their truncated sense of self and identity (a reflection of the fact that the vast majority of them are adopted, or illegitimate, or have spent a major portion of their childhoods or adolescences in institutions such as orphanages or juvenile homes) pushed them towards finding their personal fulfillment in the killings, and all their ambitions in the international celebrity that most often attends their capture.[15]

While Brady may not have murdered in order to become famous, it does seem plausible to suggest that their class position plays an important role in the way both Sadean heroes and many contemporary serial killers understand themselves. Both groups victimize vulnerable members of society as a way of increasing their own sense of self-worth and their sense of themselves as powerful beings.

Interestingly, this sense of power and control is frequently maintained even when the Sadean hero or the serial murderer suffer a reversal of fortune, resulting in either their imprisonment or death. How can the Sadean hero and the serial murderer turn their punishment, or even their death, into a positive phenomenon? In his essay on Sade, Blanchot raises the question of whether the death of Sadean heroes makes nonsense of Sade's system: "What happens to that certainty that the man of all vices will always be happy?"[16] This is where, according to Blanchot, Sade is at his most ingenious. The Sadean hero is not exempt from punishment and death, it is true, but he or she is exempt from feeling victimized by that punishment. On the contrary, Sadean heroes take pleasure and enjoyment from their punishment, just as they do from dealing out punishment. As Blanchot says, this ability to turn even the most violent and painful reversal

DAVID SCHMID

of fortune into their most triumphant moment renders Sadean heroes untouchable; they cannot be harmed, no matter what happens to them.

Opening the Gates of Janus

It would be difficult, not to mention inaccurate, to represent Brady's years in prison as some kind of triumph, and yet there is some evidence to suggest that he takes a perverse pride in being the most hated man in Britain that is not too different from Nietzsche's description of himself in *Ecce Homo* as "by far the most terrible human being that has existed so far." Nietzsche goes on to boast that "I know the pleasure in destroying to a degree that accords with my powers to destroy ... I am the first immoralist: that makes me the annihilator par excellence."[17] At one point in *The Gates of Janus* Brady describes his own situation in similar terms, arguing that his extreme isolation and the fact that he knows that he will die in prison confer certain benefits upon him and his analysis:

> The certitude of my death in captivity paradoxically confers a certainty of belief, a freedom of thought and expression most so-called free people will fail to experience in their lifetime. Unlike the merely *physically* free individual, no hellish circles of social graces and ersatz respect bind me to censor beliefs. I am not under the least obligation to please by deceit any individual whomsoever. To all practical intents and purposes, I am no longer of your world – if, as you might suggest, I ever was.[18]

What Brady claims for his writing, therefore, is both objectivity and authenticity based on his own experience, but from Brady's point of view it is equally important to understand what *The Gates of Janus* is not. Contrary to what one might expect, it is neither an apologia nor an autobiography; rather, as Anthony Metivier has noted, "the overarching purpose of *The Gates of Janus* is pedagogical,"[19] and the object of the lesson is, in Brady's words, a "dissection of what murder is really all about, from the point of view of a serial killer, for a change."[20] What remains to be determined is the role that philosophy plays in Brady's account of serial murder.

The answer to this question, as well as the key to *The Gates of Janus* as a whole, can be found in a passage where Brady challenges the very idea of serial murder: "I believe the term 'serial killer' is highly misleading, in that it implicitly suggests to the general public that murder is the paramount object or motivating urge in the mind of the killer."[21] Brady rejects this idea and instead urges his reader to consider the matter in "abstract philosophical terms," and then, Brady goes on to argue, it becomes clear that "What the average ... serial killer seeks above all is power and the will to power."[22] The fact that Brady recommends looking at serial murder from a philosophical point of view, and that he does so in explicitly Nietzschean terms, is obviously highly significant and it is also characteristic of *The Gates of Janus* as a whole. From the very beginning of the book, Brady is at pains to stress the significance of moral relativism to his own philosophical point of view, and he does so in terms reminiscent of both Sade and Nietzsche:

> Morality and legality are determined chiefly by the prevailing ruling class in whatever geographical variant, not least because a collective morality is too unwieldy and difficult to maintain. I prefer individual systems of principles rather than a collective set of precepts largely impossible to quantify or enforce.[23]

Once Brady has sounded this note of moral relativism and the primacy of individualism in philosophical matters, he returns to these points again and again throughout *The Gates of Janus*, to the extent that they become the structuring ideas of his book. On many occasions these concepts are presented so obscurely and repetitively that it makes for difficult reading, but sometimes they are presented in a fashion that is crystal-clear: "What do I believe in? I reiterate, moral relativism in all matters other than personal loyalty to chosen individuals."[24] *The Gates of Janus* is not the first book to include the writings of serial killers. In 1970 Thomas E. Gaddis and James O. Long published a biographical novel entitled *Killer: A Journal of Murder* that reproduced the writings of American serial murderer Carl Panzram (of whom more later); more recently, Brian King has edited a fascinating collection, *Lustmord: The Writings and Artifacts of Murderers*. What sets *The Gates of Janus* apart, however, is the depth of Brady's analysis and his enthusiasm for casting the act of serial murder into an explicitly philosophical framework.

Brady Evaluates Other Serial Killers

Perhaps one of the most interesting aspects of *The Gates of Janus*, however, is the fact that Brady's philosophical beliefs influence his discussions of individual serial killers, discussions that make up the second half of the book. In the process of providing psychological profiles of individual killers (and Brady's qualified endorsement of the FBI's system of profiling is another interesting aspect of *Gates*), it becomes clear that Brady disapproves of some killers and approves of others based on how closely they either do or do not match his ideas about what constitutes the philosophical meaning of serial murder. In his discussion of Henry Lee Lucas, for example, Brady criticizes the way in which Lucas was so ready to inflate the number of murders he had committed in an effort to attract attention and notoriety to himself because Brady feels that such behavior cheapens what he sees as the philosophical dimensions of the act.

If Lucas disappoints Brady, however, Carl Panzram attracts his great admiration because of the way he seems to personify Nietzschean will to power and the concept of moral relativism, as Panzram's own summary of his belief system suggests:

> In my life I have murdered 21 human beings. I have committed thousands of burglaries, robberies Larcenys [*sic*], arson and last but not least I have committed sodomy on more than 1,000 male human beings. for [*sic*] all of these things I am not the least bit sorry. I have no conscience so that does not worry me. I don't believe in Man, God nor devil. I hate the whole damned human race including myself.[25]

Brady's approval of Panzram comes through again and again in his discussion, whether in the way he describes his actions, his complete lack of remorse, or in the defiant manner of his death. As Brady says at one point of Panzram: "His beliefs and lethal philosophy of life were now irreversible: 'The only way to reform people is to kill them.' The articulate birth of a highly intelligent, homicidal psychopath, icy and incisive, divulging the incipient cancer in his youthful soul ... Nietzsche or de Sade would have heartily applauded his sentiments."[26] Through such comments, Brady in *The Gates of Janus* demonstrates why he, along with Sade and Nietzsche, are fundamental to any account of the relationship between serial killing and philosophy.

NOTES

1 Jonathan Goodman (ed.) *Trial of Ian Brady and Myra Hindley: The Moors Case* (Newton Abbot: David and Charles, 1973), p. 191.
2 Maurice Richardson, "What is One to Make of the Moors Murders?" *Observer*, May 8, 1966, p. 21.

3 Diane Goldrei, "Facing Up To Violence," *Illustrated London News*, March 11, 1967, p. 26.

4 Ibid.

5 Emlyn Williams, *Beyond Belief: A Chronicle of Murder and Its Detection* (London: Pan, 1968), p. 174.

6 Ibid., p. 102.

7 Friedrich Nietzsche, *Thus Spoke Zarathustra: A Book for None and All*, trans. Walter Kaufmann (New York: Penguin, 1978), p. 113.

8 Friedrich Nietzsche, *Beyond Good and Evil: Prelude to a Philosophy of the Future*, trans. Walter Kaufmann (New York: Vintage, 1989), p. 16.

9 Ibid., p. 132.

10 Friedrich Nietzsche, *Twilight of the Idols* and *The Anti-Christ*, trans. R. J. Hollingdale (New York: Penguin, 2003), p. 66.

11 Nietzsche, *Thus Spoke Zarathustra*, p. 58.

12 Deborah Cameron and Elizabeth Frazer, *The Lust To Kill* (Cambridge: Polity Press, 1987), p. 22.

13 Maurice Blanchot, "Sade," in *Justine, Philosophy in the Bedroom, and Other Writings*, trans. Richard Seaver and Austryn Wainhouse (New York: Grove, 1965), p. 40.

14 Marquis de Sade, "Eugénie de Franval," in *Justine, Philosophy in the Bedroom, and Other Writings*, trans. Richard Seaver and Austryn Wainhouse (New York: Grove, 1965), p. 408.

15 Elliott Leyton, *Hunting Humans: The Rise of the Modern Multiple Murderer* (London: Penguin, 1989), p. 30.

16 Blanchot, "Sade," p. 48.

17 Friedrich Nietzsche, *On the Genealogy of Morals and Ecce Homo*, trans. Walter Kaufmann (New York: Vintage, 1989), p. 327.

18 Ian Brady, *The Gates of Janus: Serial Killing and its Analysis* (Los Angeles: Feral House, 2001), p. 44.

19 Anthony Metivier, "Hypnotist, Philosopher, Serial Killer, Friend: A Critical Review of Ian Brady's *The Gates of Janus*," *Nebula* 5, 4 (2008): 175.

20 Brady, *The Gates of Janus*, p. 91.

21 Ibid., p. 85.

22 Ibid., p. 86.

23 Ibid., p. 34.

24 Ibid., p. 65.

25 Brian King (ed.) *Lustmord: The Writings and Artifacts of Murderers* (Burbank: Bloat Books, 1996), p. 169.

26 Brady, *The Gates of Janus*, p. 235.

CHAPTER 3

THE SITUATION OF THE JURY

Attribution Bias in the Trials of Accused Serial Killers

The innocent and the righteous slay thou not.

Exodus 23:7

Better that ten guilty persons escape than that one innocent suffer.

William Blackstone

It is better and more satisfactory to acquit a thousand guilty persons than to put a single innocent one to death.

Maimonides

Introduction

This chapter is not about serial killers. It's about innocent men (and they are mostly men), unjustly imprisoned men, unjustly executed men. It's about miscarriages of justice, biased juries, trial by media manipulation and public outrage. It's about unconscious situational influences on judgment. Doug Clark, a convicted serial killer, claims to be such a man. In fact, he wrote a letter to the editor of this book arguing that he was framed by his former lover and accomplice, Carol Bundy. I have read this letter, in which he lays out the case against Bundy and defends himself against her testimony. What you are about to read takes into account his side of the story.

We like to think that we are excellent judges of character and responsibility. We flatter ourselves by thinking that we would not allow irrelevant features of our environments to factor into our decisions, especially when a man's life is at stake. But in recent decades researchers in psychology, sociology, economics, and philosophy have assembled compelling evidence that seemingly trivial situational variables have immense power over our thoughts and behaviors. What if just such cues operated in the trial of an accused serial killer? What if they operated in the trial of Doug Clark?

The Case of Doug Clark

Doug Clark was convicted on January 28, 1983 of six counts of first-degree murder with "special circumstances." The jury was convinced beyond reasonable doubt that over the course of a few months he had hired six prostitutes to perform fellatio on him and, in the middle of the blowjob, shot them in the head, then raped their corpses. He was also convicted of one count each of attempted murder (the seventh woman managed to escape), mayhem, and mutilating human remains (he had used the severed head of Exxie Wilson as a sex toy for three days before discarding it in an alleyway). During the trial, he fired a series of public defenders for incompetence, briefly served as his own attorney, and called the judge a "gutless worm." He insisted throughout the trial on his innocence, claiming that his partner Carol Bundy (no relation to the infamous serial killer Ted Bundy) colluded with police to frame him. In fact, most of the evidence against him was circumstantial. Bundy's testimony was one of the primary pieces of direct evidence, despite the fact that she perjured herself in sworn affidavits, attempted to seduce the investigating detective and the judge, and admitted both to helping Clark play with the decapitated head (she cleaned it and applied makeup to make it more attractive for his necrophilic acts) and to the solo murder and beheading of John Murray, her former lover, for which she was later convicted, received 52 years to life, and died in prison of heart failure in 2003.

When Clark came up for sentencing a month later, he again served as his own attorney and attempted to make a farce of the justice system, arguing in his closing statement, "We have to vote for the death penalty in this case. The evidence cries out for it." The jury was not amused, condemning him to six death sentences. He continues to assert that he was framed by Bundy and the police, claiming that she shot the prostitutes herself in fits of jealous rage. (She admitted to being sexually obsessed with him, but said that she was the manipulated and he the manipulator.) In 1992 the California Supreme Court affirmed his death sentence. To date, his attempts to secure a retrial or commutation of his sentence have all failed, and he sits on death row in San Quentin State Prison.

Though Clark is an evidently disturbed individual with violent and bizarre sexual inclinations (he committed statutory rape with a 13-year-old, an escapade Bundy photographed), the question remains whether he was justly convicted. Most of the evidence against him was circumstantial; the decisive factor was Bundy's dubious testimony. Two authors, Mark MacNamara and Christopher Berry-Dee, have argued that Clark's guilt was not established in the trial. MacNamara wrote an article for *Vanity Fair* arguing that Clark's trial had been botched. Berry-Dee claimed in *Talking with Serial Killers* that Clark did not receive a fair trial and that he was judged not for his actions but for his ugly appearance, his foul language, and his contemptuous attitude.

I will argue neither for nor against Clark's innocence. My aim is to investigate the unconscious biases that may have influenced jurors as they deliberated whether to convict him. First, however, I discuss the situationist tradition in psychology and philosophy, focusing especially on attribution biases and their relevance to criminal trials.

Situationism and Destructive Behavior

The situationist tradition in psychology and, more recently, philosophy, examines the influence of seemingly trivial situational variables on human thought and human behavior. We often flatter ourselves, believing in our own supreme rationality, imperviousness to suggestion, and ability to carry out our plans. Most people believe they are better than average drivers, but that's statistically impossible. Most people admit that texting while driving is dangerous, yet claim that when they do it there's nothing to worry about. We seem to be masters of neither our own beliefs nor of our own desires.

Stanley Milgram found in 1963 that people from all walks of life could be led to apply massive electrical shocks to innocent victims given the right prompts. He asked people to participate in an experiment on the influence of punishment on learning, but the experiment was really about people's willingness to follow orders to harm others. Three people would participate in each run of the experiment: an experimenter, a confederate (an actor who pretends to be a subject but is actually helping the experimenter), and a subject. Through a rigged randomization mechanism, the confederate is assigned the role of learner, while the subject is assigned the role of teacher. The learner is strapped into a chair and fitted with electrodes, which are first tested on both the teacher and the learner to show that they give painful shocks. The teacher then quizzes the learner, whom he is prompted to shock after each wrong answer. Shocks start at 15 volts and increase by 15-volt increments.

Here is Milgram's own summary of the learner's reactions:

> At 75 volts, the "learner" grunts. At 120 volts he complains verbally; at 150 volts he demands to be released from the experiment. His protests continue as the shocks escalate, growing increasingly vehement and emotional. At 285 volts his response can only be described as an agonized scream.... At 300 volts the victim shouted in desperation that he would no longer provide answers to the memory test.... At 315 volts, after a violent scream, the victim reaffirmed vehemently that he was no longer a participant. He provided no answers, but shrieked in agony whenever a shock was administered. After 330 volts he was not heard from, nor did his answers reappear on the four-way signal box.

If the teacher dissents, the experimenter replies politely but confidently, with an escalating sequence of prods:

> Please continue, or, Please go on.
> The experiment requires that you continue.
> It is absolutely essential that you continue.
> You have no other choice, you must go on.

If the subject refuses once more after the fourth prod, the experiment ends. Otherwise, the experiment ends after the incapacitated learner is shocked three times at the maximum voltage of 450, which is labeled on the teacher's dial merely as "XXX."

Astonishingly, a large majority of subjects were maximally obedient; that is, they failed to disobey five times consecutively and thereby end the study early. When the experiment is described to them in detail, most people predict that almost no one will show maximum obedience and that most participants in the experiment will break off as soon as the learner starts to object. Since the participants were ordinary people, what

Milgram's situationist experiment shows is that almost anyone could be led to horrific acts of torture given the right prompting.

Another infamous situationist experiment, Phillip Zimbardo's Stanford Prison Simulation, showed that apparently normal young men could transform into sadistic totalitarians if placed in an appropriate hierarchical structure. In this study, participants were randomly assigned the role of either guard or prisoner. To heighten the sense that there was a difference between the guard identity and the prisoner identity, Zimbardo ordered two types of uniforms, one for the guards and one for the prisoners. He reinforced the distinction between guards and prisoners by forbidding the use of prisoners' names; instead, each was addressed by the number sewn onto his uniform. By the end of the study, the prisoners had so internalized their new group identities that when they were offered "parole" (i.e., the chance to exit the experiment early) in exchange for forfeiture of their stipend, most accepted; then, when their parole application was "rejected," none left the experiment. They could, of course, have simply walked out, but they identified so strongly as prisoners that leaving without the consent of the experimenter was not a live option for them.

Attribution Biases

One of the main strands in the situationist tradition is the study of attribution biases – distortions of the process of event evaluation. We can distinguish four aspects in the evaluation of an event: (1) we decide whether the event was good or bad; (2) we also decide whether someone did it (in which case it's an action) or whether it was merely an accident (in which case it's a mere event); (3) if it was an action, we must decide who did it and (4) whether the action was done intentionally. An attribution bias is defined as a distortion of any of these four aspects of event evaluation: calling something good (bad) when it is evidently not, thinking that someone is responsible for a coincidence, attributing an action to someone who did not do it, or saying that someone acted intentionally when her action was clearly not intentional.

Experimental philosopher Joshua Knobe is famous for his theory that the good or bad consequences of an action influence our decision about whether it was done intentionally. In one study he presented subjects with one of two vignettes. In the first, a corporate fat cat is told that his company is considering starting a new program that will increase profits but harm the environment. He responds, "I don't care at all about harming the environment. I just want to make as much profit as I can. Let's start the new program." In the second vignette, the new program will help the environment. The chairman's response is almost identical: "I don't care at all about helping the environment. I just want to make as much profit as I can. Let's start the new program." Even though the cases are structurally identical, experimental subjects say that in the first case the chairman intentionally harms the environment but that in the second he does not intentionally help it. Philosophers disagree whether these different responses indicate a bias in evaluative judgments or show that the ordinary concept of intentional action takes good or bad consequences into account, but everyone agrees that the results of the experiment are surprising.

Seeing Ghosts

Other surprising results bear on the other three aspects of event evaluation. In *Totem and Taboo*, psychoanalyst Sigmund Freud (1856–1939) argued that the people of ancient times and "primitive" cultures even today "people the world with innumerable spiritual beings both benevolent and malignant" and that we regard these spirits "as the causes of natural phenomena."

More recently, philosopher Daniel Dennett (in *Breaking the Spell*) and biologist Richard Dawkins (in *The God Delusion*) have also argued that unconscious biases influence our decisions about whether an event is an action or mere event. According to them, *Homo sapiens* evolved or socially developed a hyperactive capacity for agent-detection: rather than recognizing the power of chance, we attribute anything we can't explain to unknown persons and spirits. When a natural disaster strikes, we interpret it as an act of God. When someone wins the lottery, we think it was rigged. In 1755 an earthquake struck the city of Lisbon, Portugal, killing tens of thousands. Preachers throughout Europe called it an act of divine retribution for the sins of Lisbon's denizens. More recently, after Hurricane Katrina devastated the city of New Orleans, both Pat Robertson, an infamous American bigot, and Father Gerhard Maria Wagner, a Catholic priest, claimed the hurricane was a sign of God's wrath for the sexual depravity of the United States, especially its toleration of homosexuality and abortion. Freud seems to have been half-right:

not only "primitive" people but also religious zealots are prone to interpret mere events (obviously natural phenomena like earthquakes and hurricanes) as actions (the result of an agent's choice).

"Ewww … Guilty!"

In recent years researchers have shown that when people feel the emotion of disgust they are more inclined to describe someone's actions as blameworthy or punishable – even if the disgust is wholly irrelevant to the person being judged. Thalia Wheatley and Jonathan Haidt hypnotized subjects to feel a flash of disgust when they heard otherwise neutral words like "often" and "take." They then presented the subjects with vignettes in which people make moral transgressions of various types. Harsher judgments were meted out when the vignettes contained these words.

In a series of similar experiments, Haidt, along with his colleagues Simone Schnall, Gerald Clore, and Alexander Jordan, presented subjects with disgust cues then asked them to evaluate the actions of characters in short vignettes. In one scenario, subjects were placed in a room where fart spray had been liberally distributed. They of course could not have thought that the characters about whom they were reading had intentionally farted in the room just to nauseate them. It made no sense, therefore, for them to take out their disgust on the characters, yet that is exactly what they did, saying that actions non-disgusted people would describe as good or neutral were bad, that actions others described as bad were extremely bad, and assigning more stringent punishments to the characters in the vignettes.

In their next experiment, Haidt and company asked subjects to sit at a desk that replicated the worst aspects of frat-house life. On it were a discarded smoothie with unidentifiable, rotting bits of fruit lining its inside and a chewed-up pen. Next to the desk was a trash can overflowing with greasy pizza boxes and snotty tissues. These subjects, too, made harsh judgments of the characters in their vignettes, despite the fact that those characters had nothing to do with the disgusting condition of the desk.

In their final experiment, Haidt's group asked subjects to watch a clip from the film *Trainspotting* in which a character gets a bad case of diarrhea, shits into a toilet that looks like it hasn't been cleaned in decades, then – in a drug-induced fit – dives into the toilet full of diarrhea. It's a memorable scene, and one of the most disgusting in film history. And you can probably guess at this point what happened when people were asked to make moral judgments after watching the clip.

"You people are all …"

In addition to biases that influence judgments of intentionality, agency, and good and bad, people are affected by biases when assessing who performed an action. Racial and ethnic minorities are often unjustly convicted of crimes they did not commit or were not proved to commit. In the United States, over 10 percent of black men and 2.4 percent of Hispanic men (compared to just 1.2 percent of white men) are incarcerated at a given time. Black men have a one in three chance of going to jail over the course of their lifetime. There are now more black men in prison than in college. Lower-class defendants are also disproportionately imprisoned. More than half of all inmates had an annual income less than $10,000 before their arrests.

Men are often assumed to have committed crimes, are more frequently convicted of crimes of which they're accused, and receive harsher penalties than women for the same crimes. People seem to stereotype men as aggressors and women as victims, even when they know nothing about the man or woman in question. This is especially the case for sexual crimes and crimes against women. Indeed, most people assume that female rape – whether of men or of other women – is impossible. A moment's reflection on the number of orifices and devices available to wannabe rapists reveals the falsity of this assumption.

Finally, women jurors are known to vote guilty more frequently than their male counterparts when the defendant is male, when the crime is violent, when the victim was a woman, and when the crime was sexual.

"Aren't you the guy who …?"

Pretrial media coverage is another source of bias influencing jurors' determination of who performed an action. When a defendant's name and image are plastered all over the news, as often happens with sensationalized violent and sexual crimes, potential jurors may come to a decision about the guilt of the defendant before hearing the evidence presented formally in the trial. One way to avoid this bias is to relocate a trial to another city less saturated with media about the crime and the defendant. Most trials, however, are not relocated. O. J. Simpson had one of the most publicized trials in United States history, yet his trial was not relocated.

Doug Clark Again

Let us reconsider the case of Doug Clark in light of the situationist theory of attribution biases. His statutory rape of a 13-year-old, his necrophilia with the corpses of the dead prostitutes, and his appalling use of Exxie Wilson's head as a sex toy surely inspire disgust. While they are morally and legally wrong, none of these acts confirms that he was the premeditated killer. It could actually be, as he claims, that Carol Bundy was the murderer and he the mere accomplice.

Consider also the various gender biases involved. Clark's jury consisted of eight women and four men; women, as discussed above, are more likely to vote guilty in a case involving sexual violence. Clark himself is of course a man, and both male and female jurors tend to assume the worst about male defendants in crimes against women. The only other primary suspect, Carol Bundy, was a woman who testified against him while wearing a schoolmarmish outfit.

What's more, in the 1970s and early 1980s the California media had a field day covering their state's serial killers, a motley crew comprising Kenneth Bianchi and Angelo Buono (the "Hillside Stranglers" whose trial took place across the hall from Doug Clark's), Lawrence "Pliers" Bittaker and Roy Norris, William George "Freeway Killer" Bonin (a title he shares with Patrick Kearney and Randy Steven Kraft, two other California serial killers), David "Trailside Killer" Carpenter, Richard "Vampire of Sacramento" Chase, Thor Nis Christiansen, Carroll Cole, Robert Diaz, Scott Erskine, Gerald and Charlene Gallego, Charles Ray Hatcher, Ervil LaBaron, "The Original Night Stalker" (a serial killer and rapist still at large), and Randall "The I-5 Bandit" Woodfield. Doug Clark's arrest and imprisonment were highly publicized, yet his trial was not relocated to ensure a fair jury.

To this day, Clark insists that he was framed by Carol Bundy, who, he said in a recent letter to this volume's editor, was trying to copycat the murders of the infamous Ted Bundy. Prosecutors had considered charging

Clark with the murder and decapitation of John Murray, but Clark had a watertight alibi (his only one). Had he been charged, it seems likely that he would have been convicted by a wrathful jury of a seventh murder.

Conclusion

Philosopher Robert Nozick has argued that you don't know something – even when you're right about it – if you would have believed it even if you were wrong. For example, if someone bought a lottery ticket firmly believing that her number would win, and she actually did win, Nozick would argue that she still didn't know she would win because she would have predicted it even if she did not have the winning ticket.

Put yourself in the position of a woman juror in Doug Clark's trial. He has been accused of committing unimaginably disgusting acts with the bodies and severed heads of dead women. He is a man with clearly sociopathic and misogynistic proclivities. The only other suspect is a woman. All six murders and the one attempted murder had female victims. These victims were all subject to sexual aggression, having been killed while performing fellatio. You heard about Clark on the news before being selected as a juror.

Would you hesitate to vote guilty, even if you found the actual evidence against him unconvincing?

PART II

CAN YOU BLAME THEM? ETHICS, EVIL, AND SERIAL KILLING

CHAPTER 4

SERIAL KILLERS AS PRACTICAL MORAL SKEPTICS

A Historical Survey with Interviews

Why be moral? This is a question of moral motivation – what motivates us to do right and avoid doing wrong? Why avoid hurting others if it pleases you to do it? The philosophical doctrine of *practical moral skepticism* says that there may be times when no reasons, no matter how rational or relevant, motivate us to actually do good or avoid evil. Through a historical survey of serial murder, including interviews with contemporary serial killers, I will reveal the ways in which serial killers exemplify practical moral skepticism. Most serial killers whom I have interviewed are rational, and claim to know right from wrong, and yet go on to kill again and again. Throughout history, serial killers have acted on their felt reasons to stalk, attack, and murder, and these reasons override any reasons to act in a way that is kind or merciful to others.

What causes their lack of motivation to avoid evil? Some commentators suggest that the causes of violent criminal behavior and the corresponding lack of regard for ethical principles include graphic video games, the media's blurring of reality and fantasy, the breakdown of the family unit, longer working and shopping hours, 24-hour-a-day television with 300 channels of sex and violence, and so on. However, if these were the causes, then serial murder would be a twentieth-century "invention." The history I present here shows that serial killers are not a modern-day marvel and though the statistics on the prevalence of serial killers are murky at best, it appears that their numbers have not increased much over the years. On the contrary, evidence of serial murder shows that historically it often took place on a much grander scale than found today, proving that a disregard for the moral, and a failure to be motivated by "being good," is far from a modern-day phenomenon.

Moral Skepticism and the Serial Killer

Moral skepticism is a common view today. We regularly meet people who disagree with us about many "hot" issues, such as homosexual marriage, or the use of animals in medical experiments. When we come upon a view different from our own, we might argue for a bit, but we often feel that there is no way to really decide what the right answer is. We can't appeal to religion. Appeals to the Bible (or any holy book) will only be taken seriously by people who already believe in the Bible (or holy book); those from another religion will be unmoved by such reasons. We can't appeal to science. As much as we might like to, human beings can't observe *evil* – we can't develop a scientific instrument that measures it or records its presence, because it is not a physical thing. Without any way to confirm when something is good or when it is evil, it is easy to see why *epistemic moral skeptics* avoid making final judgments about problems in ethics – they don't believe that there is a way for us to come to know what is really right and wrong.

But there is another way to be a moral skeptic – one that involves actions rather than knowledge. While epistemic moral skeptics doubt that we can come to know good and evil, *practical moral skeptics* believe that we might actually know what is good, but not be motivated to do it. For example, let's say I do not doubt that it is wrong to smoke cigarettes. I know that it is very likely to harm my body, and that I could give the money spent on a pack of smokes to charity where it could feed a hungry child. Yet, knowing these things, I steal out one night and buy a pack, because it is fun to do so, or because I am addicted or subject to peer pressure. I was not skeptical about my knowledge of right and wrong; rather, I was just not motivated to do right and avoid wrong. One could make a similar argument for many vices, such as drinking too much, or doing illegal drugs, or, well, serial killing. And this is why a history of serial killing will be useful to the practical moral skeptic: the behavior of serial killers through the centuries does not show that they are confused about good and evil, or dubious about their knowledge. Rather, they are simply motivated by factors more powerful than moral codes, compassion, and kindness.

A Brief History of Serial Killers

Many would suspect that the author would start with one of the most famous killers, Jack the Ripper, the unidentified English killer of prostitutes who continues to appear on celluloid even today. Yet Jack, though often credited as the modern-day father of serial murder, is far from the first.

History does not remember many of the names and deeds of serial killers low in social station, or those without the resources to execute their murderous drives on a large scale. Thus, many historically known serial killers belonged to royalty, such as fifteenth-century killer Vlad the Impaler, and Gilles de Raise and Countess Elizabeth Bathory in the seventeenth century, who were responsible for more than a thousand murders between them. Ironically, Baron John Emerich Acton, a man with a royal title himself, proclaimed "Power tends to corrupt, and absolute power corrupts absolutely. Great men are almost always bad men." The most prolific killers in history were also "great men" whose motivation for murder and bloodlust far outstripped their motivation to run the state or protect their citizenry. These killers, left to rule their own lands without recourse, were generally not held accountable for the murders they committed, so potential punishment did not serve to motivate them to act morally.

Serial Killers of the Ancient World

The man who holds the title of "World's First Serial Killer" is found two thousand years before Jack the Ripper, in pre-Buddhist China. A member of the Han royal family, Liu Pengli was made the king of Jidong in 144 BCE by his cousin, Emperor Jing. During his reign, he set a precedent for many royal murderers who have littered history with the blood of their own subjects. The king habitually gathered a large group of slaves with whom he would pillage his own kingdom. By the end of his murderous reign, he left at least one hundred victims in his wake. The killings committed by the king and his gang were, according to historian Sima Qian, committed merely for sport, and left his subjects too terrified to leave their homes at night.[1]

The murderous raids remained unreported for several decades until the son of one of Pengli's victims told Emperor Jing about them, and Pengli was made to stand trial. The courts demanded that Pengli be executed for his crimes; however, the Emperor decided to show his cousin mercy and instead merely stripped him of his title and exiled him for the rest of his life.

Pengli was a classic psychopathic personality. This personality disorder describes people having few feelings of regret. Devoid of emotional attachment, their motivations for action are based in self-satisfaction rather than concern for others. Psychopaths need relationships, but can also see people as "obstacles to overcome and be eliminated."[2] Psychopaths are usually rational and understand the consequences of their actions. They can explain conventional moral codes easily – they just see no reason to follow them.

Locusta, a commoner by birth, worked under the guidance of Empress Agrippina the Younger and the Emperor Nero. She held great power as a poisoner. In first-century Rome, she murdered hundreds of people, including Emperor Claudius.[3] The woman's talents were used among the wealthy to dispose of unwanted family members, spouses, or lovers, yet she also used her poisoning skills for purely hedonistic enjoyment. According to Latin scribe Lucius Apuleius Platonicus, when a customer came to see her and asked about the effectiveness of her poisoning techniques, Locusta retrieved one of her slaves – kept for this purpose – and poisoned him in front of the customer. Locusta opened an underground school where she taught her art to over a hundred pupils. Locusta's poisoning spree and royal protection came to an end when Nero took his own life, leaving her unable to hide from execution.

These two ancient serial killers are described in a small handful of surviving records that teach us about this most extreme human behavior. These records suggest they had no social constraints and no fear or punishment to motivate them to stop. They had the power to fulfill their fantasies, little empathy, and violent urges. Thus, they found abundant reason to kill and no reason to abstain.

Serial Killers of the Renaissance

The end of the ancient world did not mark the end of those with high social status taking advantage of their prestige to pursue bloodthirsty ends. After a career as a noted captain in the armies of Joan of Arc, Count

Gilles de Montmorency, the Baron de Rais, led a reclusive life away from the public eye. According to the court reports, he abducted hundreds of children who had come to the castle begging for food. De Rais secreted the children into the castle, where they were sodomized or raped before – according to his accomplice Etienne Corrillaut – being killed "sometimes by decapitating them, sometimes by cutting their throats, sometimes by dismembering them, sometimes by breaking their necks with a stick, and that there was a weapon specifically for their execution, known as a braquemard"[4] (a short, double-edged sword). Much of the testimony given at de Rais' trial by his accomplices was stricken from the record by the presiding judge due to its graphic nature. According to biographer Jean Benedetti, the child victims, both male and female, were dressed in fine clothing and then taken to a secret room where they awaited their fate. At dinner, de Rais would send for the children, who were wined and dined by their host before the killer's intent was revealed. The children were often fatally wounded before the killer sodomized them; he would slice open their abdomens and play with the internal organs as they lay dying on the dining table.[5] Clearly, de Rais' motives were his sadistic and sexual satisfaction rather than moral kindness or righteousness. Hungry children did not occur for him as a reason to be caring or helpful, but only as an opportunity to satisfy his own urges.

One of the most famous literary characters was in fact based on a real serial killer. Bram Stoker's *Dracula* was named after the fifteenth-century king Vlad Tepes III (the Impaler) or Vlad Dracula (son of the Dragon). His enemies called him *Kaziglu Bey* (Impaler Prince) because he impaled his victims on large poles that littered his kingdom. As the middle son of Vlad II, Vlad III was a great warrior who ascended to the throne of Wallachia. He was a brutal and sadistic man and his claim to the throne was tenuous at best. His best defense was the sight of thousands of his enemies individually impaled and placed along the entries to his crown lands. Many of the victims were brought before the king, who would abuse and torture them before impaling them himself.

Another serial killer from the sixteenth century was in fact a relation of Vlad the Impaler. Countess Elizabeth Bathory, legends claim, would bathe in the blood of her young female victims and use the bodies for witchcraft. While there remains some doubt among modern scholars as to the motives for her actions, there is general agreement that her sadistic treatment of her servant girls directly led to their deaths. She was not motivated by moral codes, but by cruelty, and perhaps the personal power to be gained through the dark arts. Bathory's servants were sent to scour the countryside for female victims for their mistress. The 11-year killing spree came to an end on December 31, 1610, when the Countess's cousin Gyorgy Thurzo, Prime Minister of Hungary, broke into Castle Csejthe and found the dying and dead bodies of over 600 victims. Bathory's accomplices confessed under torture to their roles in procuring victims for the Countess. Their fate was met at the stake where they were burned alive. The Countess's punishment was more cruel and unusual: she was bricked into a room in the castle, where she remained until her death on August 21, 1614.

The royal status of the Renaissance killers provides insight into the corruption of power and the descent into depravity of psychopathic killers. The social mores that allow the rest of us to function in civilized society is obliterated by the psychopaths' needs to fulfill their sexual and murderous desires. Regarding de Rais, his murderous intent may have been fueled by the killings he witnessed during the Hundred Years War, when he fought alongside Joan of Arc. A more recent killer, Art Shawcross (interviewed below), saw action during the Vietnam War and claimed that the killings he saw during the war switched on something in his brain. When he returned to America following his tour, he could not switch that part of his brain off – it needed further feeding, and so he began murdering his victims. Here lies another aspect of motivation – perhaps human beings tend to become violent when they are subject to violence. Perhaps the motivation to be moral comes from living within a society with moral boundaries, and when there are no such boundaries, the human mind adapts in a menacing way to its freedom and power. If this is the case, then our reasons to act will depend on the context we are in. If we think we are in a civilized context, we will behave in moral ways, and if we believe we are in a violent context, then we are motivated to behave in violent, immoral ways.

Serial Killers of the Nineteenth Century

Andreas Bichel, who mutilated young female victims from 1806 to 1809, may have been a model for the later crimes attributed to Jack the Ripper. Known as the Bavarian Ripper, Bichel enticed young women to his home by promising to tell their fortunes with a mysterious magic mirror. The victims were knocked unconscious and stripped. When they awoke they were bound and gagged. Bichel then raped and tortured them before killing them. This psychopathic killer was a thrill-seeker who reveled in watching his victims squirm and fight against their bonds as he began the slow torture and finally the murder. Like Jack the Ripper's victims 80 years later, the girls were cut open from their pubic bone to their sternum. Yet, unlike Jack the Ripper's victims, Bichel's victims were still very much alive when the mutilations began.

Bichel was captured while fearlessly attempting to sell the blood-stained clothing of his victims in the local market, which suggests that the man felt invincible and above any law. At his trial, Bichel described the murder of one of his victims, Catherine Seidel, with relish. He remarked that he used a hammer and wedge to break open the women's breast-bones: "I may say, that during the operation, I was so eager, that I trembled all over, and I longed to rive off a piece and eat it."[6] It is documented that he would often achieve orgasm while fingering the intestines of his still-living victims following the first long cut. Psychopaths, suffering from pathological egocentricity,[7] require instant self-gratification. Coupled with their lack of remorse, this brings them motivation to act on their urges and no motivation to control themselves.

A year before Jack the Ripper began to kill, Johann Hoch began his campaign as a Bluebeard serial killer. Beginning in 1887, Hoch, born Johann Schmidt, married woman after woman, insuring them for vast amounts of money before poisoning them. Not one of his brides lived past the wedding night. He was executed for his crimes in 1906. Unlike many of his counterparts, Hoch's motive for murder was purely greed. Having received funds following the death of his first wife, he found that few questions were raised as he murdered each wife, until the final family began asking questions, which brought about his demise. Most serial killers choose their victims within a very small timeframe; the long-term stalking of a single victim is quite rare. Hoch took the time to choose his brides carefully and with much patience, selecting wealthy women with few family ties, and wooing them before proposing marriage, a union that always resulted in murder.

Jack the Ripper remains one of the world's most infamous killers. He appears in more films than any other, including Johnny Depp's *From Hell*, Alfred Hitchcock's silent thriller *The Lodger*, *The Man in the Attic* with Jack Palance, and even Sherlock Holmes' own investigation of the murders in *Murder by Decree*.[8] He has inspired countless theories of conspiracy and hypothetical solutions regarding the murders.

What type of killer would murder his victims in suburban streets, in the view of others, or along the lines of the local constabulary beats? Jack the Ripper, from all accounts, appeared to be almost invisible, if not invincible. He was almost caught by one witness, Louis Diemshultz, who was driving his pony and cart through the gates into Dutfields' Yard where the elusive killer was cutting the throat of Elizabeth Stride. Yet he still chose to find another victim in short order, to finish the job. In a time of strict moral codes, including the sexual vacuity of an entire nation, Jack the Ripper chose the most sexually explicit victims (prostitutes) and exposed them, degrading them even beyond death. The poor unfortunates, some of them the worse for drink when they met their demise, were found exposed, their skirts and petticoats pulled up to show their genitals in a most un-Victorian way.

The nineteenth-century killers' stories suggest that power continues to be one of their primary motivations. Like the royal serial killers, they sought material gain from their victims as well as perverse sexual satisfaction. The nineteenth-century killers showed a more open defiance toward commonly accepted social morality than had been seen before. Perhaps because they were not royalty (although one theory suggests that Jack the Ripper was, in fact, a member of the royal family), they were motivated to show their disdain for the ruling morality. By openly violating the rules governing society, they could show that they had power, and that they could achieve gratification in spite of the law and social disapproval.

Serial Killers of the Early Twentieth Century

One of the most unusual serial murderers in the early twentieth century has, like Jack the Ripper, inspired many films, including Hitchcock's *Psycho*, *Texas Chainsaw Massacre*, and *Silence of the Lambs*. Ed Gein, a cannibalistic serial killer from Plainfield, Wisconsin, did not have a high body count, but the mobile made of noses, the belt made of nipples, and the upside-down, hanging, gutted bodies that met police investigators have brought the killer's name to infamy. Some may argue that Ed Gein was not really a serial killer, having only murdered two victims, but had striking peculiarities – he exhumed several dead bodies and made a variety of objects from their skin, and took cannibalism as well as the desecration of corpses to a shocking level – hence his place in horror film history.

Carl Panzram boasted the murder of hundreds of victims. As a child in juvenile detention, the would-be killer saw boys treated harshly by the guards and learned to stifle his own emotions, not showing pain when he himself was beaten. This ability to distance himself from pain made murder an easy progression for the boy as he became a man. He said in his memoirs:

> From the treatment I received while there [at juvenile detention] and the lessons I learned from it, I had fully decided when I left there just how I would live my life. I made up my mind that I would rob, burn, destroy and kill every where I went and everybody I could as long as I lived. That's the way I was reformed.[9]

These chilling words describe how his moral motivations were shaped by the reformation center. Even when faced with his own execution in 1930, the killer was clearly uninterested in the moral value of any life, including his own. He hissed at the executioners, who he believed were taking too long, "I could hang ten men while you're fooling around!"[10]

A contemporary of Panzram was the sexually perverse Albert Fish. Following his arrest, Fish explained to a psychiatrist the extent of his perversions, which were so shocking that Fish was x-rayed in an attempt to prove he was lying. However, the x-rays revealed the truth, showing dozens of needles he had inserted into his perineum region in an attempt to inflict pain while gaining sexual relief through masturbation. Fish was suspected of the murders of up to a hundred children, though some argue that this figure may be an exaggeration. Growing up in an orphanage following the breakdown of his parents' marriage, Fish witnessed the abuse of many of the boys, and was abused himself. Rather than be repulsed by what he saw, according to Fish, something "took root" in his head, and he claimed that he "always had a desire to inflict pain on others" and he seemed to enjoy "everything that hurt."[11] The killer knew no bounds to his violent fantasies and fetishes. He was known to need hospitalizing following the burns he suffered around his buttocks, acquired in his attempts to set alight alcohol-soaked cotton swabs inside his anus. Fish tried almost every known sexual perversion, and according to the trial judge "some perversions never heard of before."[12] Always in pursuit of the ultimate thrill, Fish had tried all manner of societal taboos, and even enjoyed the prospect of his own execution. In 1936 a trial reporter described how "his watery eyes gleamed at the thought of being burned by a heat more intense than the flames with which he often seared his flesh to gratify his lust."[13]

This era of serial killers shows us another aspect of motivation – a delight in pain, perverse mutilation, and death that is so strong and persistent, it obscures the drive for self-preservation.

The Golden Age of Serial Killers

Serial killers increasingly made front-page news from the 1960s to the 1980s – the "Golden Age of Serial Killers." Ted Bundy, "Son of Sam" David Berkowitz, Jeffrey Dahmer, John Wayne Gacy – these killers need little introduction, and this tells us something about what motivates more "ordinary" people. Serial killers were revered as the epitome of psychopathy, both by criminal and psychological professionals and by the general public. Modern criminology was born, and behavioral scientists became the heroes and heroines of popular fiction, while the FBI became the epicenter of world research on serial killers and psychopaths. Killers were no longer locked up to await execution, but were interviewed and studied. We became openly fascinated with the deranged and the violent.

With the advent of forensic detection techniques there has been a decrease in numbers of victims per killer. But what serial killers have lost in kill rate they have made up for in sensationalist popularity. With the creation of the Internet and the ubiquity of cable TV, serial killers have become tremendously popular. They are found on the news and in bestselling books, movies, and songs. Web lists encourage their fanatical "groupies." More than thirty years after his incarceration, Charles Manson[14] still receives at least four fan letters every day. Before his execution, John Gacy's paintings sold for hundreds of dollars; now they are worth thousands. We want to own their art, write to them, read about them, and view portrayals of their lives and deeds. We are motivated to be moral, but we are also riveted by the immoral; we are motivated to watch, but not to participate.

Serial Killers Today: Conversations on Motivation

Serial killers I have interviewed have given us even clearer vision regarding their practical moral skepticism. They are motivated by fame and public portrayals, by fictionalizations, by fatigue, by anger, and more. They also question our motivations as they observe our political behavior and our sensationalist use of them as media icons. They reflect back to us a less than perfect moral image – we too are not always motivated to be kind or selfless.

Robert "Bobby" Joe Long, one of Florida's serial killers currently on death row, used our interviews to try to separate the killer from the person he is today; to show that the media had falsely portrayed him as "The Bob Thing."[15] He lost his motivation to destroy other people after the rape of his final victim, whom he released after a 26-hour assault. He had already abducted and raped a 17-year-old girl and found himself tired and unable to continue. The dual life he led – one of normalcy juxtaposed against one of murder and rape – had worn him down and he allowed the girl to escape with her life. He freed his victim and went to a cinema, where he saw federal police agents surround him. When he left the cinema, the agents followed him outside, where snipers waited on several buildings. He was arrested on the spot. Though he continues to fight his sentence, he also expresses relief that his killing spree is over. Bobby Joe Long finally became motivated to avoid evil, but he was motivated by fatigue rather than empathy.

Long also examined our motivations and the motives of the media. He talked extensively about being "freakified" by the press for his crimes. He claimed that societal perceptions of him are warped and that the crimes alone do not personify him. He believes that the media "by freakifying [him], it separated [him] from everyone else, and by doing so, it made it easier to fuck-over [him], and do whatever it is 'they' wish to do to [him]."[16] He noted that there is "no doubt you've seen this freakifying of [him]"[17] because he realizes that people listen to the media and believe what they say. For their own profit and notoriety, reporters distort who he is, with no concern as to how Long is impacted. As he disregarded the moral principle "do no harm," so the media disregard moral principles of respectfulness and truth-telling. They too are just not motivated to do the right thing.

Serial killer Ivan Milat, known in Australia as the "Backpacker Killer" for the murders of seven backpackers from 1989 to 1992, also complained about the motivations of the media and politicians in his interview. He suggested that he was being used by politicians through the press, so that they could show off how tough their policies were on crime, or how successful their new programs were. He commented that he would lose little luxuries whenever the media got wind of what he had in his cell. In one interview he protested "you can tell it is an election year – they have taken my sandwich maker off me again."[18]

New York serial killer Arthur Shawcross, who died recently, talked at length about how he was very "in control of his actions" and how his later murders were purposeful and skillful. After he was paroled, he began his murder campaign, in which he raped and killed many women, primarily prostitutes. Shawcross often talked about being the monster that one sees at night in one's sleep.[19] He explained that he usually led a normal life, but when the anger took over he became what he called a "monster."[20] He spoke of his crimes dispassionately; he saw no reason to be moved by moral rules. Instead, he loved to talk about his ability to regulate his own blood pressure while murdering his victims. This lack of passion for his victims contrasted with his pleasure and pride in his lack of emotion. He was motivated by anger and by controlling that anger with precise and careful action.

Like Long, Shawcross enjoyed his contribution to popular fiction. Long described the Dragon character in Thomas Harris's *Red Dragon* as simply "a very strange bird," one whom he related to well, adding that he felt more akin to the Dragon than to the more infamous Hannibal Lecter.[21] Many decades after his capture, Shawcross still relished the fact that Thomas Harris based parts of Hannibal Lecter on him.

These motivations actually served to help Shawcross achieve difficult things, just as the thought of a good grade might motivate us to study harder. Shawcross actually complained about how long it took to murder his victims. Several of the killer's prostitute victims were strangled during a sex act. Shawcross said, "You can't believe how long it's [*sic*] takes for them to die. I had to hold them for 4 … 5 minutes before they were finally dead. People don't understand that takes a lot of strength."[22] Australian serial killer David Birnie was a little more emotional, but also found ways to motivate himself through the difficult tasks. When asked why he did it, he responded, after a very long pause, "It is awful, very awful."[23] And yet Birnie killed many times in spite of the fact that he found it unpleasant.

The words of these killers, and the actions of their predecessors, strongly suggest that there are times when one can understand a moral code and know right from wrong, but simply not care. Practical moral skeptics claim that in the real world we are not always motivated to do the right thing; indeed, we may have strong and compelling reasons to do bad things. Just as we might spend money on frivolous pleasures, like renting a video of *Henry: Portrait of a Serial Killer* rather than sending our extra funds to charity, so Long, Shawcross, and our historical killers could reason and understand good actions. They just were motivated to act in morally depraved ways. Sometimes there is no motivating reason to behave morally.

NOTES

1   Sima Qian, *Records of the Grand Historian*, Vol. 1: *Han Dynasty*, revd. edn., trans. Burton Watson (New York: Columbia University Press, 1993), p. 387.

2   Oregon Counseling, "The Psychopathic Personality," available online at www.oregoncounseling.org/Handouts/PsychopathicPersonality.htm (accessed September 25, 2009).

3   Vicki Leon, *Outrageous Women of Ancient Times* (New York: John Wiley, 1998).

4   Jean Benedetti, *Gilles de Rais* (New York: Stein and Day, 1972), p. 114.

5   Ibid., p. 152.

6   Amanda Howard and Martin Smith, *River of Blood: Serial Killers and Their Victims* (Florida: Universal, 2004).

7   Hervey M. Cleckley, *The Mask of Sanity* (Pasadena: Textbook Publishers, 2003).

8   See Amanda Howard, *The Crime Web*, www.thecrimeweb.com (accessed September 25, 2009) for hundreds more film references.

9   Howard and Smith, *River of Blood*, p. 249.

10 Ibid., p. 250.

11 Ibid., p. 123.

12 Harold Schechter, *Deranged* (New York: Pocket Books, 1990).

13 Howard and Smith, *River of Blood*, p. 126.

14 Some may argue about Charles Manson's name here, as he is not considered a true serial killer.

15 Interview with Robert Joe Long, April 26, 2001.

16 Ibid.

17 Ibid.

18 Interview with Ivan Milat, 2003.

19 Interview with Arthur Shawcross, July 14, 2003.

20 Ibid.

21 Interview with Robert Joe Long, July 26, 2001.

22 Interview with Arthur Shawcross, May 2006.

23 Interview with David Birnie, May 2005.

CHAPTER 5

ARE PSYCHOPATHIC SERIAL KILLERS EVIL?

Are They Blameworthy for What They Do?

The Puzzle

Can you be really, really evil and still not morally responsible for the evil things that you do? Sometimes we are tempted to say no. The worry seems to be that if we deny that someone is responsible for the evil things that he or she does, then the evildoer cannot really be evil. I think this picture is mistaken, for some very interesting reasons. That's what I am going to explore in this chapter – the idea that someone can be really profoundly evil and not responsible for what he or she does. If I am right, psychopathic serial killers may well be an instance of just this sort.

(To avoid some confusion, I'll start by saying a few things that will probably strike you as obvious. Still, people sometimes run these things together when they aren't being as precise as we'll need to be. So, bear with me for a few paragraphs while I sort out some basic but important details.)

Psychopaths and serial killers are not the same thing. They can be, but they don't have to be. As I will use the term *psychopath*, this is a psychiatric category, and one that does not necessarily involve killing anyone. And indeed, many real-world psychopaths never kill anyone. Rather than killing, they only inflict the pettier miseries on people around them. In contrast, killing seems to be a pretty strict requirement for a serial killer.

Still, we should be careful because the serial killer category can be slippery. What, exactly, counts as serial killing? Some traditional criteria point to three or more murders over 30 days, with psychological gratification as an important motive. Still, we might start to wonder whether that standard can be met by lots of people we don't ordinarily think of as serial killers. Might an enthusiastic battlefield soldier count as a serial killer? How about a doctor who routinely performs euthanasia or abortion out of conviction? Could there be serial killers of non-human entities? I'm not going to try to answer these questions, interesting as they may be. My point here is merely that the category of serial killer is plausibly broad enough to include non-psychopaths. So, not all psychopaths are serial killers and not all serial killers are psychopaths.

Thus, the categories come apart. Still, I want to focus on those cases where the categories come together, where we have a psychopathic serial killer. I want to focus on these cases because I think they can help us get to the heart of some very interesting puzzles about the relationship between responsibility and other forms of moral evaluation. Or, to capture the issue in the form of a question: Does madness mean no badness?

Let me explain. Normally, how enthusiastic we are to blame people for any horrible things they do depends, in part, on how horrible the act is. If you hear me tell a rude joke, you might get irritated. However, depending on the circumstances and how well we know each other you might not say anything at all. In contrast, if I maliciously slam a crowbar into your gut, as soon as you catch your breath you will very likely say something about it. In both cases you will have very good reason to blame me, but the strength and intensity of that blame is at least partly a response to the apparent badness of the action.

On this picture, serial killing looks to be a *very morally bad thing*.[2] But here's the thing: it matters who is doing the killing. Every once in a while we hear a story of how some young kid does some or another thing that results in the death of his or her sibling. Asphyxiation, or death from lack of air, is perhaps the most common cause of accidental death among kids, and it may seem particularly heartbreaking when it was done by one young sibling to another, neither understanding what was happening. These stories are really heartbreaking. No one would deny that such cases are really terrible outcomes. But it isn't obvious that the kid who killed the other kid deserves our blame. In order to deserve blame – even for killing – the wrongdoer has to be the right kind of person, one who (roughly) understands the difference between right and wrong. So, to the extent to which kids don't understand the significance of what they are doing, they get off the hook. In general, it seems that when someone doesn't understand what he or she is doing we are prepared to absolve that person for what would otherwise be a bad act. Unless, of course, earlier that person tried to make it so he or she wouldn't understand at the crucial later time. (For example, it used to be that people would sometimes drink heavily so they would conveniently have an "excuse" for bad behavior; cultural norms on this seem to have shifted a bit, though.)

So, that seems like a good general principle: in order to be blamed for doing something bad, you have to understand that the bad thing *is* a bad thing. But what does this principle tell us about psychopathic serial killers? Do they know that what they are doing is a morally bad thing?

On the Virtues of *Philosophy Interruptus*

In the preceding section I was doing a bit of traditional philosophical stage-setting: making distinctions, clarifying terms, and saying a bit about the relationship of our concepts to one another. Here's one way of putting the philosophical project of this chapter: we are trying to figure out what we should say about something – the moral responsibility of psychopaths – when there is no clear, widely agreed method for figuring out how to answer questions like this. What we do is generate some reasons for thinking one thing rather than another. We try to figure out what general rules can explain the judgments we are confident about but might also help us understand cases where we are less confident. But we also have to be very careful about how far we take this process. In some sense, it is very easy to do philosophy. You can do it from the chair you are sitting in by just thinking about issues and trying to reason carefully. The temptation of a comfortable philosopher's armchair is to think that we can get by understanding the world without bothering to study what is already known about it. What makes this temptation particularly powerful to at least some of us is that, in some sense, we could learn quite a bit about the world without ever studying scientific research on our subject matter. That is, we could imagine different ways psychopaths might be, and then try to work through explanations of what we should think about them if they did turn out to be that way. But that's just *lazy*. When there is good evidence about how something is, we should learn it first.

Still, science doesn't answer all the interesting questions. No amount of experimental evidence will by itself tell us what to say about the responsibility of psychopaths. At least so far, science does not do a very good job settling questions of moral responsibility. So, inasmuch as we are interested in this question, we are going to need to do some philosophy. Knowing what the research on psychopaths already says gives us a leg up on doing that philosophy. So, I'm going to put the philosophy on "pause" for a moment to quickly review some of the important details about psychopaths as described in the scientific literature.

What You Don't Know About Psychopathic Serial Killers

I've found that most folks are pretty confident they know, more or less, what a psychopath is. If you don't believe me, try asking a few people what the difference is between a psychopath and a sociopath. With any luck, you'll get treated to a convoluted discussion about that person's personal theory about the difference. (Really, I recommend trying it: it is surprisingly entertaining to hear people's pet theories about this difference!) But I'm willing to bet almost none of your friends will know what the real difference is – unless, that is, your friends work in psychiatry or have some peculiar interest in psychopaths.

Don't believe me? Well, let's see what you know. Did you know the folks now identified as psychopaths used to be thought of as suffering from something called "moral idiocy?" Or that psychopaths are oftentimes incredibly charming but prone to getting the usages of words wrong? Did you know that psychopaths tend to have trouble holding down a job or staying in a relationship? Did you realize that "psychopath" and "sociopath" are different labels for the same thing?

I want to talk about that last bit – the psycho/sociopath distinction – for a moment. The history of these terms is interesting and serves as a cautionary tale for how popular conceptions of things can mislead us about the nature of things. "Psychopath" was introduced by the psychiatric community as a term to refer to people with a very specific set of behavioral symptoms that had been previously associated with "moral idiocy," "moral insanity," or "moral imbecility." There was some variation in how these terms were used, but they all shared the idea that someone thus described had the inability to recognize moral rules and to respond to them in the appropriate way. So, "psychopath" was just a new word for a category that existed in the scientific literature from around 1860 or so. But then popular culture got a hold of the term and started using it in ways that departed from the way psychiatrists and psychologists had intended it to be used. Psychopaths made good characters in stories, movies, and popular media, but the folks telling these stories were not concerned about precise medical usage. In this sense, the word is much like how "depression" or "hysterical" came to be. These are terms that started out with very specific meanings in medical contexts, but came to be popularized and to greater and lesser degrees detached from their medical usage. So, rather than running the risk of having popular usage contaminating medical practice in the case of "psychopath," a new word was introduced as a technical term to cover that category. That's how "sociopath" was born. (Later, some researchers tried to draw a distinction between psychopaths and sociopaths, but the distinction never really caught on in the diagnostic community.) However, history repeated itself. "Sociopath" made its way into the popular vocabulary and the folks who decide on categories of mental disorders (the authors of the periodically updated *Diagnostic and Statistical Manual*, a handbook with rules for diagnosing mental disorders) thought it best to try to change the label yet again. This time, though, they came up with a term that was not so catchy, so the risk of Hollywood appropriating it is close to zero. The contemporary label is *anti-social personality disorder*.

While all this was happening, some researchers (notably, Robert Hare) came to think that there is a population of people who imperfectly overlap with those diagnosed with anti-social personality disorder. Hare and others took up the old term "psychopathy" to refer to this population. For our purposes, what is important is that there are some striking features to this group. First, they tend to have very bad impulse control and this seems to be correlated with some important differences in the brain. Second, psychopaths seem incapable of experiencing shame and guilt, and they don't respond to depictions of harm in the way we do. Third, they have great difficulty recognizing and drawing distinctions between rules that are somewhat arbitrary ("conventions") and rules that are widely recognized as "moral" or less arbitrary. (More on this in a moment.) Finally, there is no known effective treatment for psychopathy. This is to say, we currently have no way of fixing those defects of the brain and the habits of behavior that account for psychopathic behavior.

This last bit – about the "unfixable" nature of psychopaths – is important. It is important because part of what needs fixing in psychopaths is their apparent inability to experience emotions that are necessary for us to regulate our moral lives. If psychopaths can't experience guilt or shame, then the prospect of experiencing these emotions can't affect what they do. If they don't have aversion reactions – the "ick!" or "I don't want to see that!" reaction – to depictions of harm (e.g., a mutilated limb), then these things don't structure their behavior. But these reactions are precisely how many of us come to acquire and hold on to our diverse moral convictions and our sense of what is right and wrong. So, even if psychopaths were otherwise completely like us, they would be at a severe disadvantage when it comes to regulating their own behavior. (For that matter, it puts *us* at a disadvantage when we try to encourage their good behavior and discourage their bad behavior.)

The distinctive psychological profile of the psychopath isn't limited to an absence of remorse, shame, or aversion to the perception of harm. As I noted above, it also includes an important inability to recognize the difference between what psychologists call "conventional" and "moral" rules. (I put these terms in quotes to mark the fact that these are labels; it is an open question whether these labels accurately capture any Real Moral Rules, whatever those turn out to be.) Conventional rules are rules that we (often collectively) make up or stipulate. Laws are generally like this, and so are the rules of many games and social interactions. In the US it is ordinarily wrong to drive on the left-hand side of the road. However, if there were no law against it or we didn't already have some rule in place, it would not be wrong to drive on the left-hand side of the road (provided you could do so without putting yourself or other people at risk). Similarly, the rule in football that each team can have no more than 11 players on the field during a play is conventional. Leagues could change it if they decided to (indeed, some high school leagues use an 8-person rule).

Conventions cover a lot of our interactions. They are, however, in some sense "local" or bound to particular places and contexts. The rules governing driving, game-playing, manners, and so on are all tied to particular places, times, and groups of people. There are, however, some rules that don't seem so straightforwardly conventional. Rules about injuring other people seem to be like that. We don't need to find out what the local rules are for certain kinds of actions. If you were parachuted into a random country without knowing anything about the local people, you could be pretty confident that it would be wrong to walk up to the first person you meet and sucker punch 'em for fun. Pretty much anywhere, it is wrong to hurt people "for fun" or "just to see." This difference – one where certain forms of rule-breaking are always bad – is an important one, marking out what some psychologists call "moral" rules. So, we might put the difference this way: "conventional" rules rule out things *because* we (or some relevant group of us) say so, whereas "moral" rules rule out things regardless of whether or not someone says so.

My point is *not* that there is necessarily a real difference in these rules. At the end of the day, maybe it will turn out that all rules are arbitrary or that there is no fundamental difference between "moral" and "conventional" rules, as psychologists have characterized them. That would be interesting. However, the point I'm trying to make doesn't depend on whether or not there is a particularly fundamental or deep difference. My point is just this: you and I recognize that there is an *apparent* difference. And it is the ability to recognize *that* difference – the on-the-face-of-it difference between "moral" and "conventional" rules – that psychopaths lack.

The inability to distinguish between these kinds of rules means that psychopaths are in a tough position – they can't recognize when they are breaking rules that matter a lot to us (whether or not those rules reflect the *true ultimate nature of morality*, whatever that turns out to be). It is sometimes tempting to think that maybe they know something we don't know or can't admit. But that is to misunderstand, to confuse blindness for knowledge. It isn't that the psychopath knows the rule but realizes some dark secret that the rule is bogus. Rather, the psychopath is *blind to the rule in the first place*. The psychopath can't even see what we are talking about – that there is, at least on the surface, a big difference between hurting others and eating your chocolate cake before the entree has arrived.

Why do we think they are blind in this way? Well, according to researchers who study these folks for a living, if you offer a psychopath a reward for trying to sort rule-breaking of conventions from rule-breaking of moral cases they simply can't do it. And if you try to explain the difference to them, they will think you are trying to pull a fast one on them. Let me explain.

It is hard to get inside the head of a psychopath. To get a sense of what his or her world must look like, at least with respect to "moral" rules, you would have to imagine a scenario where people were trying to convince you that there is a hugely important difference in lots of everyday actions that seem all roughly the same to you. For example, they might tell you that there are some ways of getting out of bed that are okay and others that aren't. And, we might imagine, every attempt to explain when the rules hold or don't turns on the supposed significance of some invisible feature of the world – *mrah*, let us call it – that you don't really get, that never plays a role in your feelings and thinking, and that doesn't seem particularly important even when it is explained to you. In the scenario we are imagining, I suspect it would be hard for you to directly care a lot about *mrah* because you wouldn't ever really be sure when it is there and why it matters. Sure, you get that people talk a lot about it and seem concerned about it, but as far as you can make out, this looks really random and arbitrary. If someone asks you to distinguish between the *mrah*-causing actions and the non-*mrah* causing actions you couldn't reliably do it. Indeed, you might start to think they were trying to pull the wool over your eyes, controlling you for their own purposes by making up a difference and pretending that everyone can see it.

I don't know if that helps. But *mrah* is just "harm" spelled backward. And harm seems to be an important thing that psychopaths just don't understand very well. Even when they get what counts as harm, notoriously they have a difficult time caring about it. However, harm just is what makes a lot of things really, genuinely bad (at least, as far as we're concerned). Blindness to harm is thus a serious problem for them and us. If you can't see it, it is hard to learn to respond to it even if everyone else seems to be doing so. In the case of psychopathic serial killers, it may be impossible for them to recognize and respond to the badness of killing, just as it would be tough for you and me to respond to someone's frantic worries about the *mrah* that we are doing as we go about our daily life, pursuing our desires and trying to achieve our various goals.

Back to Philosophy

Even if we accept that there is something importantly different about psychopaths, these facts don't settle whether or not psychopathic serial killers can be blamed for any wrongdoing they commit. To figure that out, we need to do some philosophy.

As I noted before, on the one hand we tend to think that serial killing is pretty obviously the kind of thing that seems blameworthy. On the other hand, we also seem to think that not just anyone can be blamed. When we blame someone, we seem to presuppose that they were able to understand the nature of what they were doing, that it was in some important sense morally bad. This, though, is exactly where the scientific study of psychopaths is a useful complement to our philosophizing. As I was discussing above, psychopaths seem to lack the ability to recognize the moral significance of what it is that they are doing, at least when it comes to harming others. So, if our earlier proposal was correct – that blaming requires a kind of understanding on the part of the wrongdoer – then it looks like psychopaths, even psychopathic serial killers, aren't really the right sorts of beings to be on the receiving end of our blaming. They are surely doing really bad things. But rabid dogs, hurricanes, floods, and viruses can bring lots of harm to the world without being morally responsible in the ordinary, full-blooded sense of the phrase.

If all this is right, we ought not (morally) to blame psychopaths for harming others. That means that psychopathic serial killers aren't, properly speaking, blameworthy for what they do.[3] I'm not saying it would be easy for us to stop blaming psychopathic serial killers for their killing. And I'm not saying we would have no reason to remove them from society. On the contrary, we have some of the very best reasons to remove them from society! They are a threat to us and nothing we or they can otherwise do will keep them from victimizing us. So, those threats need to be addressed in effective ways. In this, though, the appropriate reaction seems closer to quarantining, or what medical personnel do with people suffering from dangerous, highly infectious diseases. We have good reason to keep ourselves and the disease apart, but the disease and its carriers are themselves unfortunate pieces of nature gone wrong. They are not anything we rightly can make a target of our blame, resentment, and indignation. We might feel these emotions, of course, but there is some sense in which they are misfiring or inappropriately directed.

At any rate, that's what seems to follow from the available scientific evidence and the bit of moral theorizing we did at the start. At this point, though, things get very tricky. You could think this outcome is so bad that we need to revisit the moral theorizing. Sometimes philosophical arguments land you in places that suggest the argument must have gone wrong at some point. We can't rule out this possibility, but I do think there is a further concern floating around here that, if addressed, might make this conclusion seem more sensible and less bleeding-heart pansy than it surely seems.

Psychopathic Serial Killing and Evil

Let's start with the idea that there is something especially horrific about serial killing, something that puts it beyond the reach of excuse by medical diagnosis. To see what that might be, I think it helps to invoke a different moral category, distinct from blameworthiness. I want to talk about evil.

The term *evil* gets used in a lot of ways. Sometimes people use it as a bombastic substitute for "morally bad." Sometimes it gets used in a coldly cynical way, as a way of characterizing our enemies when we want to mobilize social or political support for our fights with those enemies. But there is a sense of evil that picks out a special kind of psychology, different from run-of-the-mill moral badness. It is that sense of evil we invoke when we say something like "kicking puppies is bad, but putting them in an operating blender and laughing about it is just plain *evil*." Although doing this to puppies is certainly comparatively worse than kicking them, at least sometimes the point of invoking the idea of evil is to say more than blending puppies is extra bad. *Evil* marks out a kind of person or a kind of motivation that is qualitatively different than ordinary moral badness. Hannibal Lecter is evil in this special sense. Maybe Agent Smith in the *Matrix* movies is like this, and certainly Emperor Palpatine from the *Star Wars* movies is along these lines. Although he's a bit more complicated, the Joker in *The Dark Knight* might fit the bill.

In this usage, "evil" is a category that picks out people or actions that desire to see other people harmed for no reason beyond the desire itself. To be evil in this sense is to want to see others harmed for no further reason. This is very different than wanting to harm people so as to bring about world domination, the arrival of utopian political order, or ordinary compliance with the powers that be. In all these cases, the desire to harm people is just a means for accomplishing some other task. The genuinely evil person, in the special sense at hand, wants to see people harmed for no further reason – the desire to see that harm done is all the reason there is for wanting to harm others.

I think it is an open question whether there are many (or any) people who are actually evil in this sense. However, if there are such people I would not be surprised to find that serial-killing psychopaths fit the bill. For example, perhaps a psychopathic serial killer finds fascinating the idea of dissecting a living person, fails to see any objections to doing so beyond the risk of getting caught, and proceeds with the business of torturing and killing people. On my view, this would be evil.

Here's an interesting feature about evil in this sense: it doesn't require that the evil person be responsible for being evil. That is, our evil, psychopathic serial killer need not be responsible for being a psychopath or for any of the things he or she does at all. Evil – profound, genuine, really superbad evil in the sense we've been talking about – just doesn't require responsibility. In this sense it is like being a jerk or a tightwad. These are bad things to be, but your being these things doesn't require that you be responsible for your jerk-ish and tighwad-ish behavior. Maybe you are a jerk because of a brain tumor, or maybe you are a tightwad because of low blood sugar. For all that, it would still be true that you are a jerk and a tightwad.

Now I don't want to pretend that knowing the origins of how you became a jerk or tightwad might not affect our reactions to your behavior. If we know the origins of these things it can affect how we regard the fact of your being a jerk or a tightwad. We might be less willing to blame you, or more likely to explain away your behavior to our mutual friends. Still, many of us would be less willing to hang out with the jerk or to ask for money from the tightwad, regardless of how these defects of character were arrived at.

Coming back to evil, then, I think evil is one of those descriptions of people that is (1) inherently condemnatory (no one wants to be *genuinely* evil, a *true* jerk, or a *real* tightwad) without (2) taking a stand on how that condemnatory nature came to be. It is a bad way to be, and in the case of evil, a really, really bad way to be. There is good reason for us to have a visceral, strongly negative reaction to the evil person and his or her deeds – such people have interests that are strongly at odds with the basic terms of our living together. So we want them expelled, destroyed, or otherwise expunged from our lives when we are convinced that they are among us.

If all of this is right, then we can explain why the non-responsibility of psychopathic serial killers should leave us a bit unhappy. The worry that I noted above was this: focusing on the fact that such predators are not responsible seems to mean that we must abandon our moralized reactions to them (e.g., indignation, resentment, and so on). Any account that concludes with this reaction to psychopathic serial killers must therefore be wrong. What the foregoing remarks on evil help us to see, though, is that this reaction is too quick. While psychopathic serial killers may not be morally responsible for harming others, they might well count as genuinely evil. Nothing about their non-responsibility would affect whether or not they are truly evil.

Matters are complicated in part because our attitudes towards evil are oftentimes wrapped up in the assumption that the evildoer is also responsible for what he or she does. But as I suggested above, that need not be the case. Sometimes evil is as evil does, and that can be enough.

NOTES

1 My thanks to Shaun Nichols and Dominic Murphy for many and several discussions about psychopaths over the years, and to Stephanie Vargas for feedback on this essay.
2 If, however, you are an American undergraduate or similarly contrarian soul, you might be tempted to deny this claim. Perhaps you think morality is relative

in some or another way. Or, maybe you think that morality is merely some invented story we teach people for the purposes of social control. Or, perhaps you think there is some convoluted reason why serial killing turns out to be, on balance, a morally wonderful thing. That's fine, because you can play along anyway. When I use the words *moral* and *morally responsible* and *blameworthy*, you can just think this after each of those terms: *according to the way ordinary people around here think*. The puzzles I am interested in and what we should say about them can be raised on any view that admits we have moral concepts, regardless of whether those moral concepts are all they are cracked up to be.

3   What about free will, you ask? Don't psychopaths have free will? It depends on what you mean by free will. If free will involves an ability to understand the moral significance of what one does, then we should think they lack free will. If free will doesn't require this power, then psychopaths might well have free will. In that case, though, our free-willing psychopaths will still lack something else, a power required for moral responsibility (i.e., the ability to understand that what they are doing is morally wrong).

CHAPTER 6

SYMPATHY FOR THE DEVIL

Can a Serial Killer Ever Be Good?

Can murder be good? And is it possible for a murderer to be a good person? Put aside the one-time murderer and the reluctant murderer. Dark waters beckon us deeper: to delve into the mind of a serial killer, the murderer who kills for pleasure or need. Let us consider the murderer who kills as his way of life, kills as part of who he is, and kills to maintain his "equilibrium" – as what comes "naturally" to him.

Repugnant as it may seem to even consider such questions, we need to challenge our comfortable moral presumptions. Surprisingly, it may be possible for a serial killer to be good. Philosophy often has surprising results. We might believe, with Aristotle, that a person who commits evil deeds, lives an immoderate life, and participates regularly in violent crime is someone who cannot really be happy and flourish as a human being.[1] But Tony Soprano, from HBO's popular television series *The Sopranos*, is a Mafioso who was arguably a flourishing human. Likewise, Dexter Morgan, from Showtime's television series *Dexter*, presents us with a serial killer who makes us question our blanket condemnation against murder. He is an anti-hero we champion; a coldblooded killer we never want caught.

Dexter on Trial

If we rely upon our basic moral intuitions, we readily condemn Dexter. He is, after all, a serial killer. I contend that Dexter deserves a fair trial before we morally condemn him. In this essay we shall provide Dexter his day in court: as defendant in a trial of ethics, rather than law. Ought Dexter to be ethically denounced for his actions? Or should we exonerate him? While a criminal trial hinges upon motive, opportunity, and forensics, an ethical trial hinges upon bringing various ethical theories and tests to bear on the person in question. I will ethically evaluate Dexter Morgan against such touchstones, and show him to be a serial killer who is morally excusable – and, perhaps, even morally praiseworthy.

You, the reader, will be a member of our ethical jury. I will compare Dexter to several traditional philosophical moral standards. Like a member of a criminal jury, you will evaluate the evidence presented – comparing Dexter's life and deeds against the theories that appear on the witness stand. Some witnesses will appeal to you and others may strike you as non-credible or absurd. Like a criminal juror, you are free to dismiss some witnesses and their theories as crazy or irrelevant. And like a criminal juror, you will take all the evidence presented and make your decision about Dexter's morality. Making philosophical judgments is commonly done in this way, so you will be practicing being a philosopher throughout this essay: evaluating arguments, working with concepts, and drawing conclusions based on reasons. Philosophy is the courtroom and ethical theories are the evidence. You deliver the verdict.

The goal of this ethical trial is not to convince every reader to celebrate Dexter's homicidal lifestyle. Rather, the goal is to convince a common jury pool of reasonable people that Dexter's character is morally excusable and perhaps even morally good. By "reasonable" I mean the commonsense person who acknowledges that the world is one of moral grays rather than black and whites, and who already recognizes that there are not necessarily moral absolutes. After all, if one allows for killing in self-defense or in defense of one's children, then one might also allow for a serial killer to murder killers who would prey upon the rest of us.

I will not visit every alleged transgression perpetrated by Dexter throughout the Showtime series. It will be simpler and more philosophically interesting to focus on the general premise of the series: Dexter is a serial killer who exclusively kills murderers. This is a common philosophical strategy – we decide whether or not the action, *in principle*, is good or evil – and then we do not need to examine every action that conforms to the principle.

Four Ethical Tests

During his ethical trial, Dexter will be evaluated via four ethical tests. The Utilitarianism Test asks if Dexter maximizes happiness, overall. That is, does Dexter produce the greatest amount of happiness for the greatest number of people? The Kantian Test asks if Dexter's actions are rational and universalizable, per the *categorical imperative*. That is, can we take the notion of killing killers, and make it a law that everyone ought to follow? The Virtue Theory Test asks whether Dexter can be considered a virtuous human being. To be virtuous, one must strive for personal excellence and function well as a human being. The Social Contract Test asks if you, the reader, would "hypothetically consent" to Dexter's actions. That is, if you were behind a "veil of ignorance" where you didn't know your fate, would you want Dexter patroling your neighborhood, acting as a dark shepherd protecting against the wolves that would devour you or your loved ones – a dark shepherd of lambs who would otherwise go to slaughter?

I will argue that Dexter passes all of these ethical tests and as such should be exonerated as an ethically good individual – or, at the very least – as a morally permissible killer.

Dexter Dreams Darkly: An Overview of Showtime's Dexter Morgan

For the uninitiated, Dexter works as a forensic blood-spatter analyst at the Miami-Metro Police Department. In his free time, he methodically stalks and kills murderers. Particularly, Dexter visits a brand of dark "justice" upon those who have escaped the net of our legal system, either by evading capture or being acquitted due to legal technicalities. Dexter ferrets out who these murderers are, confirms their guilt, stalks them and renders them unconscious, indicts them of their crimes upon wakening (often spurring a gallows confession), and then kills them. Expertly,

Dexter always makes sure to leave no trace, witnesses, or body: he dismembers the corpses into garbage bags, which he dumps into the ocean from his sailboat.

Dexter's targets have killed multiple innocents, without regret or remorse, meanwhile escaping all retribution and justice. Dexter ensures that these murderers pay for their crimes against humanity. Though Dexter is motivated by the homicidal lusts of a serial killer, he is constrained by an ethical code: The Code of Harry (taught to him by his father, Harry Morgan). Dexter abides by this code in deference to his deceased father, but also due to his own recognition that his prey are deserving monsters, even if he is a monster as well. While Dexter may represent a dark hand of justice, we should be clear: justice is not always his primary motivation. Dexter possesses a lust to kill, which he sates by killing killers.

Peculiar for a serial killer, Dexter is a family man – or at least appears to be. Though Dexter is emotionally disassociated, he seems close to his stepsister Debra – a detective for the Miami-Metro PD – and admits that he is "fond of her." Dexter ultimately commits himself to his longtime girlfriend Rita, who later becomes his wife. Though Dexter initially considers Rita to be part of his facade, a "beard" that conceals the true monstrous face beneath, Dexter progressively betrays feelings of affection, protectiveness, and perhaps even love for Rita.

To Rita's children – Astor and Cody – Dexter plays father figure. He feels very protective of them, which reflects in his wrathful condemnation of murderers whose victims are children. Dexter's protectiveness toward children perhaps stems from his horrific childhood experience, when he and his brother witnessed the violent death of their mother and were then left for dead in a shipping container. This highly suggests that the *sociopathy* that Dexter and his biological brother embody is due not to a malfunction in their brain physiology, but to trauma in their childhood.

Last, and primary in Dexter's life – even if just in memory – is Harry, Dexter's deceased adoptive father. Harry adopted Dexter after he and other police officers discovered him, blood-soaked, in the shipping container. As Dexter grew up, Harry discovered Dexter's sociopathic tendencies and trained him to channel his homicidal needs so that he would only kill remorseless murderers. Harry taught Dexter to hone his techniques and *modus operandi* so that he would never be caught. Dexter is very respectful of his father and deferential to the code Harry set out for him. Not only is it Dexter's Ten Commandments, it is the only barrier, they both realize, to keep Dexter from turning into an avaricious and unrestrained monster. Beyond respect and reverence toward his late father, Dexter ultimately betrays some glimmerings of feeling toward him: "If I were capable of love, how I would have loved Harry."

Killing to Maximize Happiness

The easiest ethical vindication of Dexter's killings arrives via *utilitarianism*: an act is ethical if it maximizes overall happiness. An action that makes many people happy is a good one, even if it makes one person unhappy. Killing society's predators, then, might be morally good by preventing the future torture and slaughter of innocent people. Utilitarianism denies that any act is intrinsically wrong, even killing: an act is only *instrumentally* wrong if it fails to maximize happiness. Simply phrased: the ends justify the means.

The famous contemporary example known as the "Ticking Time Bomb" might serve as a template by which to illustrate utilitarian reasoning. Imagine that a rogue CIA agent (similar to Jack Bauer in the television series *24*)[2] has captured a known terrorist, and has him in the room of an abandoned house. The agent knows that the only way to prevent a hidden bomb that the terrorist has planted from exploding in New York City, killing thousands, would be to torture the terrorist to the point of death. Imagine, in addition, that the rogue CIA agent has reliable intelligence that the terrorist deliberately targeted and killed several innocent American citizens prior to his being captured. While we might reject that the Ticking Time Bomb scenario justifies torture and killing generally, we still might acknowledge that, in this case, torturing and killing a terrorist to prevent innocent deaths is morally permissible. The terrorist is already unrepentantly guilty of multiple murders, and he will readily kill several more innocent people if he is not stopped by an action that is, almost without exception, immoral. This is the exception.

Utilitarianism will advocate torturing and killing the terrorist in order to save the innocent lives that he would have taken. Though killing, in general, tends to be counterproductive to maximizing happiness, this case is the exception to the rule. It is clear that the killing of the terrorist, for whatever harm it will perpetrate, will effect the vastly greater good.

Is this moral reasoning not the same in the case of Dexter? Dexter kills an unrepentant multiple murderer who will surely kill more innocent people in the future. Both Dexter and the CIA agents are "rogue" – acting contrary to institutional prescripts, yet both actions seem morally justifiable in similar ways. Killing one evil person to prevent him from inflicting additional suffering and death to a number of innocent people is an ethically justified killing (at least by the lights of utilitarianism).

What would you do, if you had the following choice: you could decide to call or not call the local police to prevent the killing of the terrorist? Would you make that call? Or would you allow the rogue CIA agent to torture and kill the terrorist in order to prevent the bomb explosion from killing thousands of innocent people? If you, as a member of our ethical jury, would not place that phone call, then is seems you condone the actions of the CIA agent. By the same logic, Dexter's actions would also seem to be condoned. Both Dexter and the rogue agent kill a guilty person as the only effective way to save multiple innocent lives. By condoning the torture and killing in the Ticking Time Bomb case as morally permissible, one would seem to provide a moral pardon for Dexter as well.

Kant's Dark Champion

If Dexter is to be lynched by an ethical theory, a philosopher would suspect Kantian ethics to be the hangman. Yet when it relates to retributive killing for the murder of innocents, Immanuel Kant (1724–1804) not only condones killing, but clearly endorses it as a moral imperative. Consider his example of a hypothetical island society that decides to dismantle itself:

> Even if civil society resolved to dissolve itself with the consent of all its members – as might be supposed in the case of a people inhabiting an island resolving to separate and scatter themselves throughout the whole world – the last murderer lying in the prison ought to be executed before the resolution was carried out. This ought to be done in order that every one may realize the desert of his deeds, and that bloodguiltiness may not remain upon the people; for otherwise they might all be regarded as participators in the murder as a public violation of justice.[3]

Dexter, then, represents Kant's just executioner. By killing the murderer, the murderer is respected as a rational being: we apply his own rule of action reciprocally back to him. Deem it the dark side of the golden rule: if we are to do unto others as we would have them do unto us, then, by the same logic, if we do *into* others, we would have them do, similarly, *into* us.

That is, not only should we refrain from inflicting upon others if we ourselves would not wish to be inflicted upon, but by the same token, we should actively inflict upon the individual what he or she would himself inflict upon others.

After all, the golden rule says it's *irrational* to treat others in a way we would not want to be treated; it would be inconsistent. As a rational being, I must recognize that there is nothing special about me that would justify treating others in a way I would not wish to be treated myself. The murderers Dexter targets are rational beings who kill not out of stark insanity or raving lunacy – they know what they are doing. The rule Dexter acts upon – to kill others for his own ends – is a rule we must apply back to him.

Dexter seems, at times, guided by this dark golden rule. In several cases, Dexter kills the murderer with the same type of weapon they employed to kill their victims: a silverware dinner knife, a machete, and so forth. Dexter appears to recognize that such reciprocation of "an eye for an eye" is justly appropriate.

One might impugn Dexter's motivation, of course. According to Kant, an action needs to be performed with the appropriate motive: killing, for instance, should not be driven by emotional vengeance, but by a rational recognition that the murderer's rule of action ought to be respectfully applied back to him. Yet Dexter acts out of homicidal obsession rather than impartial retribution. Dexter, though, does recognize that the infliction upon his "victims" aligns with just retribution, as Kant prescribes. Dexter allows himself to vent his homicidal needs only upon those deserving. In this way, Dexter is abiding by Kantian motivation in constraining himself to only killing killers. Perhaps Dexter is not solely motivated to act out of rational recognition of moral obligation, yet how many of us are? At worst, Dexter is amoral, according to Kantian ethics, not immoral. But perhaps Dexter passes Kant's categorical imperative better than that: after all, Dexter restrains his feral emotions in following the rational law set before him in the Code of Harry. While Dexter's predation may be a mishmash of sociopathic need and rational recognition of moral duty, his restraint in choosing his victims, and the way he kills them, is in rational accordance with Kant's own prescripts toward capital punishment.

Serendipitously, Dexter's homicidal duty even solves a challenge to Kant's dark golden rule. Consider the dilemma Kant's reciprocal rule leaves us: If the killer should be, in turn, killed, who should do the killing? Though we demonstrate respect to the killer by applying his rule of

MATTHEW BROPHY

action back to him, doesn't this violate our own rule of action? Imagine, for instance, that Kant's island society is constituted entirely by pacifists. Would not Kant's prescription that the killer be killed violate the moral commitments of the pacifist citizens, even if they recognized that the killer ought to be killed? Most of us, while not pure pacifists, still feel some moral commitment against killing another human being. It seems an unfair moral burden for any citizen to shoulder that they should have to kill a murderer, when it violates that citizen's own personal moral commitment not to kill others. Who among the citizenry ought to shoulder such a ghastly weight? Uniquely, only Dexter is positioned to kill the murderer without having to sacrifice his moral integrity or commitments; in fact, it satisfies rather than undermines his life projects and commitments. Dexter serves society in washing its bloodguilty hands, without necessitating other citizens to bloody their own.

A Virtuous Devil or a Moral Monster?

Virtue theory doesn't peddle in ethical absolutes, but prescribes that individuals practice and develop character traits befitting well-functioning human beings, so that they may have the best chance of thriving. These character traits are found in moderation. To have deficiencies or excesses in such traits is to have vices. Vices inhibit human beings from functioning and flourishing in their lives.

Dexter starts out as a youth festering with vices. He is excessively cruel (he tortures animals); he lacks empathy and social affiliation. He is not moderate at all and has to develop a character that is more functional. As an adult, Dexter struggles to overcome these obstacles, and through the television series he appears to progress. Successively, the coldbloodedness of Dexter thaws – at least toward those for whom he ought to care. Despite his initial deficiencies in empathy, Dexter appreciates and ultimately appears to love his girlfriend, Rita, and feels protective of her children. He is fond of his sister and is respectful (perhaps even loving) of his deceased stepfather, Harry.

While some of Dexter's virtues may be anemic, they are not absent – and they are ever-increasing over the course of our time with him. While Dexter starts out in a deficit of virtue, he seems to be deliberately aiming at the good life, even if he doubts that he will ever be capable of achieving it. At one point in the series, Dexter feels liberated from his need to kill – it no longer consumes him. It appears as if Dexter had reached a point of moderation in his character traits through his deliberate struggle to control his homicidal lust. Even Aristotle himself might be proud of the progress Dexter has made through aiming at the good life.

"What would Jesus do?" is a common mantra among many Christians. Such inquiry stems from virtue ethics: how one becomes virtuous is to strive to emulate the virtuous person. Dexter's mantra is "What would Harry do?" Dexter strives to do right by Harry's code and to do as Harry would have wanted him to do: to walk the best path available to him. Though Dexter is far from virtuous himself, he strives to emulate an individual who is virtuous (or at least is far closer to virtuous than many).

That a serial killer could flourish seems a big pill to swallow, but Dexter does appear to grow and flourish. While Dexter views himself as a malfunctioning monster, he flourishes in his professional career and personal life. He is a successful and well-respected blood-spatter specialist, a favorite of the police lieutenant, Maria LaGuerta. Dexter is a veritable virtuoso at his job and engages in spatter analysis as if it were an art. With lasers, threads, and other tools, he almost dances in reenactment of what the Jackson Pollack-esque blood patterns signify regarding how a victim was killed. Similarly, in his methodical stalking and killing of murderers, he feels in his element, and even enjoys classical music as he makes preparations for their deaths. In his personal life, Dexter is committed to Rita, a girlfriend (and later wife) who vibrantly loves him; he is looked up to by Rita's children, and he is admired by his stepsister, Debra.

Yet a hollow man can appear flourishing while being internally empty. Dexter often describes his enviable life as a veneer, from which he receives no satisfaction. He claims to be play-acting so as not to raise suspicion as to what lies behind the curtain. Dexter does come to recognize, however, that no man is an island, not even a sociopathic killer. In the last episode of the second season, Dexter admits that he needs people in his life. This admission suggests that he is not just going through the motions, but is emotionally invested in the people around him, and that he gets something significant from his relationships with them.

Besides his emotional and creative sides, Dexter is contemplative: his thoughtful narration spans the length of any given episode. Dexter is living the examined life far more than most, one of contemplation and restraint. He follows the Code of Harry in rational recognition that the path he walks is a tightrope, and if he does not abide by the code, he may sink into the darkness and become an unrestrained, vicious monster.

A malfunctioning monster might be a prosecutor's description of Dexter: an inhuman, coldblooded killer. Dexter is indeed violent, ferocious, cruelly efficient, cold to his victims, but are these automatically vices? Virtue and vice are somewhat relative to the individual and his or her role in the culture or group.

Seen myopically, Dexter may strike us as a malfunctioning individual, but if we view Dexter as a soldier in our midst, protecting us, we can see his "vices" as virtues. To function well as a soldier, one needs to have some emotional disassociation in order to survive, yet at the same time be fiercer than the common person. Only by being callous toward killing the enemy can Dexter, or any solider, manage to carry on in protecting innocent others from harm. Only by being ferocious can he be successful.

We should not judge Dexter by the rubric of a typical citizen: Dexter is a warrior of our society and needs to be assessed on a sliding scale. I realize that this suggestion is contentious and provocative. Admittedly, it will take far more argument than we have space for here, to establish Dexter as a virtuous warrior. I do, nonetheless, believe a cogent argument could be made that Dexter would best be judged by the virtues of the role he occupies – similar to the specific virtues a soldier ought to have, in Plato's *Republic*, in contrast to the differing virtues a ruler or producer ought to have. I contend that by functioning as a soldier, Dexter – in part – enables his own republic to function and flourish, as well as its citizens who comprise it. He protects his society from enemies, not outside city walls, but hidden in their midst.

Hypothetical Consent: Would You Want Dexter in Your Neighborhood?

We are afraid of Dexter – or at least what he represents. But we should not let that fear affect our moral judgment. We must take a step back and ask ourselves whether or not we would want to have Dexter in our own neighborhood. This question relates to social contract theories, generally, that justify governmental and individual actions based on the notion of hypothetical consent. Consider the example of your local police department. While you may not have ever explicitly consented to having a local police department, you rationally *would* consent to its existence, as you want to be protected against criminals, and you recognize that having order enforced is in your rational self-interest. The local police department, therefore, is legitimate because you would hypothetically consent to its existence and function. As a taxpaying citizen, if you were given the option to decide which of two societies in which to live – one with a local police department or one without – you would rationally choose the former.

Now imagine that you can live in one of two nearly identical neighborhoods; the only difference is that Dexter patrols the streets in the first, but not in the second. Know that both neighborhoods will be riddled with its share of active rapists, molesters, and murderers who evade capture. Put yourself behind what philosopher John Rawls calls a "veil of ignorance," where there are certain things you do not know: you don't know the crime rate of the neighborhood, the person you will be in that community, or what loved ones you will have (though certainly you will have loved ones). Which of the two neighborhoods would you choose to live in? Be assured, by the constraints of the hypothetical example that Dexter represents, that Dexter would be your protector in the first community and pose no harm to you; rather, he would eliminate the killers who might otherwise kill you, your spouse, your friends, your children.

Imagine that you or your loved ones could very well be the future victims of the murderers whom Dexter would preemptively kill. Then ask yourself with rational, self-interested honesty if you would endorse having Dexter on patrol, discovering and killing these murderers, thereby preventing the suffering and death they would perpetrate upon innocents.

Consenting to this hypothetical question is not an endorsement of putting Dexter on the government's payroll, or funding a "protective assassin" position with community money. Dexter is an independent and lone agent, a guardian in the shadows, protecting citizens against monsters who kill.

Consider a related question: If you had the opportunity to anonymously submit damning evidence against Dexter, thereby guaranteeing that he would live his life in prison without parole, would you do so? If your rational self-interest leads you to conclude that you would rather allow Dexter to remain free – protecting you and your loved ones by killing the murderers – then you privately consent to his actions, even if you are to deny complicity in them.

We can imagine analogs to Dexter in our government: black-op CIA or military operatives who assassinate vicious, known dictators and terrorists who would otherwise kill innocent people. Yet your individual endorsement of Dexter is less ethically complex than endorsing secretive governmental operations. And governments' motivations tend to be less pure than Dexter's – and their detrimental effects far more chaotic and bloody.

Closing Arguments

Dexter may be a killer, but he is righteous in his dirty deeds. Every predator Dexter kills is guilty of murdering innocent people in the past, and would kill many more in the future. Dexter is not a monster, though he does suffer some emotional deficits from an unimaginably traumatic childhood. These deficits he progressively struggles to overcome. Dexter abides by a moral code – the Code of Harry – which helps him aim at the good life, one of retributive justice curbed with self-restraint. And though a coldblooded killer, Dexter's heart thaws through his relationships with his stepsister as well as Rita and her two children. Dexter's development is sure to continue throughout the series: in season three, Rita discovers that she is pregnant with Dexter's child. Dexter is a soon-to-be father. There is no question that Dexter will refrain from harming the loved ones in his life. Rather, he will fiercely protect them as a father, husband, and brother. Further, he will protect all citizens from the predators who prey upon the innocent.

While we might find Dexter frightening, more frightening are the predators he eliminates. And while we may want to condemn Dexter as a monster, he is our monster: we want him in the darkness, hunting the wolves that would devour us, protecting us so that we can sleep, safely, through the night.

NOTES

1 Aristotle, *The Nicomachean Ethics*, ed. and trans. David Ross (Oxford: Oxford University Press, 1998).
2 R. Cochran and J. Surnow, *24*. Fox broadcasting company (television series, 2001).
3 Immanuel Kant, *Philosophy of Law* (1796), trans. William Hastie (Edinburgh: T & T Clarke, 1887), p. 198.

PART III

DANGEROUS INFATUATIONS
The Public Fascination with Serial Killers

CHAPTER 7

THE ALLURE OF THE SERIAL KILLER

The only sensible way to live in this world is without rules.

The Joker[1]

The Allure of Monsters

Question: Dante's *Divine Comedy* is made up of three books (or canticles), the first of which is called the *Inferno*. What are the names of the other two books?
Dante's *Divine Comedy* is considered one of the greatest works in world literature. Yet few can name all three of its books, and fewer still have read the whole thing. Most people who read it read only the *Inferno*, and in fact the structure of the *Inferno*, with its ever-deepening circles of Hell, is a mainstay of common culture. Why do the other two books, the *Purgatorio* and the *Paradiso*, receive far less attention? It's because with their respective images of waiting interminably, and of peace and plenty, they aren't vivid and exciting; they're boring. But gruesome horror is vivid and exciting. This is what the *Inferno* contains – indeed, mostly consists of. So now the question becomes: Why is gruesome horror exciting? As mysterious as this question is, there's a bigger, more disturbing mystery: What is it in our nature that finds the monsters responsible for such horror alluring? The particular monster we are interested in is the serial killer.

That monsters are alluring is not in doubt. Nothing else explains their appearance throughout human verbal and written art. There is Humbaba, the monstrous giant in the Gilgamesh epic, dating from before 2000 BCE. Homer's *Odyssey* (written perhaps as early as 1100 BCE) is abundantly supplied with monsters, from Polyphemus the Cyclops, through the Laestrygonians (a tribe of giant cannibals), and finally to Scylla and Charybdis. The Old English epic poem *Beowulf* recounts one of the most interesting monsters, the mighty and terrifying Grendel. Over a period of many years, he attacked and ate dozens of the Danes of Heorot Hall, only to be finally bested by Beowulf, the hero of the Geats. All of these monsters systematically hunted and killed humans over a stretch of time – they were all serial killers.

The allure is just as powerful in real life. The Roman emperor Nero was an extravagant tyrant, ordering the executions and torture of perhaps hundreds of people, including his own mother. He was also fond of viciously persecuting Christians. He remains a source of inquiry and curiosity. Jack the Ripper first appeared in 1880s London, and is still an important subject of movies, books, and historical detective work. This work continues because the Ripper's identity remains unknown. In fact, "Jack the Ripper" is an alias given to the serial killer by a letter sent to the London Central News Agency.[2] The Son of Sam, Ted Bundy, and all the other modern serial killers grip our imaginations. We are horrified by their killing, but cannot look away.

Plausibly, serial killing monsters show up in our art because they show up in real life. And they are alluring in our art – when they are, which is often – for one reason: the artists make them alluring (Hannibal the Cannibal from the movie *Silence of the Lambs* is the Platonic ideal of such an alluring monster – he is urbane, intelligent, charming, and eats his victims). Other alluring serial killers include Sylar, Jigsaw, Jason, Dexter, and Ghostface from, respectively, the television shows/movies *Heroes*, *Saw*, *Friday the Thirteenth*, *Dexter*, and *Scream*, as well as Aaron Stampler, from William Diehl's books *Primal Fear* and *Reign in Hell*. But these artistic constructs we enjoy watching and reading about are just that, *constructs*. Why would artists render serial killers alluring? Are any actual serial killers alluring? How do we square our horror of them and our revulsion at their killing with any allure?

The answers to these questions, which we explain below, reveal how complex humans' thoughts and emotions about serial killers are. There is more than one answer at work, and, as one digs deeper, a surprising answer emerges: that what is actually alluring is the *idea* of the serial killer, but only when that idea is contemplated from a certain, specific, safe reference frame that allows *both* the positive and negative emotions

ERIC DIETRICH AND TARA FOX HALL

associated with serial killers to be experienced at the same time. There is nothing more stimulating than surviving a brush with death, that threat to the one thing we all hold most dear: our lives. The feeling of being threatened when someone dangerous has power over us makes our hearts pound in our chests from fear. It is only when that feeling is coupled with the *safe* boundaries of the silver screen or written word that it becomes irresistible.

Explaining the Allure: First Look

Serial killers in real life may not be as alluring as fictional ones, but they are at least fascinating in a terrifying way. A significant part of this fascination comes from the *mystery* serial killers represent and our deep human need to minimize mysteries. We all ask, "Why would anyone stalk and kill one human after another?" This behavior is bizarre, senseless. So to assuage our terrified fascination, we seek reasons.

Humans require reasons, or explanations, for everything, from why the sun comes up and goes down to why the stars appear in recognizable patterns in the night sky to why people get sick and die. It is easy to see why such explanations are needed: they provide control, prediction, and, emotionally, they reduce fear. In fact, one crucial function for human religions, from the beginning, was (and is) making a dangerous, mysterious world seem *humanly* rational. Gods, who were a lot like people only stronger and magical, controlled everything. Gods controlled the seas and rivers, the weather, the sun and moon, the stars and planets, and even the afterlife. A well-known example is one Western explanation of why spring returned every year (it was caused by Persephone's return from the underworld, where she was the consort of Hades). Therefore, explaining what happens in the world is important, especially so if what happens negatively affects us. But to this day, we cannot explain serial killers' behavior. And lacking this explanation matters a great deal, for serial killers are responsible for a significant proportion of murders in the United States. According to Kenna Quinet, the number of victims of serial killers ranges anywhere from around 350 to almost 2,000 a year (there are roughly 16,000 murders in the US in a typical year).[3]

Wanting to explain deadly events is clearly a rational want. In seeking explanations of deadly events, including serial killers, humans feel a certain amount of curiosity. One cannot seek explanations for things without somehow being drawn to the thing to be explained, even if that thing is extremely dangerous or repugnant, such as why prison rape occurs. Curiosity always has a positive emotive component; it is the sort of thing that feels good, at least somewhat, when satisfied, like discovering the reasons for the bright pastel colors of a sunset. Hence, we are drawn to serial killers in order to explain them, which we must do if we are to avoid them, or remove them from society, or prevent them from occurring. Our being drawn to them is innate, it is funded by our curiosity. This explains part of the allure of serial killers: we are just curious about them for perfectly rational reasons: we'd like to reduce the danger and horror they impose. This curiosity-driven allure is such a rational course of action that it is common throughout the animal kingdom. Even animals with quite small brains engage in such behavior. For example, some species of fish do what's called "predator inspection." The fish, while eating, notice that something dark looms up ahead of them. It might be a large predator fish or the legs of a fish-eating bird, or it might be some floating moss or a log. Swimming away from food every time something dark looms up ahead is a good way to starve to death because it happens often. The fish have to stay and eat. This is clearly a situation where more information would be very helpful, yet the only way to get more information is to swim a bit closer to the looming dark thing and inspect it for the telltale signs of being a predator (which the fish apparently know). The fish's strategy is: if it appears to be a predator, then quickly swim off, otherwise, keep eating. Of course, the risk to gathering this extra information is that the dark looming thing might in fact be a predator, in which case the fish have just swum closer to it. Risky behavior for the sake of a good meal: it was ever thus.

Stalking the Deeper Reasons

But there's more to be explained here than just our need to understand and cope with serial killers. We still have to explain why serial killers are often central characters in our most horrifying movies, some of which are as deservedly famous as any movie can be (e.g., Alfred Hitchcock's *Psycho*). We begin explaining this by noting that humans engage in some quite peculiar behavior relative to other animals: we egregiously violate what is called the *hedonistic assumption*. This assumption says that for the most part animals will approach what is good and avoid what is bad. Of course, all curious animals violate this assumption to some small degree (see above). But humans are strange in the extent to which we violate it. Humans go far out of their way to find and engage in activities that are obviously aversive, things that from a purely rational perspective should be avoided. Examples include horror movies, fear-inducing rides like roller coasters, and dangerous extreme sports, like parachuting, bungee jumping, and mountain climbing. Dangling from half-inch hand- and footholds on the edge of a sheer rock wall with only a thin rope to prevent a climber from a fall of four thousand feet is exhilarating precisely because death is so close. No other animal engages in such reckless thrill-seeking.

The key to this odd behavior seems to be that humans experience both positive and negative feelings *at the same time* when exposed to aversive things.[4] Such *co-activation* (as it is called) means that just because we are frightened doesn't mean we aren't also enjoying ourselves. Indeed, some of the most enjoyable moments of an event may be the most frightening, such as the moment a parachuter jumps from a plane out into the air. Co-activation provides a positive correlation between opposite feelings, e.g., fear and pleasure. Andrade and Cohen, the authors of the psychological study that revealed the surprising fact that humans experience negative and positive emotions at the same time,[5] use co-activation to *partially* explain why people go to horror movies. The idea is that our feelings of excitement and pleasure so closely co-occur with being frightened that we view the latter as causing the former. Hence, we seek out aversive actions.

Closing in for the Kill

However, we say "partially explain" because there is one other crucial ingredient that is needed: a *protective frame*. That is, moviegoers and other thrill-seekers usually won't experience any positive emotions together with their negative emotions unless there is some sort of mindset they can enter where the danger to them is seen to be not real, or greatly minimized, or something they are confident they can deal with.[6] Hearing the Joker ask "Why so serious?" on the screen is riveting and exciting. Hearing him whisper it to us in the dark of our bedroom just as we are falling asleep would be utterly terrifying.

Serial killers in the real world obviously don't allow for a protective frame. So it looks like an explanation of their allure based on co-activation founders here. But in movies, books, and other media a protective frame does exist. The serial killer on the screen is up there on the screen. He can't get to us; we are perfectly safe. So we feel safe to be scared to death.

Removing Empathy

Andrade and Cohen's full explanation of the allure of celluloid serial killers seems to work. Within a protective frame, we are free to enjoy being afraid. But the protective frame does something else, too, something disturbing. It removes any *empathy* with the victims (to further help remove such empathy, serial killer movies and slasher movies in general almost always portray victims as thoughtless risk takers, selfish hedonists, etc. – in short, someone not deserving our empathy). Andrade and Cohen point out: "high levels of cognitive empathy (i.e., perspective taking) can significantly reduce people's ability to experience positive affect when facing negative stimuli." This is the key. When a protective frame removes empathy, it removes the grounding of a sense of morality and ethics. Abstraction sets in. Victims become just prey, and the monsters become more than monsters. This loss of a moral sense opens up a path to a deeper, more satisfying explanation of the allure of the celluloid serial killer, and, ultimately, of the real one.

To sum up what we have so far, the only allure of real (non-celluloid) serial killers we've uncovered is the one associated with our curiosity about them, which in turn arises from our rational need to explain and cope with them. The allure of celluloid serial killers is due to the fact that, inside a protective frame, our empathic sense and hence our morality towards the killer's victims vanishes, and we are left with our feelings of pleasure caused by excitement and fear, i.e., negative emotions co-activating positive ones.

The Prison of Rules

Feeling empathy for others is the basis for morality and ethics. Morality is usually defined as *other-regarding behavior*, behavior based on empathy. That is, morality's essence lies in taking another living being's welfare seriously. Often, such a morality flows freely and naturally from each of us to

ERIC DIETRICH AND TARA FOX HALL

those we interact with. But many philosophers have noted that this natural tendency isn't enough. Relying only on it is not a good way to infuse enough of the needed morality into the world. Such philosophers have suggested that morality manifests itself as a *requirement* on each of us who seeks to be a moral person. Thus, morality must be taken further, to the point where we are *required* to take another's welfare as seriously as our own. However, once we are inside the protective frame, this requirement vanishes because others' welfare becomes non-existent. Indeed, we can say that within the protective frame there are no *others*, there are just ourselves and *objects*. The question emerges, then, is it moral to enter a protective frame? This question takes on an edge because with loss of a moral anchor within a frame, other aspects of the serial killer can come to the fore. And some of these other aspects are alluring in perhaps much more dangerous ways.

To get at this, we start from a new direction. Human beings are immersed in rules – it would be hard to overstate how immersed. Our species really should be called *Homo oboediens* – the rule-following human. Rules form the girders of all our highly structured groups, communities, societies, and cultures. Actually, cultures *are* just collections of rules, which those of us within a culture learn and internalize. Languages, essential to being human, are intricate rule-following productions of sounds. All of our religions are repositories of rules controlling the most intimate aspects of our lives: who we can marry, who we can have sex with and when, what we can eat and when, who we must kill, when we should kill ourselves. Games, ubiquitous in human cultures, are impossible without rules. Art, poetry, music, dance – are all based on rules, and all are meaningless shapes and noise without them. Even the great rule-breaking art requires rules to break. Cubism and Dadaism in painting and the visual arts, the poetry of e. e. cummings, the later writings of James Joyce, 12-tone music, or any "music" by John Cage (his famous composition 4' 33' is three movements of noteless music – the audience is meant to hear the sounds of the surrounding environment while it is being performed) – all of these wouldn't even exist if it weren't for rules. Finally, science is not only profoundly rule based, but exists solely to unearth the rules that govern the universe and all things in it, none of which could exist without rules.

The vast majority of these rules are *implicit*. Stopping at stop signs and red lights is due to following explicit rules. But most other rules operate implicitly, controlling us without our conscious involvement. We effortlessly learn these implicit rules and they effortlessly control us. Very often, this control makes life on planet Earth better than it would be otherwise.

Yet, in spite of the role in our lives of this vast matrix of rules, humans are also individual *selves*. And herein lies the problem. Rules, by definition, require everyone to obey them. Indeed, rules' reason for being is this very obedience: rules are about both *control* and *homogenization*. Under such conditions, it is hard to be a self, for one's self tends to merge completely with the rule-governed masses. Selves wind up struggling to exist as selves. To win this struggle, or to even not lose it, requires *public self-assertion*, usually in the form of rule-breaking. Why *public* self-assertion? Because selves derive their selfhood in large measure by defining themselves relative to others. This is true throughout much of the animal kingdom. For example, it is not possible to be the dominant alpha male or female in some group without also asserting one's independent selfhood. Back to humans, great athletes can't win Olympic medals or break world records unless they first distinguish themselves from the crowd. New music, art, trends, or inventions can't come into being unless the creator breaks out on his own in new directions.

This means that the crucial commodity for the self is *freedom*; the self requires freedom for its existence. Rule-breaking is asserting or grasping freedom by breaking out of the chains imposed by all the rules we have to follow. The self's search for this freedom is epic and costly, a fact noted by many throughout the ages. From the story of Icarus to *Catcher in the Rye*, the struggle to be a self figures prominently in great literature and other art, where it is revealed as a struggle of ultimate importance. We quote e. e. cummings: "To be nobody-but-yourself in a world which is doing its best, night and day, to make you everybody else – means to fight the hardest battle which any human being can fight; and never stop fighting."[7]

Humans struggle to be both selves and rule-followers. We all both seek and eschew freedom, and suffer the consequences of this struggle. The importance of this can be seen by noting that the sum of all human rules still leaves room for assertion of one's self. Even military organizations leave room for some self-assertion. Personalities shine through in the form of speech patterns, stated beliefs, and goals. But it's not enough.[8] So rules, while good in many ways, are also bad because they make it hard to be a self. Very often, therefore, we break the rules. Usually, we just dip our toes in the sea of rule-breaking: we drive a little over the speed limit, we lie, we dress inappropriately, we use unsuitable language, we buy a Harley. Every so often, a few of us step up to our ankles in that sea. And sometimes, a tiny number of us swim far out into it ... with deadly results.

In this battle between asserting one's self and merging one's self with the rule-following collective, serial killers stand as an avatar of ultimate freedom. They appear so unbound by the rules of civilized society that they wantonly commit one of the few acts regarded as wrong in all human cultures: they murder. And as a final declaration, they murder for their own personal reasons.

This view of serial killers as alluring individuals arises in those of us who are not serial killers and who are not in any immediate danger from one; in other words, in those of us who are in a protective frame – a frame of physical and psychological distance. Moreover, we think that this view of serial killers as ultimate avatars of freedom is not explicitly conscious in most people. It works behind the scenes, generating allure and causing people to be drawn not to serial killers *per se*, but to the *idea* of serial killers (and then, only certain ones).

There is one other aspect of this cause of the allure: all of us who follow the rules and struggle to be moral want to know if the rules have any substantiality, any genuineness. Many of us fear that the rules are just a thin veneer of modern civilization. But part of us also hopes for this. We want to know how thin the veneer is and how much force it would take to break through. To quote another alluring killer, the Joker, as he refers to all of us: "You see, their morals, their code, it's a bad joke. Dropped at the first sign of trouble. They're only as good as the world allows them to be. I'll show you. When the chips are down, these civilized people, they'll eat each other. See, I'm not a monster … I'm just ahead of the curve."[9] So, we sit down with our favorite serial killers from fiction – the Joker, Grendel, Jigsaw, Hannibal, and the others – and we try to figure out if they really are monsters or not. Our rule-following part believes that their ultimate freedom is purchased at a great and terrible price, proving that such freedom is false and worthless. But our deeper, inner selves long for their freedom, if only to stay ahead of the curve.

Conclusion

In our usually unacknowledged desire to break free from society's rules, we not only condone the celluloid serial killer's actions, we champion them. We have taken real killers and transformed them into sympathetic heroes and put them in our stories. A moral question arises: Should we be making art celebrating serial killers?

A deep irony exists here, of course. Real serial killers are not free at all. They kill for pathological reasons that push them along like a raging torrent pushes along whole trees and gigantic boulders. Moreover, real serial killers kill real people, not just those who "deserve" to die, as in the stories. They are not the heroes we idealize them as; they don't kill to escape boundaries, they kill to maintain their own perverse boundaries.

For most of us, sitting down with a real serial killer would not be an artistic, philosophical experience, but rather a terrifying, repulsive one. Yet, within a protective frame, safe and secure, we transform the serial killer, already an object of deep curiosity because of his or her fearsomeness, into an icon, an avatar. We revel in this transformation, exploring our darker side that longs to know what it feels like to be the one giving the orders instead of taking them, doing everything we want to, impervious to the consequences.

NOTES

1   *The Dark Knight*, dir. Christopher Nolan, Warner Bros. Pictures, 2008.
2   Philip Sugden, *The Complete History of Jack the Ripper* (New York: Carroll and Graf, 2002), pp. 260–70.
3   Kenna Quinet, "The Missing Missing: Toward a Quantification of Serial Murder Victimization in the United States," *Homicide Studies* 11, 4 (2007): 319–39.
4   That we humans simultaneously experience conflicting emotions when violating the hedonistic assumption was unexpected, but we do.
5   Eduardo Andrade and Joel Cohen, "On the Consumption of Negative Feelings," *Journal of Consumer Research* 34 (2007): 283–300.
6   Ibid.
7   e. e. cummings, "A Poet's Advice to Students," in *A Miscellany*, ed. George James Firmage (New York: Agrophile Press, 1958), p. 13.
8   At least it's not enough in Western cultures. Some Asian cultures differ, notably Japanese culture. In general, different cultures vary considerably in the importance they ascribe to the self. However, in cultures that ascribe less importance to the self, it is not clear whether selves exist in any lesser degree in individual humans or if, rather, the selves are repressed by obedience to the rules. See Ulric Neisser and David A. Jopling, *The Conceptual Self in Context* (Cambridge: Cambridge University Press, 1997).
9   *The Dark Knight*.

CHAPTER 8

DEXTER'S DARK WORLD

The Serial Killer as Superhero

In the first episode of *Dexter* (the Showtime series based on characters created by Jeff Lindsay) we watch a well-dressed man leave an elegant charity event, walk alone to his car, get in, and start the engine. Faster than we can see, a wire flips over his head and jerks his neck tight against the headrest. It is a scene familiar to every moviegoing and televiewing American, only one thing is wrong: the perpetrator is the series hero, Dexter Morgan.

Other familiar images follow. The men drive into a silent, desolate bayou illuminated only by the car's headlights, and Dexter drags the man into moviedom's standard abandoned building. Dexter is as chilling and malevolent as any of the countless others we have seen in this role. When the man shuts his eyes, refusing to look at the evidence of his own crimes, Dexter shouts, "Look, or I'll cut your eyelids off."

The man begs for his life. "I couldn't help myself. I couldn't. I –" He falters. "Please! You've got to understand."

"Trust me. I definitely understand," Dexter replies with a wicked smile. "Ya see, I can't help myself either." He pauses. "But children! – I could never do that ... I have standards." He then proceeds to drug the man, secure him to a table, draw a drop of his blood for a keepsake, and carefully cut his body into pieces.[1]

This, then, is Dexter, a television hero who engenders deeply conflicting feelings in his audience. A remorseless and cold-blooded murderer, he nevertheless has standards. He is also a friendly guy and a regular Joe, who, as he confides, will while away a Sunday with his girlfriend Rita and her children and then "kill a man, dismember him and be home in time for Letterman."[2] The contradictions in Dexter make us uncomfortable. We see the evil in him, yet we can't help liking him.

And as we think about him and our conflicting feelings about him, we find ourselves lost in our own murky bayou. We thought our basic ideas about human nature, good and evil, and people's role in society had a solid foundation. Now all around us we find philosophical quicksand.

Dexter is a cold-blooded killer, but his murders help to save innocent lives: how do we assess the morality of that? Something in him drives him to kill: are evil impulses part of the basic human makeup even of the best of us? And what of Dexter's attempts to mask his true nature by feigning feelings he does not possess: is that not fundamentally dishonest?

Why Do We Love Dexter?

The key to drawing viewers into these dilemmas is the way the program enlists our sympathy with Dexter. For one thing, he tells the story himself, as first-person narrator, thus placing the viewer squarely inside his mind. He describes his feelings and shares his fears and anxieties in a way that makes it hard for us to turn away from him. His frankness and apparent sincerity win us over. Dexter readily admits, of course, that his life is a pose, that he has learned well how to ingratiate himself, to pass himself off as a sincere, caring person. It may be that this is just what he's doing with us. But if so, the strategy works.

For we take Dexter's side in the trials he faces. At the most basic level, we root for him to escape detection, and this reaction alone might give us pause. Normally, we hope the serial killer in a story will be caught. That seems natural. Or perhaps it is a sign that we are on the side of good and against evil. Then what does it say when our allegiances are reversed?

We might tell ourselves that this is a mere trick of literature. Since this is Dexter's story, told from his point of view, we adopt his perspective. If the same story were told from the point of view of a detective on Dexter's trail, we would then root for his capture. We might also raise the issue of Dexter's standards: Harry's Code.[3] Dexter only kills people who have themselves committed murder and have escaped punishment for their crimes because his father, Harry, taught him to control his murderous

SUSAN AMPER

impulses by only killing killers. If he is in fact a dispenser of justice, we might say that rooting for him still puts us on the side of good. Of course, viewers may not consciously puzzle out these ideas; even so, the dilemma is there to unsettle us.

Moreover, our empathy for Dexter goes deeper than merely hoping he does not get caught. As Dexter grapples with life, we witness his struggle and sympathize. We can see ourselves in Dexter: his feeling of alienation, his wry take on the people around him and their incomprehensible behavior. But this is scary. If I identify with a serial killer, what does that say about me? And then, what does it say about others? My next door neighbor, the repairman who comes in my house, the cop on the beat, my son's teacher: do they also identify with Dexter?

Without doubt, serial killers, both real and fictional, fascinate us. A Google search for "serial killers" returns 18,500,000 entries. Top attractions include "Stories about Famous Serial Killers and Murderer Cases" on www.trutv.com/library/crime/, serial killer details on www.all-serialkillers.com, Wikipedia's list of serial killers by country, and YouTube's top ten serial killer videos. Ted Bundy, Charles Manson, Jack the Ripper, Jeffrey Dahmer, Son of Sam, and the Zodiac Killer continue to captivate. The serial killer has become a profitable marketing device, and Ed Kemper, Henry Lee Lucas, and Ed Gein have been turned into cultural icons. These real-life models for Michael Myers, Norman Bates, Jason Voorhees, and Hannibal Lecter are reimagined villains for a world haunted by the specters of war, terrorism, and violent crime.

People's fascination with these figures, while worth exploring in its own right, is quite different from our attraction to Dexter. Even the most engaging and personable of fictional killers, Hannibal Lecter, holds for us only the attraction of the cobra: his grace, cunning, and deadly efficiency may enthrall us, but we do not identify with his struggle or hope that his wounds will be healed. Among real and fictional serial killers we seek in vain a model for Dexter.

Dexter Morgan: Superhero

In fact, the literary figure Dexter most closely resembles is the comic book superhero. Like most superheroes, he is an orphan of traumatic origin. After witnessing his mother's murder by chainsaw at the age of three, Dexter is raised by foster parents who, like Superman's Ma and Pa

Kent, hide his identity while teaching him how to survive in an alien world and how to harness his unique nature and "use it for good." As an adult, Dexter, like other superheroes, brings criminals to justice, operating outside the law, usually at night.

Three other characteristics of superheroes are central to the themes of the genre: the hero's secret identity, alien nature, and dark side. The superhero is an outsider by nature and his behavior – even his crime fighting – puts him outside the confines of ordinary human society. Through the years superheroes increasingly have inhabited a dark frontier world where motivations and morality are far from clear. Dexter shares the superhero traits, as the series shares the comics' thematic concerns. The interplay of these traits provides the content, too, of the philosophical issues the program raises.

Dexter disguises himself as a mild-mannered blood-spatter analyst for a great metropolitan police force. In a workplace teeming with testosterone, he is a non-threatening presence, a nerd bordering on a cipher. This is precisely his plan. Like Superman's secret identity, Dexter's is designed for concealment. Just as Clark Kent is the last person anyone would suspect of being Superman, so Dexter seems a downright preposterous candidate for the Bay City Butcher.

The traditional rationale for maintaining a secret identity, however, is to protect people who are close to the superhero: friends or family who might become targets for villains. Dexter's mask is designed instead to protect Dexter. He has been taught since childhood the absolute necessity of hiding who he really is. The primary goal is to escape detection for the murders that he will irresistibly commit, but a more basic imperative is to hide his alien nature.

For as much as a superhero who comes from a distant planet, or has been bitten by a radioactive spider, or exposed to cosmic rays during a space mission, Dexter is abnormal. His "birthplace," he tells us in the episode "Born Free," is the cargo container in which he saw his mother dismembered with a chainsaw. That experience has so warped him, his foster father explains, that Dexter will never be like normal people.[4]

Hiding who he is becomes his strongest instinct. When his girlfriend's mother says, "So, Dexter, tell me everything there is to know about you," Dexter answers silently, "You have made me your sworn enemy, evil woman." In the same episode, "See-Through," Lila, a woman he is becoming involved with, says, "You're going to tell me all your deepest, darkest secrets!" For most people this would be a welcome invitation to intimacy. Dexter's response is to end the relationship.[5]

SUSAN AMPER

Dexter is not just different; he is, at the core of his being, evil. His instincts are to kill people, cut them into pieces, and collect their blood for his trophy case. We know superheroes have a dark side, but this is extreme. Harry himself, in an unguarded moment of relief when Dexter passes a psychological evaluation, exults that the doctor did not see "the monster inside you." He corrects himself, but the truth has been spoken.[6]

Dexter and the Viewer

These qualities in Dexter – his feeling of being different, his evil impulses, and the secret identity he assumes to hide them – provide the content of the philosophical issues that the series explores. What makes these issues real and urgent to the viewer is the way the program evokes conflicting feelings for Dexter. Our problem is that while we do see Dexter as abnormal and even monstrous, we can't help identifying with him. In the episode "Crocodile," Dexter says, "I'm the outsider looking in."[7] We know what that's like. Dexter fakes behavior he doesn't feel in order to fit in. Been there. Scene after scene, we find Dexter, the psychopath, acting and thinking just like us.

A flashback scene in the episode "Love American Style" shows Dexter as a teenager mowing his lawn. A girl his age walks up along the sidewalk. They exchange hellos, and as Dexter keeps mowing, the girl walks along next to him. "Do you need any help?" she offers.

"Naw," he replies, offering a simple factual answer to what plainly was not a simple question – and continuing to mow.

Nervously, the young girl perseveres. "So, are you going to go to the spring formal?"

At last, Dexter stops. He turns to her in utter bewilderment. "Why would I want to do that?" he replies, and at this the crestfallen girl turns back the way she came.

Harry has overheard the conversation and admonishes Dexter. "She wanted you to ask her to the dance, Dexter."

"That's not what she said."

"Well, you have to learn their signals," Harry explains.[8]

Here, as in many such sequences, Dexter's reactions actually seem *more* natural than the learned behavior that is accepted as appropriate. Often, the anomaly makes us laugh. In the episode "See-Through," as Harry preps him for his psychological evaluation, Dexter keeps giving answers that are sure to raise alarms. As the time for the testing nears, Harry settles on a simple strategy: "Whatever you think is right is wrong. He asks you a question, I want you to think of your answer first, then tell him the exact opposite, okay?"

We cut to the psychologist asking his questions. "Does it make you angry when your teachers tell you what to do?" *No.* "Are you often bored?" *No.* "Have you ever killed an animal?" *No.* In Dexter's lies we recognize the reality of a 12-year-old boy.

Much of this humor is gentle, a good-natured tweaking of the artificiality and hypocrisy that is part of everyday life. But underneath lies a darker humor. For Dexter keeps reminding us why he plays this game: because his real self is unacceptable – alien and monstrous.

This darker humor is clearest in the context of Dexter's oft-expressed fears of intimacy. Because he does not feel real emotions, he says, he has learned to fake them. As an adult he needs a girlfriend – in order to appear normal. He actually feels just as he did as a teenager: he would prefer solitude. But what would people say? "Lives alone, quiet, keeps to himself." That won't work. "Might as well put a sign on the door that says, 'Serial killer lives here.'"

Deliberately, he chooses a woman whose abusive relationship with her estranged husband has left her psychologically damaged. She will be less likely to see Dexter for who he is. And there's a bonus that Dexter appreciates: her experience has left her unready for sexual intimacy. Rita's unhappy experience makes her and Dexter's relationship an uncomfortable subject for humor. We take it seriously when Dexter laments in episode 1, "I don't know what to say to my girlfriend when she needs reassuring." But in a later report on their relationship, he says, "She wants to take it to the next level. She doesn't realize: I don't have a next level." Viewers laugh out loud – and wonder what's so funny.

Dexter vs. Dexter

The most serious problem with Dexter's pose – and ours – is that it entails a denial of one's true self. Substituting socially appropriate behavior that we don't feel for our true emotions is an assault on our own integrity and authenticity.

Existentialist philosopher Jean-Paul Sartre (1905–80) describes a waiter who self-consciously adopts the role of waiter; he deliberately walks like a waiter, talks like a waiter. Sartre condemns such role-playing. Social roles, conventions, even moral systems, he argues, all are arbitrary, external to the individual human being. We live in absolute freedom to choose our own behavior. We cannot point to social rules or a moral principle and say, "I had to do what I did."

This freedom, however, is anguishing. We are left without any guide or compass, nothing to base our actions on, or blame them on. Since all actions are free choices, we cannot escape our personal responsibility for everything we do and its consequences. We would like to latch onto a moral code, a belief system, something to give our lives meaning and direction. But to do so is to deny our freedom and the responsibility that goes with it. This is precisely what Sartre's waiter does. He is free and he knows that he is free – because he knows that he is acting – yet he chooses to bind himself to arbitrary convention. This, for Sartre, is "bad faith."

Like the waiter, Dexter knows that his behavior is just an act. But Dexter offers an interesting twist. He calls attention to the fakery, mocks it. And invites us to do the same. The strategy is designed to ease the conflict that comes when we see how artificial certain behavior is and engage in it anyway. It is one of the most characteristic behaviors of our time. For this is the age of air quotes, of self-irony. "This is the part where I play the diva," says an overbearing manager – who then proceeds to act like a diva.

With such ironic self-reference we deliberately separate ourselves from our own behavior. That person who is trying to ingratiate himself with his boss or colleagues – that's my Clark Kent, not the real me. The behavior, in effect, tries to get around Sartre's criticism. He demands that we recognize and accept that social conventions have no true validity. Well, I'm doing that. You see, I'm laughing at the conventions. The real me is not denying my freedom: I'm using that freedom to expose the conventions themselves. The problem is, Sartre might reply, that you only accomplished this by dividing yourself into two people.

Dexter himself, though he resorts to the strategy, clearly feels it tearing at him. The role he is forced to play is not just an inconvenience or a joke. It is a denial of his very self. Harry's Code itself – the bedrock principle of Dexter's existence – what does it demand, but that Dexter destroy not just anyone, but people exactly like himself?

The ultimate case is his own long-lost brother. No mere biological brothers, Dexter and Brian are kindred souls. Dexter is filled with admiration for the artistry of this murderer, and when he meets Brian's alter ego – a sensitive and charming physician – Dexter bonds with him as with no other person in his life. This soulmate Dexter must extinguish. In the final episode of the first season, he finally traps his brother, takes him to Brian's own killing room. Strapped to a table, the older brother makes it clear that in killing him, Dexter is also killing himself. When Dexter says that he wishes he could set Brian free, Brian replies, "You're the one who needs setting free little brother. Your life is a lie."

"Sorry, I can't hear you anymore," says Dexter, as he slits his brother's throat. "But you're right."

Some viewers may feel less of a connection with Dexter's self-loathing than with his feeling of being an outsider. Yet his fear and revulsion at his own murderous impulses draw on a timeless view of the human condition. "The heart of man," the Bible tells us, "is evil from his youth." And Dexter's situation fits closely the ideas of Sigmund Freud (1856–1939) about human nature and the development of civilized society. In his conception, human life involves a conflict between the id and the superego. The id refers to our basic urges – an amoral, insatiable, egocentric drive for self-gratification. This drive is a fundamental part of our nature that cannot be eliminated, but must be restrained, or individuals would be out of control and civilization would be impossible.

The superego opposes the id and seeks to control it. If the id is the child, the superego is the father. It may also be thought of as representing the moral order or the conscience. The impulses of the id cannot be destroyed, but rather must be directed and channeled into acceptable, productive behavior. Human life is thus a never-ending conflict between one's aggressive id and the superego that seeks to control it.

Dexter's situation fits this model closely. His instinct to kill represents the id. His father works to control the instincts. Harry's Code channels Dexter's lust to kill so that he only kills murderers and not the innocent.

Freud's concept of human nature is out of fashion in today's culture. It is poles apart from most of the popular psychology that fills the bookstores and the airwaves. Where Freud and *Dexter* posit fundamental, inescapable conflict inside us, today's gurus see unbounded potential. Nothing can hold us down or back if we will diligently maintain a positive attitude. This modern viewpoint is embodied in the character of Dexter's colleague, detective Angel Batista. He subscribes wholeheartedly to the New Age concept that all things will come to those with positive thoughts, and he never fails to offer this advice to others. "You've got to think positive," he tells Dexter in "It's Alive." "Because whatever we think creates the world around us." And later: "Don't forget: tell the universe what you need." Meanwhile, Batista himself is miserable. His wife has thrown him out and rebuffs his attempts at reconciliation. He tries to date, but can find no interest in other women. It doesn't occur to Batista that all his self-help books have gotten him nowhere, but to Dexter and to us the irony is plain.[9] With Batista as with Dexter himself, the program sides with Freud's viewpoint. The dark side of human life is not some imaginary ghost we can talk ourselves out of: it's real and it's not going away.

Dexter's Ethics

Viewers who might not consciously weigh the pronouncements of Sartre or Freud nevertheless do find themselves trying to sift their attitudes, and judgments, of Dexter. He may be a serial killer, viewers are apt to think, but that doesn't make him a bad person.

The most obvious ethical problem viewers must confront is the fact that Dexter kills people in cold blood. In his defense it may be said that, in accordance with Harry's Code, he kills only people who have killed and only when he is absolutely certain of their guilt. Whether that makes it right is a very vexed question. Is his behavior right because he punishes the guilty who would otherwise escape justice, or is it wrong because it violates the laws that protect us all? Some would argue that the ends – the punishment of the guilty – justify the extra-legal means. *Utilitarian* philosophers, including Jeremy Bentham (1748–1832), James Mill (1773–1836), and John Stuart Mill (1806–73), argued that that action is best which brings the greatest happiness to the greatest number of people. Defenders of Dexter might well argue that when a serial killer is killed his unhappiness is far outweighed by the happiness of the people he would otherwise kill, and their families.

Seeking to formulate a rule, or test, for whether behavior is moral, the rationalist philosopher Immanuel Kant (1724–1804) devised what is known as the *categorical imperative*. "Act so that the maxim of thy will," the principle states, "thou canst will to be law universal." In simple terms, Kant is asking, "What if everyone did it?" According to Kant, your action is moral if you can honestly wish that everybody in such circumstances would act this way. A person acting fairly or generously could wish that everyone would do as he has done. But a person acting to benefit himself at the expense of others could not rationally wish for others to do the same.

A defender of Dexter could say that his behavior meets Kant's test. Dexter is killing psychopathic killers in order to prevent them from killing again.

It is reasonable to say that everyone in this situation should act this way. But Kant's imperative can be tricky. Dexter's behavior may pass Kant's test when you describe it the way we just did, but what if you describe the same behavior in a different way? Dexter goes outside the law to punish people who he is certain are guilty, but the courts have found innocent. Most people would not agree that everyone should do this.

Significantly, Dexter himself does not claim that his behavior is right, describing it rather as an accommodation necessary for his survival. He did not set out, like other superheroes, to combat crime. He kills because something in him compels him to kill; he confines his killing to other killers so that he will be able to live with himself. Indeed, while Superman fights "for truth, justice, and the American way," Dexter's goal is more limited and self-interested. His guiding principle, given to him by Harry, is "Don't get caught."

Dexter's Dark World

From whatever angle we approach Dexter, we end up uncertain, ambivalent. We cannot condemn his vigilantism, nor can we fully accept it. We sympathize, even identify with his insincerity; we know it's a matter of survival, not an attempt to bamboozle people, or get ahead, or score. And yet we can't help feeling that faking his emotions, especially in relation to his girlfriend Rita, is just not right.

Through it all we keep coming back to the view of a man who is struggling to cope. Dexter didn't choose the life he was given; living it requires constant effort, difficult choices, and painful soul-searching. He does what he can; sometimes he does what he must; but all in all he seems to be trying his best.

This view of him reflects very well the ethics of the day. If earlier ages emphasized obligations to others – called people to duty, to meeting their obligations to God, family, country, community – today people are more called on to work out *their* problems. We are enjoined to make the best of our lives, not to give in or give up – to require more of ourselves, to face problems rather than avoid them, to make decisions and live with the consequences, and to move on. Being our best selves is today's measure of virtue.

This new measure of virtue reflects the darkness the series shows us. What more can we ask of a person, the program seems to say, given what we are up against in this world. The video sequence that runs under the opening credits shows us this world. In it successive sinister-seeming close-ups are revealed as parts of Dexter's morning routine. Blood trickles down a man's skin and drips into an immaculate white basin: Dexter has cut himself shaving. A knife pierces flesh tightly wrapped in plastic: he's preparing steak and eggs. Strings get cinched tight: he's lacing his sneakers.

The sequence does more than merely suggest the violence that dwells almost at the very surface of everyday life. The images themselves – a tightening of the laces, the shirt stretched tight against his face – we recognize them. In their dark context they are part of us; we have absorbed them, largely from *entertainments* which we have avidly sought out. Like so much in Dexter, we see, we recognize, we laugh.

It's a dark and nasty world – not "out there" as we usually say, but inside us. We should be judged accordingly. Superman was invulnerable: he could afford to be noble. Dexter, and we, face a harsher reality. Trying our best is the best we can offer.

But we don't feel good about this new standard. We feel how far it is from our highest ideals, and the contradiction, like the conflict raging in Dexter, will give us no peace.

NOTES

1 "Dexter," *Dexter* 1.01, Showtime, October 1, 2006.
2 Ibid.
3 "Born Free," *Dexter* 1.12, Showtime, December 16, 2006.
4 Ibid.
5 "See-Through," *Dexter* 2.04, Showtime, October 21, 2007.
6 Ibid.
7 "Crocodile," *Dexter* 1.02, Showtime, October 8, 2006.
8 "Love American Style," *Dexter* 1.05, Showtime, October 29, 2006.
9 "It's Alive," *Dexter* 2.01, Showtime, September 30, 2007.

PART IV

A EULOGY FOR EMOTION
The Lack of Empathy and the Urge to Kill

CHAPTER 9

KILLING WITH KINDNESS

Nature, Nurture, and the Female Serial Killer

Introduction

Until 1978, when police in suburban Chicago discovered the moldering remains of several dozen teenaged boys in the fetid crawl space of a pudgy building contractor named John Wayne Gacy – who eventually confessed to 33 murders – the largest number of victims dispatched by a single American serial killer was 31. This earlier killer, like Gacy, was a classic criminal psychopath who led an outwardly respectable life while secretly indulging in wholesale torture and murder, a sadist who achieved the heights of sexual ecstasy by inflicting slow suffering and death on helpless victims. Before Gacy laid temporary claim to the dubious distinction, the *Guinness Book of World Records* listed this long-forgotten psycho-killer – who operated in the closing decades of the nineteenth century – as our country's most prolific multiple murderer. Her name was Jane Toppan.

That a woman was America's long-reigning champion of serial homicide comes as a surprise to many people, particularly those who continue to believe the hype about Aileen Wuornos, the hard-bitten Florida prostitute who, having shot seven male motorists in the course of a year, was widely touted as "the first female serial killer in history" and subsequently immortalized in the Oscar winning movie *Monster*. To some extent, the insistence that only men are capable of such enormities is a sexist assumption that cuts across political lines, being shared by social reactionaries (who persist in seeing women as the "weaker sex"), middle-class liberals (who idealize women as less prone to violence), and radical feminists (who tend to see their sex as morally superior to the male). There is a famous (if happily outmoded) riddle about a boy who – having been badly injured in a car accident that has killed his father – is rushed into the emergency room, only to have the surgeon exclaim, "I can't oper-ate on him – he's my son!" The inability of the average person in the not-very-distant past to realize that the doctor is the boy's mother is precisely equivalent to the continuing failure among the general public to recog-nize that the sadistic sex-killer of 31 victims might be a woman.

It is also true, of course, that Wuornos represented something of an anomaly: a female predator who killed in the random, assaultive style of male serial stalkers like the Zodiac and David "Son of Sam" Berkowitz. Relatively few female psycho-killers have conducted their homicidal sprees with guns or knives. Nor are there any known examples – at least in modern times – of female mutilation-murderers who have engaged in the kind of horrors perpetrated by the legendary Whitechapel monster, whose victims were subjected to hideous post-mortem butcheries. As Camille Paglia puts it, "There is no female Jack the Ripper."[1]

This fact, however, does not mean that only men are capable of serial murder. Rather, it suggests that men and women tend to perpetrate serial homicide in different ways. The contrasting cases of John Wayne Gacy and Jane Toppan are instructive in this regard. Both these individuals were subjected to extreme, unrelenting humiliation as children – a com-mon factor in the backgrounds of sociopathic killers. Both grew into adults who cultivated jovial, outgoing public personas. (Gacy liked to dress up as a clown and entertain hospitalized children, while Toppan's bubbly personality earned her the nickname "Jolly Jane.") Their homi-cidal methods, however, were radically different. Gacy trolled for his vic-tims – young drifters, hustlers, and runaways who were brought back to his basement lair, overpowered, handcuffed, then tortured, raped, and garroted. By contrast, Toppan, a private nurse, preyed on family mem-bers and friends, poisoning them slowly and deriving voluptuous pleas-ure as she watched them subside into an agonizing death.

Gacy's style of murder – rapacious, promiscuous, penetrative (or what Freudians call "phallic-aggressive") – is typical of the male serial killer, whether homosexual (like Gacy) or (more usually) heterosexual. By the same token, Toppan's conforms to the standard picture of female serial murder, which often seems like a grotesque, sadistic travesty of intimacy,

ELIZABETH SCHECHTER AND HAROLD SCHECHTER

nurturing, and love: not the savage violation of a stranger's body but the tender administration of a lethal potion to a loved one.

That there appears to be a rough correlation between these two brands of serial murder and the stereotypical distinctions between male and female sexual behavior raises a provocative question. In the never-ending debate over the source and extent of sex differences, philosophers, psychologists, cultural anthropologists, and others have examined a wide range of phenomena, including attitudes towards work and family, propensities towards jealousy and anger, investment in children, mate preferences, and performance on tests of emotional and verbal and spatial reasoning. And though aggression and crime have also been studied, no one, to our knowledge, has specifically considered the subject of serial sexual homicide. Is there light that can be shed on the controversial issue of gender differences by considering the phenomenon of female serial murder *vis-à-vis* the analogous atrocities perpetrated by men?

Female Nurture and Human Nature: Some Philosophical Background

The quest to understand *human nature* is one with a very long history in both Eastern and Western philosophy and religion, from Aristotle (384–322 BCE) and Confucius (551–479 BCE) to Hinduism and Judeo-Christianity to Freud and the behaviorist psychologist B. F. Skinner. As the psychologist Steven Pinker begins his own book on the subject, *The Blank Slate*, "Everyone has a theory of human nature."[2]

The debate about our common nature, and indeed whether and in what sense such a thing even exists, is deeply related to the so-called "nature/nurture" controversy. Speaking broadly, the two sides in this debate are *nativism* and *empiricism*. Contemporary nativists believe that the human mind is innately endowed with a large number of psychological mechanisms:[3] for example, a language acquisition system that enables young children, though not their parents or their teenaged siblings, to rapidly and easily acquire any language they hear spoken around them – or a "cheater detection module," designed to detect violations of social contracts.[4] Thus, while nativists believe that learning from experience of course accounts for a great deal of human mentality and behavior, they maintain that the human mind is nonetheless structured from birth to seek out and attend to particular experiences, and not others, and to learn particular things from those experiences, and to respond to them in particular ways.

Compared to nativists, contemporary empiricists posit a much less rich innate psychological endowment in human animals, and attribute the psychological traits and behaviors that people exhibit throughout their lives to forces in their environments – especially their social/cultural environments – to a much greater extent. In one famous longitudinal study, for example, young American men in the 1950s ranked "good financial prospect" in a marital partner as the second-to-least important out of eighteen possible characteristics, while "good cook/housekeeper" and "chastity" came in at relatively important eighth and tenth places, respectively. By the 1990s, the rankings had changed dramatically. "Good financial prospects" now came in, at thirteenth place, as more important to men than either "good cook/housekeeper" or "chastity" (fourteenth and sixteenth places, respectively). Also, by the mid-1990s, both sexes agreed that "mutual attraction/love" was the most important characteristic in a spouse – up since the 1950s from third place for men and sixth place for women. Although mate preferences are highly evolutionarily significant, biological evolution could hardly have operated upon them so quickly. But it is not difficult to think of the social, cultural, and political transformations that occurred in America during the second half of the twentieth century that would account for this sea-change in values.[5]

Citing findings like these, empiricists tend to emphasize the psychological differences between people, especially different cultural groups. For empiricists, while human culture is rich and fascinating and deeply explanatory of human life, there is little that is interesting to be said about human nature in general. Indeed, to the extent that empiricists are willing to speak of human nature at all, they really only speak of our astonishing natural malleability, our ability to become whatever the contexts of our lives have made us.

In contrast, nativism has always been associated with the belief in a robust and shared human nature: with the belief that there exists a set of deep facts about human psychology, facts that are in a very real sense universal – whatever important and fascinating psychological differences might also exist between us. But there is one important exception to the universality of the nature that nativists attribute to our species. Throughout history, many of the most famous and influential accounts of human nature have assumed, or implied, or asserted outright, that there is no such thing as human nature, singular, and that there is instead a male (human) nature and a female (human) nature.

♟ ELIZABETH SCHECHTER AND HAROLD SCHECHTER

(Though, unsurprisingly, historical accounts typically viewed male human nature as particularly and gloriously human.)

The commitment to distinct male and female natures is a feature of some contemporary work on human nature as well, particularly some of the work falling within the category of *evolutionary psychology*. Evolutionary psychology is an interdisciplinary research program that attempts to explain patterns of human behavior in terms of *evolved psychological adaptations*. Much of the work in evolutionary psychology deals with psychological traits that are claimed to be truly universal evolved adaptations (such as, again, a language acquisition system or a cheater detection module). But some work in evolutionary psychology deals with "sex-typical" traits: traits that are claimed to have evolved under the unique selective pressures that faced ancestral women in particular, or under the unique selective pressures that faced ancestral men. This work suggests that while we may mostly all share a common nature, a distinction can nonetheless be drawn between male and female human nature, and each of these needs separate elucidation.

Interestingly, some of the sex-specific psychological adaptations posited by evolutionary psychologists – such as an adaptation disposing men, more than women, to feel that they "own" or have a right to control their partners' sexuality[6] – conform or at least bear some resemblance to prevailing gender stereotypes. (Though it's worth noting that these theorists have argued just as strenuously for a number of sex-specific adaptations that fly in the face of popular "wisdom" about women and men – such as the notion that cheating is a "guy thing," since women are naturally monogamous.[7] For this reason, those parts of evolutionary psychology that deal with sex differences are often derided (usually, but not always, by empiricists) as no more than old school gender essentialism dressed in modern scientific garb.[8]

That some scientific hypotheses about sex differences bear a resemblance to dominant gender stereotypes, however, doesn't necessarily mean that they're false. Some stereotypes may contain at least a grain of truth, even if the truth is always far more subtle and complicated than any stereotype.

Female serial killers are interesting in this context for several reasons. First and most obviously, their very existence radically violates some sweeping beliefs about women that still have a very good deal of traction in our culture. Second, while some of these stereotypes about women may be no more than stereotypes, some of them have been given, albeit in revised form, recent defense by legitimate scientists. But female serial killers are perhaps particularly interesting because they simultaneously violate and conform *to* these stereotypes. Indeed, we think it is possible that the phenomena of male and female multiple murder provides *some* modest support for claims of innate sexual difference – but not necessarily the differences you might expect.

Female Serial Killers: A Typology

Female serial killers tend to fall into one of several categories, though the lines between them are sometimes blurred.[9] As a homicidal healthcare worker who dispensed death to her trusting patients, Jane Toppan, for example, conforms to the type that students of serial murder – resorting to the tabloid style that the subject invariably invites – call "Angels of Death." At the same time, since her victims included close family members like her foster sister, she bore similarities to the kind known as "Black Widows," a term that refers to women who murder a string of husbands, along with anyone else they perceive as an obstacle to their own happiness, such as inconvenient children and bothersome siblings.

A particularly appalling example of the latter variety of psychopath was America's nineteenth-century "arch-murderess" Lydia Sherman, who killed three husbands in succession, as well as six of her own offspring (ranging in age from nine months to eighteen years) and two stepchildren. All were dispatched with arsenic-spiked food, drink, and patent medicine, and suffered the prolonged torments produced by that particular (and, at the time, widely available) poison: unbearable nausea, uncontrollable vomiting and diarrhea, excruciating abdominal and muscle cramps, convulsions.

Another common type of female serial murderer is the woman who, as part of a "killer couple," actively engages in sadistic lust-murder as a form of sex play. Typical of the breed was Carol Bundy (no relation to her notorious namesake, Ted). An overweight, severely myopic 37-year-old who had suffered from a lifetime of psychological and sexual abuse, Bundy fell under the thrall of a predatory sociopath named Douglas Clark and became an eager participant in his increasingly depraved activities. Her complicity in Clark's atrocities reached a pitch of perversity when he brought home the head of one of his victims, a 20-year-old streetwalker named Exxie Wilson. Throwing herself into the unspeakable spirit of her lover's "games," Bundy applied cosmetics to the decapitated

♠ ELIZABETH SCHECHTER AND HAROLD SCHECHTER

head and gave it a pretty hairdo, after which Clark took it into the bathroom for some necrophiliac fellatio.

We would like to note two features of these cases. First, despite the differences between these common types of murderesses, female serial murderers arguably constitute what philosophers call a *natural kind*. A natural kind is a collection of things that are grouped together in virtue of some natural similarity or commonality. The grouping must not be *artificial*; it cannot be dependent upon human interests and concerns. Rather, the elements in the set should instead be grouped together on the basis of some natural and important features that they all share with each other and not with other elements outside the set.

Primates are a good candidate for being a natural kind, since all primates naturally share some important traits; most obviously, they are all descendents of a single common ancestor that no other animals are the descendents of. But house-pets are not a natural kind, even if cats and dogs and parakeets and goldfish are the non-human animals that we love most in the world, for this is not a natural grouping of things. (Note that while this latter grouping of animals may be informative, it is informative about us, and not about the actual animals in the set.)

Female serial murderers appear to constitute a natural kind for several reasons. There may be a single (albeit no doubt complex) developmental trajectory to the phenomenon; female serial killers tend to kill in certain kinds of ways (either indirectly, through their partners, or covertly, via poisoning and smothering); they tend to choose similar victims (their own children, their unsuspecting husbands, their elderly charges, their ailing patients), and victims with whom they have a certain kind of personal relationship. And meanwhile the phenomenon differs from that of male serial murder in some important respects, especially, as we have suggested, in their choices of victim and preferred methods of killing.

A second feature we would like to note is that, from the perspective of the debates aforementioned in the *Female Nurture and Human Nature* section of this essay, there is a deeply paradoxical quality to all the cases mentioned above, since they all simultaneously undermine and reinforce prevailing stereotypes about gender. On the one hand, the very notion of female serial murder undermines the common conception of women as the "gentler sex." That it does this is revealed in the way people – including journalists, jurists, and even judges – commonly attempt to deny that the moral depravity of the female serial killer equals the male's: by suggesting, optimistically, that the angel of death might really have been a mercy killer; or by excusing the female member of a killer couple as not really a sexual sadist herself, but as merely highly suggestible or overly eager to please her male partner – is there anything a woman won't do for love? – as if she herself were just another helpless victim of that evil, male monster.

Or, accepting that the female serial killer is a murderer, many may still insist to themselves that at least poisoning isn't nearly so brutal as stabbing to death. But what lesser evil can this more "feminine" method of killing signify, when a slow death by poisoning is *more* agonizing than a sudden death by stabbing? And when the poisoner, unlike the shooter or the stabber, has hours and days in which she could but does not suffer a change of heart and call for a doctor – or at least cease administering the poison? Long hours and long days, also, in which she can delight in her victim's ceaseless suffering and her own power over it?[10]

And so the female serial killer is commonly denied, or merely ignored, as something of a conceptual impossibility. (Just as a female doctor was treated as a conceptual impossibility not so long ago, as the riddle in the introduction to this essay testifies to.)

Yet, at the very same time, there is *something* unsettlingly "feminine" about the killers described above. It is as though, in the female serial killer, we see a dark, grotesquely distorted version of traits that have been traditionally associated with women: fatal care-taking, lethal nurturing, depraved romantic devotion. In confessing her atrocities, Carol Bundy often came across as a hideous caricature of a little girl playing with dolls. ("We had a lot of fun with her," she said in reference to Exxie Wilson's severed head. "I made her up like Barbie.") Even Elizabeth Bathory – the legendary fifteenth-century "Blood Countess" who reputedly bathed in the blood of slaughtered virgins as a way of retaining her youth – exemplifies a stereotypically female trait: the lengths to which women will go in the interest of personal beautification.

Of Poets and Monsters: Our Common Nature

There is a limited parallel to be drawn between the image of femininity that female serial killers project and the image of masculinity projected by their male counterparts. The male serial killer is often a loner stalking the city streets, driven by blood-lust, on the prowl for casual sex with an anonymous stranger, a prostitute, his sexual thrill ultimately erupting as a fit of rage. In the male serial killer we find a grotesquely exaggerated

ELIZABETH SCHECHTER AND HAROLD SCHECHTER

image of masculinity. But there is an important difference between an exaggerated image and a distorted one.

With respect to prototypically male patterns of serial murder, the entire phenomenon, even at its deepest level – the ruthlessness, the incredible egotism, the willingness to go to any lengths for one's own sexual gratification, the complete lack of feeling for other people – presents a heightened, monstrous image of what is still recognizable as *masculinity*. (We are of course not saying that anything close to this actually characterizes most men; we aren't speaking of men or of maleness *per se* here, but of what is called "masculinity," or at least dominant conceptions of it.) Thus we may be shocked and horrified by the atrocities of a male serial killer: a man did *that*? But we are not shocked to learn that the atrocities were perpetrated by a *man*.

In contrast, there is an incredible tension between the image of femininity that the female serial killer projects and the image of femininity that she simultaneously violates. The tension is so great in part because people have tended to view the psychological traits that are absent in such a woman as inseparable from, as even responsible for, many of the socially crucial tasks that are still predominantly "women's work": the tending of the infirm, the forging and maintenance of romantic relationships, the careful preparation of the family meal. In fact, even some contemporary work on innate differences between the sexes has proposed that women's greater tendency to shoulder significant care-taking responsibilities is rooted in their purportedly greater degree of natural empathy and humanitarian concern, and so forth.[11] But female serial killers seek out those same "care-taking" responsibilities – and the romances, the marriages with children – without possessing any of the more basic emotional traits that we want to believe *motivate* those behaviors in the normal case.

Thus, while female serial killers and male serial killers may both constitute distinct natural kinds, *serial killers*, male and female, are arguably such a kind as well.[12] For while, at one deep level, the various types of female serial murder possess some characteristically "feminine" aspects, at another level, the most basic nature of the act – the ruthlessness of it, the incredible egotism, the willingness to go to any lengths for one's own sexual gratification, the complete lack of feeling for other people – presents, once again, a monstrously exaggerated image of masculinity.

Or perhaps of humanity. For some of the traits these monsters possess in abundance – cruelty, self-absorption, sadism – unfortunately appear widespread in our species, and not only in men. Consider a mother like Marybeth Tinnin, who got so high on the attention and sympathy she received following the natural death of one of her children that she went on to secretly murder and then publicly grieve eight more. (Munchausen syndrome by proxy, Tinnin's affliction, is an overwhelmingly female phenomenon.) Consider the phenomenon of so-called indirect aggression (spreading malicious rumors, ostracizing, belittling), the preferred form of bullying for girls[13] – though most recently epitomized by the adult Lori Drew, who "cyber-bullied" her daughter's peer, 13-year-old Megan Meier, into hanging herself. Remember that, as soon as they were permitted to, (white) women *did* join the Ku Klux Klan. (And remember also that long before they were permitted to stand alongside their fathers and husbands, they sewed their hooded gowns, as Carol Tavris points out in *The Mismeasure of Woman*.[14]) Consider that, as Jean Elshtain documents in *Women and War*, imperialistic fervor has struck not just male politicians and soldiers but also the women who bore them, these "givers of life."[15] (As one American woman wrote to her local paper, in enthusiastic support of the bombing of Hiroshima: "When one sets out to destroy vermin, does one try to leave a few alive in the nest? Certainly not!")

Fortunately, egotism and cruelty aren't the only traits we possess; generosity and compassion are also real and also widespread. But it is difficult to look at the sheer quantity of evil in the world and not conclude that much of this darkness is born in us. And that we are born with it.

Some readers may be astonished, or even offended, by the suggestion that serial murder reflects anything about human nature. Serial killers are of course exceptional in various ways. But so, too, is a Martin Luther King Jr., or an Emily Dickinson, and yet few would object to the claim that visionaries and geniuses shed some light on our kind, even though the vast majority of us never approach such insight or accomplishment or sheer feeling for the world. What rankles is the claim that monsters, too, have a human nature. But they do: some of the very traits that make them monsters are still recognizably and uniquely human. This is why we suggest that they, too, male and female, speak a part of the truth about us all.

NOTES

1 Camille Paglia, *Sexual Personae: Art and Decadence from Nefertiti to Emily Dickinson* (New Haven: Yale University Press, 1991), p. 247.
2 Steven Pinker, *The Blank Slate: The Modern Denial of Human Nature* (New York: Viking, 2002), p. 1.

ELIZABETH SCHECHTER AND HAROLD SCHECHTER

3   Nativism is also typically associated with the claim that certain concepts are innate in our species – for example, the concept of *quantity*, or of an *agent* – and even that humans innately represent certain information about the world – for example, that a ball rolling towards a wall will hit the wall and stop or roll backwards rather than pass through it unimpeded. See Richard Samuels, "Nativism," in John Symons and Paco Calvo (eds.) *The Routledge Companion to Philosophy of Psychology* (London: Routledge, 2009), pp. 322–35.

4   On the possibility of a "cheater detection module," see Leda Cosmides and John Tooby, "Cognitive Adaptions for Social Exchange," in J. H. Barkow, L. Cosmides, and J. Tooby (eds.) *The Adapted Mind: Evolutionary Psychology and the Generation of Culture* (New York: Oxford University Press, 1992), pp. 163–228.

5   David Buss, Todd Shackelford, Lee Kirkpatrick, and Randy Larsen, "A Half Century of American Mate Preferences: The Cultural Evolution of Values," *Journal of Marriage and the Family* 63 (2001): 491–503.

6   Margo Wilson and Martin Daly, "The Man Who Mistook His Wife for a Chattel," in J. H. Barkow et al. (eds.) *The Adapted Mind: Evolutionary Psychology and the Generation of Culture* (New York: Oxford University Press, 1992), pp. 289–326.

7   David Buss, *The Dangerous Passion: Why Jealousy Is as Natural as Love and Sex* (New York: Free Press, 2000).

8   For a nativist's critique of some of the science of innate sex differences, see for instance Elizabeth Spelke, "Sex Differences in Intrinsic Aptitude for Mathematics and Science? A Critical Review," *American Psychologist* 60 (2005): 950–8. Scientific defenders of innate differences between the sexes deny that they are guilty of gender essentialism for several important reasons. The most basic is that they believe that any interesting innate psychological differences between the sexes will be merely statistical; there will be many more differences among men and among women than there will be (average) differences between men and women. Another is that contemporary nativists don't believe that an innate predisposition will lead inexorably to the behavior that it disposes one towards. We, for instance, suggest that there is some sort of innate drive towards violence in our species, but in plenty of places and cultures, many people go their entire adult lives without ever acting violently. And we certainly don't believe that because human violence is natural it is somehow morally okay, much less that it ought to be decriminalized; "natural" isn't a synonym for "good." (Anyway, prohibitions on violence are also quite natural to our species.)

9   For a comprehensive guide to serial murder, see Harold Schecter, *The Serial Killer Files: The Who, What, Where, How, and Why of the World's Most Terrifying Murderers* (New York: Ballantine Books, 2003).

10 See Patricia Pearson, *When She Was Bad: Violent Women and the Myth of Innocence* (New York: Viking, 1997) for extended examples and discussions

of female violence and of the ways in which this violence is commonly misperceived. Also see Ann Jones, *Women Who Kill* (New York: Ballantine Books, 1980) for further detail: when judges and jurists finally do become convinced of a female murderer's guilt, they often subject her to even harsher punishment than the average man who has committed a similar crime receives, presumably because the female killer is viewed as even more of an aberration than the male killer. She is punished, in effect, not just for having committed the crime itself, but also for having violated her "feminine role" in committing it.

11 Simon Baron-Cohen, *The Essential Difference: The Truth About the Male and Female Brain* (New York: Basic Books, 2003).

12 Compare: *Homo sapiens* and *Pan troglodytes* (the common chimpanzee) are both distinct natural kinds, but they both belong to the single kind *primate*, as well.

13 Rachel Simmons, *Odd Girl Out: The Hidden Culture of Aggression in Girls* (New York: Harcourt, 2002).

14 Carol Tavris, *The Mismeasure of Woman* (New York: Simon and Schuster, 1992).

15 Jean Bethke Elshtain, *Women and War* (New York: Basic Books, 1987).

ELIZABETH SCHECHTER AND HAROLD SCHECHTER

CHAPTER 10

IT PUTS THE LOTION IN THE BASKET
The Language of Psychopathy

Creepy tone and cadence aside, as a philosopher studying the reasons for the moral judgments we make, few lines of pop culture dialogue intrigue me more than those spoken by James "Buffalo Bill" Gumb in the film *Silence of the Lambs*. Standing above a dry well, peering down at his soon-to-be next victim, Buffalo Bill (so called because he "skins his humps") instructs young Catherine in her duty, saying, "It rubs the lotion on its skin. It does this whenever it's told." Granted, after years of cultural allusions and parody, these lines have lost some of their horrifying impact. And yes, Buffalo Bill is a fictional (though fact-based) character. Nevertheless, these lines of dialogue are a wonderful template for how we judge serial killers, how we think of them, and what we assume about them and the parts of human nature they lack. Of course, it is conventional wisdom to think of serial killers as emotionally detached or distant from their victims, so Buffalo Bill's reference to Catherine as "it" appears straightforward – he is psychologically imbalanced or impaired, he does not see her as human but inanimate, which implies he feels no guilt in killing her to make his skin-dress. Yet, this explanation leaves me wanting.

Why, exactly, do we feel repulsion at the objectifying of Catherine? What methods are available to classify Buffalo Bill's pathological behavior? What standards of human conduct and human nature has Buffalo Bill violated, and where do these standards come from? Ultimately, why do we find him so morally abhorrent? To answer these questions, I evaluate Buffalo Bill through philosopher Jürgen Habermas's notion of *communicative rationality*, and I get there in three steps.

First, I show that current clinical and psychiatric classifications of Buffalo Bill are too narrow, in part because they fail to answer fundamental questions about our moral expectations of human behavior that might explain our repulsion. Human beings expect others to treat them in at least minimally moral ways. For instance, no one wants to be forced into death, particularly murdered. Even in those extremely aberrant cases where someone has asked to be killed, asking is quite different from having someone sneak up uninvited to lop off your head. When we want to die – like with suicide, assisted suicide, or "praying" for death – we intentionally opt for death, and this is quite different from having that option chosen for us. The point is that the expectation not to be "unexpectedly" killed is a moral expectation grounded in our human nature and our deep-seated human traits. If so, then when these expectations are not met – like with Buffalo Bill – our repulsion stems from a violation of some deep-seated human trait, like communication, as we shall see.

Second, I connect this current lack of moral grounding to confusion in the fields of psychiatry and psychology regarding the difference between *antisocial personality disorder* (ASPD) and *psychopathy*.[1] As we shall see, there is a dispute about whether these two disorders are different kinds of disorders, different degrees of the same disorder, or even just the same disorder, full stop. For those who think they are different kinds of disorders, ASPD manifests through behaviors like repeated lying, reckless disregard for others and self, and lack of remorse, while psychopathy manifests through personality traits like lack of empathy. The difference is that ASPD is strictly about how we act, whereas psychopathy is about inherent and entrenched reasons or conditions for one's actions. It is my argument that the reasons for the actions of psychopaths can be traced (at least in part) to deficits in deep-seated human traits like communication, as reflected in personality traits, like the inability to feel for others. In other words, human beings are designed in a certain way, they have a certain human nature, if you will, and these designs are our deep-seated human traits, like how we are designed to communicate with one another by taking the other's perspective, not something other animals appear to do. Personality traits, then, are the *personal* ways we confront and engage these human traits – even though we probably do this without reflection. This is like playing a sport where there are rules we must follow, but within the rules we can play as we see fit; however, deviate from the rules, especially fundamental rules, and the sport ceases to be. If I grab the ball in my hands and proceed to run around the field, I am no longer playing soccer. Similarly, humans are constructed with certain capacities and traits, or a nature; we can play within these boundaries to create our unique personalities, but if we bend these deep-seated boundaries too far, our humanity fades. This is what happens to psychopaths.

Therefore, third, I argue that by grounding our evaluation of people like Buffalo Bill in something fundamental about human nature, such as a deep-seated trait like communication, we shift the focus from behaviors to the reasons behind them and provide a moral explanation for psychopathy. As such, our repulsion for Buffalo Bill's words to Catherine is generated by our recognition that he has an impaired communicative rationality, a core capacity of humans. This means our repulsion is a recognition that Buffalo Bill has lost (or never had) a major part of a human capacity we expect all humans to have. Essentially, humans are designed as communicative beings; we are by nature geared towards understanding one another through perspective-taking, where we can anticipate one another's response because we are designed to capture the other's perspective – cognitively, a very complicated and complex process. This is how we gain our capacity of empathy, something Buffalo Bill is missing.

Why a Moral Grounding

When someone is diagnosed with a disorder, more than their psychological state is being assessed. When we listen to Buffalo Bill's dialogue and declare "That dude's crazy," or more professionally "He has ASPD" (the current stand-in for psychopathy), we are making moral claims that are grounded in an understanding of human nature. Psychological assessments of Buffalo Bill's behavior invoke a notion of pathology (or abnormality); this suggests a *presupposed normative assessment of human behavior*. Think of it this way: if you say he's crazy, you can only do so based on some standard of how humans ought to behave. This suggests you know what it means to be human and have standards (hopefully that are defensible) for proper human behavior. We call these standards *norms*.

Imagine one day I wake up to find my dog Ballu unable to stand on his legs. I automatically panic because I know this is not how a dog ought to behave; Ballu is violating a norm of dog behavior through this abnormal exhibition. How do I know this is abnormal? Over time, through our observations of dogs, and then our contemplation and debate on these observations, we established a definition of the proper nature of dogs. Of course, we add to and subtract from this definition – which becomes the basis of our *normative assessment* – when we learn new things about dogs, but nonetheless, we establish criteria for their proper behavior by referring to this definition. This is the same thing we do with humans – though admittedly, it has proven more complex and controversial because we have trouble agreeing on the definition and the source of the norms. Regardless of where the norms come from – they could be handed down from cultural traditions, or religion, or pronounced by science – they are telling us something about what it means to be human and how we ought to behave, and these are ultimately moral claims.

Why is Buffalo Bill's behavior abhorrent? More specifically, why is Buffalo Bill's "conversation" with Catherine abhorrent? These questions lie at the center of our declaration that his behavior is clinically pathological. They are not questions, however, answered in psychological assessments – they are merely assumed to have been already answered. When the clinician steps in to evaluate Buffalo Bill, she assumes – likely without consciously knowing so – that the behaviors she is evaluating are unacceptable. She works with accepted norms – "If patient A exhibits these behaviors, he has X disorder" – that become disguised as pathological disorders. This suggests that before the clinician starts studying behaviors to see if they "fit" a disorder, even before she establishes a group of behaviors *as* a disorder, she imagines (or contemplates) some behaviors as not normal. The dilemma, however, is whether she assesses these behaviors with an explicit understanding that she is judging people based on a concept of proper human nature, or whether she does so with no, or maybe only implicit, acknowledgment of these norms.

To explain this, let us turn again to the example of my dog. Do we say, "Hey, dogs that do not walk are not good or healthy dogs," or do we say, "Dogs are animals that are designed to walk on four legs, so they ought to be able to walk based on this nature"? What separates the two declarations is that the latter makes an explicit acknowledgment of the base-level norms, as grounded in an assessment of the dog's nature, while the former – even though it may arise from this grounded assessment – does not pay heed to it *explicitly*. To put it one way, by smuggling in the norms without acknowledging them, we never address the source of the disorder in our concept of human nature. At best, we can follow the actions of those before us and label certain behaviors as unacceptable, even though we may be able to say nothing more than, "For the good of society, people should not act this way." At worst, we may end up mislabeling behaviors, oversimplifying disorders, overestimating the numbers of people with disorders, and underestimating those with truly pathological conditions. Even more, we may end up missing the grounding reasons for our repulsion towards certain behaviors because we never acknowledge the deep-seated human traits that are being violated. Put another way, potentially too many people display the behaviors listed, while potentially too many others have traits not easily categorized in behaviors. When our judgments become limited to behaviors alone, as opposed to traits or conditions, the abnormality of disorders like ASPD is distorted with categories that are overly broad and under-conceptualized.

Put still a different way, when we establish a disorder, do we back into the norms, or do we come at them head on? For instance, at ground zero of constructing a disorder, do we imagine behaviors as problematic, or do we imagine personality traits, conditions, and deviations from human nature as problematic and work our way back to the behaviors? For example, to get ASPD as a disorder, do we first see certain personality traits, affective conditions, and states of mind that deviate from human nature and our deep-seated traits as abnormal, and then make the move to behaviors that display these various traits and conditions? Or, do we collect behaviors into categories of normal and abnormal based on traditional patterns of thought in psychology and medicine?

If you look at the diagnostic criteria for ASPD, you can see some of Buffalo Bill's behaviors there.[2] He is deceitful, lies, acts aggressively, and lacks remorse for his behavior. But there is certainly no indication why these sorts of behaviors are pathological; it is simply assumed from the beginning we ought not employ them.[3] We often assume norms of behavior without question. Sure, some assumptions about norms work out to be harmless. For instance, assuming that lying is bad turns out to be a good assumption. But assuming that women ought not vote, or that African Americans should be slaves, turn out to be pretty darn terrible assumptions. It would be advisable, then, especially when thinking about psychological pathologies, to think about the norms informing our categorizing of behaviors.

There is something about the lines Buffalo Bill speaks that is abhorrent beyond ASPD, something that intuitively tells us, "Hey, that's not the way people should *ever* speak to others." Perhaps our abhorrence of his lines is built into our human nature and is simultaneously assumed and ignored when we pass clinical and popular judgments on those we find abnormal. It is assumed in that we classify Buffalo Bill's behavior as pathological; it is ignored in that we do not acknowledge the source of this classification, both because we do not address the root of why this behavior is abnormal, and because we *only* address behaviors. By not making such moral groundings explicit, our judgments are that much weaker and harder to defend. In other words, if we do not know the root of why we believe something beyond, say, the traditions of a profession like psychiatry, we will have an awfully difficult time defending what we believe when challenged. For example, if I ask you why lying is unacceptable, and you say, "Because it is" or "Because people should not do it," then you are following a rule blindly. Of course, when pressed about lying, most of us can find at least some moral reason against it. The problem, however, is that we all too often follow rules blindly that in hindsight have questionable moral grounding – like believing women should not vote, or African Americans ought to be slaves.

Traits versus Behaviors

There is a dispute among mental health professionals about how to classify antisocial tendencies and whether to classify psychopathy as a separate disorder from ASPD.[4] Some psychiatrists and researchers challenge the notion of ASPD as a separate disorder, suggesting it relies completely on behaviors without looking deeper into the person and understanding one's emotional and interpersonal traits. After all, one can behave in a rigid manner because one is angry, or afraid, or obsessive-compulsive; or one can be friendly because one likes people, or one wants to swindle them, or because one is overly dependent. In short, behaviors do not always tell us what is going on inside someone's mind. Consequently, when you diagnose someone with ASPD through an examination of her behaviors alone, you miss something important in the understanding and classification of the disorder.

How about an example of traits versus behaviors? Many of us lie, but we do not all lie for the same reasons. I might lie to not hurt another's feelings, you might lie to avoid punishment for something you regret doing but did anyway, and Ted Bundy lied because he wanted to lure young women into situations of vulnerability so that he could brutally torture and kill them. All three of us lied, but we did not do so for the same reasons. For most of us, the act of lying does not represent a deep, disturbing moral flaw. For us, lying is a behavior that is momentary; and while it might reveal something about our inner state of emotions and motivations, it does not suggest that we have personality traits like Ted Bundy. Traits are constant states (or dispositions) inside of us that come out in behaviors at moments when the trait is jolted into action; it is a condition inside of us – a tendency of thought and emotion. While traits come out in behaviors, the same behavior in different people might happen because of different traits. They come out under specific conditions, through a series of varying and diverse behaviors. Consequently, to suppose that one can infer a person's traits by simply reducing them to narrow behaviors on a list does not seem to follow.

As an example, one of Ted Bundy's traits was a lack of empathy for others, particularly women, and his lying was part of the manifestation of this trait. The other manifestation was his killing of women, especially in the manner in which he did it. Again, the killing or murder of others can happen for many reasons. You can kill for self-defense, out of momentary rage, because you are careless or reckless, or because you enjoy killing. As far as we know, Bundy killed because he enjoyed it, because it gave him a rush and a sense of power over others. These motivations are different from those of others who kill. This means that traits are complex; they are hard to spot and identify through surface observation; and they are woven deep into our psyche.

This is at least one reason ASPD came to subsume psychopathy as a disorder: traits are not easy to spot. When a clinician sits down with a patient, it is arguably easier and more efficient to look for behaviors that fit a list – like lying – than to look at behavioral patterns, measure them against the patterns of the larger population, consider them in reference to norms, and make logical inferences about the patient's motivations. But while ease and efficiency matter, do they matter enough to challenge the moral and clinical significance of traits? Also, just think of the financial and social costs of over-diagnosing some people and under-diagnosing others. Distinguishing between ASPD and psychopathy means that the estimated 1 percent of the population with psychopathic traits does not get lost within the larger category of ASPD. Do we want psychopaths, those with deep-seated traits of deviation, to go undiagnosed? As Robert D. Hare, a well-regarded researcher on psychopathy, writes, "it is the egocentric, cold-blooded and remorseless psychopaths who blend into all aspects of society and have such devastating impacts on people around them who send chills down the spines of law enforcement officers."[5] This seems reason enough to reconsider the diagnosis of psychopathy.

At present, ASPD amounts to nothing more than a list of behaviors seen frequently in the general population, and certainly in my student body – reckless disregard for safety, lack of remorse for mistreating others, consistent irresponsibility, impulsivity and failure to plan ahead – oh no, looks like many of my students (and sadly, sometimes me). I assume most of my students are not psychopaths, so the time of mental health workers would be better spent finding those who are and treating them (if possible), instead of over-diagnosing the population.

My reasons, however, for paying heed to traits, and distinguishing between ASPD and psychopathy, go further. As mentioned above, Buffalo Bill has indeed committed some of these actions classified as ASPD, but those actions alone should not be our urge to call him psychopathic, or even antisocial. It is that the actions committed came from personality traits we find most devoid of humanity and fit a continual pattern of behaviors that point to psychopathy. He did not just kill one woman, he killed several; and his actions demonstrate he did so without any regard for their human value, considering them as purely means to his ends, believing his need for their skin more important than their lives. Even more, his lines to Catherine lack any empathy, any recognition of her humanity, and this matches the pattern of his wider actions. When he speaks to her, she is a skin-suit in need of slaying; he does not recognize her as an interlocutor in a conversation; it would seem he is incapable of proper communication. If Buffalo Bill is a psychopath, is it because he is missing the capacity to follow the logic of communication built into our nature?

As philosopher Jürgen Habermas tells us, *communicative rationality* – which differs from *instrumental rationality* – is a deep-seated human trait that is made up of processes like perspective-taking and reciprocity – the building blocks of empathy.[6] Habermas says that communication has an internal logic; just think of the rules and procedures we must follow for communication to take place. While each culture might have specific ways of communicating, they all share common denominators that are inescapably linked to our human nature. Communicative rationality is the innate reasoning capacity we have to understand others and to have them understand us. This is different from instrumental rationality, which is our capacity to make goals and strategizing how to achieve them. Communicative rationality is the logic of understanding; instrumental rationality is the logic of strategy.

Without the rationality of communication our humanity crumbles because we no longer can empathize with others, or take the perspectives of others, or reciprocate their intentions. When this happens, we have, if all things line up, psychopathy. Psychopaths do not necessarily lose their humanness or ability to function in human society, as someone like Ted Bundy shows, but they have difficulty exercising capacities that are essential to their humanity or for fitting into human society without continued deception, lying, manipulation, and cunning. What Buffalo Bill's lines to Catherine give us, then, is a window into his communicatively irrational mind; this helps explain his further actions, and also our repulsion. Seen from this perspective, his actions repulse us because of what they say about his personality traits (and thus his lack of certain deep-seated human traits) and his inability to rationally interact with others. We are, as Habermas puts it, communicative beings, and when we lose this capacity, like Buffalo Bill, we slip into mental illness, because we can no longer do what others expect from us, and interestingly, what we expect from ourselves, all things being equal. This means when you say, "Gee, that Buffalo Bill is not right in the head," there are cognitive reasons for this response that go beyond the source of the traits. Indeed, there are several possible sources for Buffalo Bill's traits: he might have physiological head trauma or he might have been severely psychologically abused as a child. But we do not grow repulsed by the possibility that someone has damage to a region of the brain or was once abused psychologically. We abhor the manifest behaviors and personality traits that signal someone is incapable of the human conduct we expect from them. It is the violation of our moral expectations that repulse us.

Primates, Communication, and Serial Killers

We often think of ourselves as isolated individuals who could walk away from society at any time we desire. We might think of ourselves as independent, as uninfluenced by others, as making our own decisions, as fully responsible for our own lives. Philosophers in the modern Western tradition often consider human beings this way, as *autonomous* and fully independent decision-makers. But this point of view seems to suggest that living in a society is optional and that we evolved from solitary creatures without a need for interaction, communication, and the other aspects of culture. Frans de Waal, who has spent several decades studying primate behavior, suggests that "there never was a point at which we became social: descended from highly social ancestors – a long line of monkeys and apes – we have been group-living forever."[7] At the root of his statement, de Waal is confronting a long-standing notion that humans are isolated agents out for maximizing self-interest. This idea of human nature as asocial, individualistic, and free from the bonds of others, seems contrary to evolutionary theory and lots of empirical evidence that says we are by nature social and interconnected with others.

Yet, de Waal's claim is actually even stronger. He says not only are we naturally social creatures, but the accompanied capacities like reciprocity, empathy, and perspective-taking evolved too and form continuity with our primate ancestors.[8] It is beyond our scope here to debate whether animals actually have morality; instead, I want to work in the other direction. If capacities like empathy were part of our evolution – and de Waal's primate tests strongly suggest that we at least evolved the elemental forms of these capacities long ago – then morality is not simply a veneer over our selfish genes; it is, rather, a reflection of our deep-seated human traits.[9]

There is, however, another way to strengthen this argument. As we have seen, communication is not just a minor mental process; it is a form of rationality unlike other rationalities. When we are instrumentally rational, we have a task we want to achieve and we plan to make that happen. This is why serial killers should not be considered irrational, as they are often instrumentally rational. Some of them – like Ted Bundy – are anything but irrational in this respect; he was very good at planning and devising to reach his goal of killing young women.

Communicative rationality, however, is something different; this is rationality with the primary function of mutual understanding, not task achievement. With much of Western thought wrapped up in the metaphysical notion that humans are isolated agents, rationality has often been conveyed as merely instrumental. But if de Waal and Habermas are right, and we have always been social creatures utterly connected to one another through communication, then communicative rationality might play a larger role in our behavior than previously thought.

Think of communicative rationality this way. Human beings, as social beings, are designed to understand others (what Habermas calls the *telos* of understanding, the Greek word for "end"), illustrated by such examples as coordinating mutual wellbeing, developing ways to overcome difficult conditions, manipulating environs, solving problems and disputes, procreating, raising offspring, celebrating achievements and losses, securing identities, protection, and so on. Even when we are physically alone, we are never without others; they remain in our thoughts, in our reflections, in our deliberations of conscience. Communicative rationality is a capacity – like walking – that comes to us naturally in time (assuming there are no impairments). Like walking, which requires other smaller capacities such as muscle coordination, foot movements, and balancing, communicative rationality requires other capacities too. For communicative rationality, we need to have at least *perspective-taking* and *reciprocity*. Perspective-taking is the process of thinking through someone else's situation. For example, when I ask "How are you?" and you respond "Terrible!" I might worry because I take your perspective and imagine the possible reasons for your exclamation; this I can only do when I see you as a full human being just like me. Reciprocity is the process of giving back to others what they give to you, or vice versa. For example, when you take my perspective in a conversation, I should do the same in return. Reciprocity guarantees conversations go in both directions, a key to human coordination and understanding. Perspective-taking and reciprocity are bedrocks to any moral system because without them we cannot appreciate other people as people just like us, and so we cannot value their thoughts, emotions, or lives. These capacities are the foundations for feelings of empathy. Therefore, communicative rationality is a common denominator of all moral systems.

When our communicative rationality begins to disintegrate, the loss of perspective-taking and reciprocity becomes apparent in our awkward, even frightening dialogue, as our ability to interact with others begins to dissolve. Like Buffalo Bill, we cannot take the perspective of others if we don't think of them as human or equal, and we ask from them things we are unwilling to give back in return – all of which is reflected in our communication. Think of the horror film *The Strangers*, where the murderers never communicate with their victims, save for one short reply at the end. Or take the infamous serial killer Richard Ramirez, who said, "I told one lady to give me all her money. She said no. So I cut her and pulled out her eyes." There is no perspective-taking here, no reciprocity, no empathy. Or how about serial killer Edmund Kemper, who when asked what he thought when he saw a pretty girl walking down the street replied, "One side of me says, 'I'd like to talk to her, date her.' The other side of me says, 'I wonder how her head would look on a stick?'" His words, his dialogue, show us his communicative irrationality, his lack of empathy, his deep-seated disconnection from others. Maybe minor disturbances in our communicative rationality lead to ASPD, but major disturbances lead to psychopathy. The dissolution of perspective-taking and reciprocity means we can no longer empathize with others; we see others as objects incapable of giving us perspectives and unworthy of reciprocity. As a result, our ability to moralize and understand moral systems dissolves too.

If we are social creatures, that evolved accordingly and with certain social proclivities; and if these social proclivities gave way to fundamental capacities like perspective-taking and reciprocity; and if these capacities are part of all moral systems; and if these capacities are embedded in the larger, more complex capacity of communicative rationality that allows us to interact with others – then stunting, impairing, or injuring this capacity could have grave consequences for our moral reasoning, our empathy towards others, our ability to appreciate another's perspective, our ability to reciprocate another's kind gesture, or our ability to see another as human. Clearly, if this line of reasoning holds, loss of communicative rationality could amount to psychopathy, as some define it. Since this rationality is communicative, its clearest expression might come through dialogues with others. Is this what we see when Buffalo Bill says to Catherine, "It rubs the lotion on its skin. It does this whenever it's told." Is he showing his communicative irrationality, his loss of reciprocity and perspective-taking? If so, then perhaps our repulsion at his dialogue is our own communicative rationality kicking in, letting us know he is violating our moral expectations.

NOTES

1 For a readable history of psychopathy, see John Seabrook, "Suffering Souls: The Search for the Roots of Psychopathy," *The New Yorker* (November 10, 2008): 64–73.
2 American Psychiatric Association, *Diagnostic and Statistical Manual of Mental Disorders*, 4th edn. (Washington: American Psychiatric Association, 1994), pp. 645–50.
3 Seabrook, "Suffering Souls."
4 Robert D. Hare, "Psychopathy and Antisocial Personality Disorder: A Case of Diagnostic Confusion," *Psychiatric Times* 13, 2 (Feb. 1, 1996): 39–40; quote at p. 5.
5 Ibid.
6 On sanity and communication, see Jürgen Habermas, *Moral Consciousness and Communicative Action*, trans. Christian Lenhardt and Shierry Weber Nicholsen (Cambridge, MA: MIT Press, 1990), p. 100. For an overview of his theory, see Jürgen Habermas, *Inclusion of the Other*, ed. Ciaran Cronin and Pablo De Greiff (Cambridge, MA: MIT Press, 1998), pp. 3–46.
7 Frans de Waal, *Primates and Philosophers* (Princeton: Princeton University Press, 2006), p. 4.
8 Ibid, pp. 30–1.
9 Ibid, p. 21.

CHAPTER 11

ARE SERIAL KILLERS
COLD-BLOODED KILLERS?

One of the reasons we are so fascinated by serial killers, both real and fictional, is that we are trying to figure out why they are different from us. There is a branch of philosophy known as *moral psychology* which investigates what psychological factors make us moral or immoral beings. Moral psychologists are not focused on questions like "what is the right thing to do?" Instead, they are interested in why some people are able to act on their moral principles and others fail to do what they think is right. Moral psychology offers us two theories to explain why some people kill repeatedly while most of us never do: (1) *lack of empathy*, and (2) *lack of impulse control*. This essay critiques the lack of empathy explanation.

In Cold Bold: The Moral Psychology of Fictional Serial Killers

When we look at some of the best-known fictional serial killers we see the same moral psychology presented over and over again. Let's start with Hannibal Lecter. Lecter is portrayed as a brilliant doctor with both a very keen understanding of the human mind and cannibalistic urges. In the movie version of *Red Dragon*, we see him as an occasional consultant on serial killer cases even before his incarceration; and in both the books and other movies in which Lecter appears as a character he is consulted by the FBI for insight into other serial killers.

The idea of the brilliant, manipulative, and ultimately remorseless serial killer is not unusual in serial-killer fiction. Catherine Tramell, the character played by Sharon Stone in the two *Basic Instinct* films, is incredibly skilled at getting people to do what she wants. She seems to regard her lovers as tools that she can toss aside when they are no longer useful. Similarly, Tom Ripley, who first appeared in Patricia Highsmith's *The Talented Mr. Ripley*, is a very sharp individual who will kill whenever it is necessary to achieve his goals. Tramell and Ripley are so skillful at manipulating people and covering their tracks that neither is ever brought to justice. And we get the impression in the film *Red Dragon* that Lecter was only caught as a fluke. Even though he's captured, Lecter is able to manipulate his way out of maximum security and live the remainder of his life on the lam.

All three characters are very intelligent, cold and calculating, and seem to lack any concern for those they've killed. In the movie version of *Red Dragon*, Lecter kills a musician because he was off-key. According to the picture presented by these characters, what seems to be missing is *empathy*.

I Think I'll Eat Your Heart: The Lack-of-Empathy Explanation

However, "empathy" has a number of different meanings that would suggest very different deficiencies in our serial killers. Some people use "empathy" as a synonym for compassion, remorse, or some other feeling. When people say that serial killers lack empathy, it appears they mean it as more than a placeholder for some emotion. For the claim to be philosophically interesting, there must be something distinct about empathy. In psychoanalysis, empathy refers to the ability to understand what someone else is feeling (in a clinical sense, without any accompanying emotions). In social psychology, empathy refers to a vicarious emotional state that is being felt because of someone else's situation. In discussions of literature, empathy often refers to a feeling of attachment or connection to the character that gets us involved in the story. The list could go on, but for our purposes three general notions of empathy seem relevant: understanding, vicarious feeling, and connection. Good philosophers

ANDREW TERJESEN

separate out the different definitions of a confusing term and evaluate them one by one, and that is what we will do now.

Which of these kinds of empathy do our fictional serial killers lack? It might be tempting to say that they lack the ability to understand what someone else is feeling. However, if that were true, then they would be very bad serial killers. One thing Lecter, Ripley, and Tramell have in common is a masterful grasp of the human mind and its emotional states. If they could not understand how others feel, they would not be very good at manipulating them. Moreover, Lecter does torture some of his victims as punishment. If he did not know they were suffering, he would not be able to torture them successfully, or take satisfaction in it.

Okay, so maybe they do have empathy in the form of understanding, and instead it is empathy in the sense of connection that they lack; as a result they are not affected the way we are affected when we see someone suffering. But in philosophy, we should be able to give some account of *why* they are not affected the way the rest of us are. If the answer is simply that they lack empathy in the sense of the ability to form attachments, then this would not really tell us anything. What we learn is that serial killers are different from us because serial killers are different from us; they are not affected as we are by someone else's emotions because they react differently. This is called *circular reasoning* in philosophy, and no explanation can be circular and still useful or interesting. (In addition, especially in the novel *Hannibal*, Lecter seems to form a genuine emotional attachment to Clarice Starling, so he *does* respond as we do!)

The philosopher John Deigh argues that psychopaths lack what he calls *mature empathy*.[1] He acknowledges that serial killers must be able to understand what others feel (and even respond as we do) in a basic way. What Lecter, Ripley, and Tramell lack is the ability to see other people as being individuals like themselves. Mature empathy is a specific kind of connection reflecting our ability to connect with beings as having similar worth as ourselves. People who lack this kind of empathy don't see people as having plans and goals that are worth respecting. Instead, people appear to them as tools which they can manipulate to achieve their own goals. Deigh's take on the problem of *psychopathy* fits with the way we usually talk about serial killers – they are cold-blooded manipulators. But we encounter the same problem of circular reasoning. To simply say that serial killers are unable to see others as people does not really tell us how they are different from us. It answers the question by putting off the hard work: what does it mean to not be able to connect with others as people?

Dexter and the Extreme Lack of Understanding

One possible explanation for being unable to connect with others is not being able to understand how others think. If someone doesn't react in a way you can understand, they don't seem to be a *real* person. A good, recent example of a fictional serial killer that gives us insight into how this must work is Dexter Morgan. In the novels (beginning with *Darkly Dreaming Dexter*) and the television series, he seems to have trouble empathizing (in the sense of understanding).

In his internal narration, Dexter describes himself as completely devoid of emotion and repeatedly insists he is without feeling. His seemingly emotional responses are all part of an elaborate act that his adoptive father, Harry Morgan, taught him so that he would fit in with everyday people. Interestingly, Dexter's problems with emotion seem to be a two-way street. Not only does Dexter have to fake feeling emotion, he seems to have difficulty understanding it in others. As he says at one point in the television series, "I can kill a man, dismember his body and be home in time for Letterman. But knowing what to say when my girlfriend's feeling insecure? I'm totally lost." Dexter's dealings with his girlfriend Rita are filled with awkward misunderstandings based on Dexter's lack of understanding of what should be obvious to any normal person. A good example of this is his attempt to initiate sex with Rita while she is sobbing as she watches *Terms of Endearment*.

Harry's training seemed to be as much about getting Dexter to recognize the meaning of the emotional reactions of others as it was about Dexter exhibiting signs of the emotional reactions people would expect to see. Harry Morgan thinks that it is important for Dexter to do this so he would "fit in." This reinforces the idea that we connect with people when they appear like us and expressing emotion is an important part of who we are as people. Real-life serial killer Ted Bundy, probably the most "normal" of all serial killers, claimed that he had difficulty reading the emotions of others and felt disengaged. Of course, we have to take this with a grain of salt, as Bundy had possible ulterior motives for depicting himself as mentally deficient.

Is this then the key difference between serial killers and the rest of us: Serial killers cannot be affected by the emotional reactions of others – they can't see them as people – because they lack the ability to recognize the emotional states of others? This fleshes out Deigh's idea that serial killers lack mature empathy by giving us a mechanism

ANDREW TERJESEN

malfunction that explains this deficiency in serial killers. They have trouble walking a mile in someone else's shoes.

However, this also flags a basic problem with Deigh's moral psychology. There seems to be another group of people who also lack the ability to comprehend the emotional states and thoughts of others, those who are diagnosed as having *autism spectrum disorder*. In fact, there is good evidence that autistics also have difficulty seeing others as persons with their own distinct sets of goals and desires. But, it would be absurd to suggest that every autistic is a potential serial killer. Even if serial killers have trouble comprehending or experiencing the emotions of others, or lack mature empathy, that is not sufficient to make them serial killers. Something else must play a role in their behavior. Let's leave the fictional accounts and consider the moral psychologies of some real serial killers.

The Hot-Blooded Reality: Sex, Rage, Fame

Describing Dexter Morgan (or Ted Bundy) as emotionless is actually misleading. When Dexter tells Sgt. Doakes that he doesn't feel anything, Doakes retorts, "Who's lying now?" Dexter is able to experience emotions like affection, rage, and loyalty to his family – even his urge to kill seems to be something that could be classified as an emotional response. He has problems dealing appropriately with these emotions, but he does not lack them. Let's ignore the revelation in the novel *Dexter in the Dark* that his "Dark Passenger" is actually a supernatural entity suppressing Dexter's emotions. For our purposes that only solidifies a point that someone like Dexter just can't exist in the real world. Although people have speculated about it, Thomas Harris has never officially identified someone as the model for Hannibal Lecter. This is probably because no flesh-and-blood being could behave in as cool and calculated a manner. Real serial killers must operate differently.

Emotion often lies at the heart of real serial killings. Jeffrey Dahmer, for example, seemed to act out of sexual desire mixed with shame over those desires. It's not even clear that he wanted to kill (as Dexter does) as much as he had perverse desires to preserve these men and experiment with their bodies. Nor is Dahmer the super-smart serial killer who eludes the police by his wits. The homophobia of two police detectives did more to help him evade the law than Dahmer's intelligence. People ignored a lot of signs (especially the decomposing smell) because they didn't want to delve too deeply into *that* lifestyle (or maybe they assumed that homosexuals were just weird). John Wayne Gacy seems to have had similar issues and motivations, although he did a much better job of maintaining a mask of normalcy.

Dennis Rader, the BTK Killer in Wichita, was by his own admission motivated by sexual desire and obsession. In a 1978 letter about his crimes he refers to the "sexual relief" of killing someone and being turned on by his actions. Rader also seemed to be motivated by a desire for fame, as he corresponded with authorities and even complained that his killings were not being recognized as the work of a serial killer. Like Gacy, Rader maintained a "normal life" for over thirty years. Once again dispelling the myth of the super-smart killer eluding police, he became a person of interest when he sent a floppy disc that contained identifying information to the police. He had asked the police if they could trace a floppy disk and they (as anyone should expect) lied to him and told him it was impossible.

There is a long list of serial killers, like Gary Ridgway (the Green River Killer) and Arthur Shawcross (the Genesee River Killer), who seem to have been motivated by a hatred of women and took out their aggressions on the women they abducted and killed. Or a list of those who were simply angry at society. Though it is disputed, there is good reason to think that John Allen Muhammad, one of the Beltway Snipers, was motivated by a hatred of the US government. Given all the evidence from real-life serial killers, it seems wrong to think of them as dispassionate and lacking all human connection. Still, while the lack of empathy might not be what makes them serial killers, maybe their other emotions would not overwhelm them if they had some empathy for their victims. Let's explore this idea further.

My Evil Just Happened to Come Out: Empathy Inhibits?

What kind of empathy would stop us from acting on violent or paranoid fantasies? It does not seem like the ability to understand what someone is feeling would have any effect on a serial killer's homicidal impulses. After all, many of these real-life serial killers were sadists who took pleasure in their victims' suffering, so they must have understood that they were suffering. Perhaps what serial killers lack is the ability to vicariously experience the emotions of their victims, the most common way we think

ANDREW TERJESEN

of empathy. In that case, when a killer is strangling a victim they know they are hurting them but they don't feel it.

One moral psychological view, known as *moral internalism*, claims that we can't really make a moral judgment unless we experience the *wrongness* of the action. So even though someone might say "strangling people hurts them" and "hurting people is wrong," moral internalism suggests that serial killers don't really believe it is wrong unless they feel the pain they're causing. However, there are some reasons to be skeptical of the idea that serial killers are different from us because they lack the ability to vicariously feel their victim's pain.

To begin with, it is entirely plausible that someone could feel the pain they're causing and continue to cause it. In everyday situations we seem able to override these vicarious reactions. For example, a parent or a doctor could experience the pain of a child getting a shot and still go through with the shot. In this case, it seems like other concerns enable us to override our experience of their pain; but why should we be any different than the serial killers who think they are on a mission or want to hurt the person as an act of revenge? Since serial killers seem to act out of rage, sexual desire or frustration, or hatred, it seems impossible that they lack the ability to experience emotions vicariously.

The emotional part of our brain is not neatly divided. If you have some emotions, you can experience all of the rest (though not necessarily with the same frequency as everyone else). But if you know what fear feels like, then some of that old fear will resonate when you see the signs of other people feeling fear. Psychologists call this phenomenon *emotional contagion* and we all have experienced it, like when excitement or agitation sweeps a crowd. Serial killers might not have the full range of emotional experiences that normal people have, but I would think that the emotions of someone being killed would connect with anyone. Serial killers would need to overcome this response and that means they had to have a reason to do so that is separate from this kind of empathy.

There is still one form of empathy that serial killers might lack. Serial killers might lack connections with fellow humans. Everyday people, on the other hand, feel some basic connection with others so that when we see someone hurt we are moved by a desire to help that person. Empathic connection breeds concern. But again, we are confronted with circular reasoning. To say that someone lacks connection for their fellow human beings does not tell us anything about why they do not feel that connection. Even worse, we can find examples of serial killers who are motivated precisely because of their ability to connect with their fellow human beings.

Serial Killing Because They Care? "Angels of Death"

There have been a number of serial killers dubbed "Angels of Death" who were nurses who killed terminally ill or elderly patients. Charles Cullen claimed that he killed patients in order to spare them from going into respiratory failure or cardiac arrest. He said he overdosed these patients as a way to end their suffering and to prevent them from becoming "de-humanized" by hospital personnel. In this case, an enormous amount of empathy in the sense of connection with his patients (and arguably empathy in the sense of understanding and experiencing vicarious emotion) led Cullen to kill dozens of patients. His empathy did not inhibit his actions; if anything, it seemed to have facilitated them.

Donald Harvey, another self-professed "Angel of Death," who claims to have killed almost a hundred patients, also insisted that he was motivated by empathy for the sufferings of terminally ill patients. What all of this suggests is that it is a bit premature to conclude that a lack of empathy (in any of its forms) is why serial killers give in to their homicidal impulses. However, this does not mean that empathy is irrelevant to what makes serial killers tick. Instead of determining whether or not people will be serial killers, empathy seems to affect how they go about being serial killers.

Serial killers with exceptionally low empathy – who do not seem very connected to their fellow human beings or do not do a very good job of understanding others – are more likely to act directly on their violent urges. They bludgeon or strangle their victims. Getting so close to a victim makes it unavoidable that the killer will be assailed with images and emotional expressions that would overwhelm most ordinary human beings.

"I didn't want to hurt them, I only wanted to kill them": Empathic Dissonance

The preceding quote from David "Son of Sam" Berkowitz suggests he had enough empathy that he was averse to causing people pain even when he attempted to end their lives. To normal people this seems a twisted kind of logic, but we don't have the moral psychology of a serial killer. This way of thinking is the product of small vestiges of Berkowitz's empathy trying to counteract his homicidal urges.

Most serial killers rely on methods that distance themselves from their targets. The Beltway Snipers and the Son of Sam shot all their victims (and the Zodiac Killer shot most of his victims first). Shooting people is a far less intimate act than choking or hitting them. It's possible for one to act quickly so that there isn't time to take in the amount of suffering being caused or rethink what is being done. Another distancing method serial killers might choose is to select a victim they can't relate to, like someone of another race or gender, or a member of a group that society marginalizes, like the homeless or prostitutes. This way it's easier to overcome any normal empathic reactions they have (and the evidence seems to be that they would have some reaction, just not enough to stop them from killing).

Indirect methods, like poisoning or overdosing someone on pain medication, are associated with angels of mercy. It's not surprising that people who seem to be very high-empathy – caring about the plights of strangers – would find a way to kill that would not expose them to visceral emotion. Their victims die relatively peacefully, so the killer is not disturbed by their pain when they die. Miyuki Ishikawa, a Japanese midwife who is estimated to have killed about a hundred babies, chose the most indirect method of all when she began her killing spree: she refused to take care of the infants. If she was, as she claimed, an "angel of mercy" who couldn't bear the suffering of her orphaned charges in 1940s Japan (when the availability of social services was low), then abandoning the infants may have been the only action she could have taken to end their lives.

The idea that most of us have an aversion to directly causing harm has been evidenced in a recent study by the moral psychologist Joshua Greene.[2] In his experiment, people were given two dilemmas to respond to. In the first, participants were presented with a runaway trolley that will kill five people unless you flip the switch and redirect the trolley so it only kills one person. Most people agreed to flip the switch. In the second example, participants were asked if they would push one very heavy person onto the tracks in order to stop the trolley from killing five people. In this case, most people thought it was wrong to push the person onto the tracks, and the emotional parts of their brains were much more active. We won't kill someone, even to save other people, when that someone is close to us physically – our empathetic response kicks in.

The extent to which serial killers can (or allow themselves to) feel empathy affects how they act: in terms of how they kill, how often, and so on.

The important thing here is that what makes them kill is not simply their lack of empathy. This is why I include the caveat "allow themselves to feel," as it seems clear that some serial killers realize that they would have difficulty going through with their actions and do what they can to make it easier on themselves. What I want to suggest here is that the evidence points to serial killers being motivated by emotional urges that are independent of any kind of empathy they feel. If Ted Bundy had more empathy for his victims, he probably would have killed them in a more impersonal manner, but it wouldn't have stopped him from killing. Empathy is not the answer.

The Serial Killer Next Door?

Philosopher Jeanette Kennett has proposed a non-empathy based explanation.[3] Kennett bases her argument on studies of diagnosed sociopaths, though sociopaths aren't all killers. Many of them live very normal lives with the occasional lapse into larceny, deceit, and so on. Kennett points out that many of these sociopaths seem to have trouble in assessing risks. A number of serial killers exhibit less development in the prefrontal cortex in the brain, which is associated with risk assessment, decision-making, impulse control, and the ability to abide by social norms; but these need not be separate functions. People who are poor at assessing risks would do a poor job of controlling their impulses, because they would not consider the consequences of following that impulse. In the civilized world, people behave according to rules, laws, or etiquette because they fear the consequences of acting improperly; our fear helps preserve social conventions. But if one does a poor job of assessing the risks of getting caught and the effects of punishment, then one might be more willing to flout social convention.

According to Kennett, the problem with psychopaths is that they are unable to form a conception of themselves as individuals with long-term plans and goals. Rather than mapping out their lives, they live moment to moment. The difference between someone who lies and steals on a regular basis and a "normal" person is that the lying thief does not consider that these actions might undermine their long-term plans and relationships if their lies are exposed and people stop trusting them.

Many serial killers are described as aimless and drifting and in some cases are literally drifting across the country. Or they embark upon a

ANDREW TERJESEN

killing spree that does not last too long. And even those who seemed to have held it together for a very long period of time, like Dennis Rader, end up acting recklessly, which is how they get caught.

This seems a much more accurate picture of a serial killer (compared to the cold and methodical fictional killers like Hannibal Lecter and Dexter Morgan). Serial killers may differ from us in terms of their impulses, but they don't have to (there are many people from abusive backgrounds who share the rage of these serial killers but don't become killers). Instead, a serial killer seems to be the result of violent and destructive urges combined with the inability to think through the consequences of their actions. Most serial killings seem to be hasty and products of the "heat of the moment." More often than not it seems that impulse overwhelms long-term consequences.

Though it might not be comfortable to think about, most of us have probably experienced the kinds of overwhelming impulses that strike these killers at some point in our lives. However, we recognize that these impulses cannot be allowed to run free – they threaten our jobs, our family, and everything else we've spent our entire lives building. So while someone might do something that makes us so angry that we wish them dead, we don't grab a knife and start stabbing. And even those who do, there's still a chance they'll be unable to complete the act, or if they do actually kill somebody it is not something that happens enough times to fit the definition of "serial killer."

In this version of the moral psychology of serial killers, the role of empathy is more incidental. Empathy has an effect, but its absence is not the root cause even when coupled with violent urges (after all, you regularly resist the urge to kill your boss, even when it seems like there is no human connection to be made at all with that soulless corporate drone). Empathy does not even seem to inhibit serial killers; what it does is shape how they act. This makes sense if you can imagine yourself having trouble controlling your impulses. What if you had difficulty consciously stopping yourself?

In this essay problems have been pointed out with the lack-of-empathy explanation (not the least of which is that there is a number of different things it could refer to), whereas the lack-of-impulse-control explanation seems very promising in light of all that we've considered. Still, it's up to you to be a good philosopher and weigh the arguments and evidence to form your own ideas about the moral psychology of killers and non-killers. But these ideas should be defensible by arguments and not merely reflective of a popular view of human nature.

NOTES

1 John Deigh, "Empathy and Universalizability," in Larry May et al. (eds.) *Minds and Morals: Essays on Ethics and Cognitive Science* (Cambridge, MA: MIT Press, 1996), pp. 199–220.
2 Joshua Greene et al., "An fMRI Investigation of Emotional Engagement in Moral Judgment," *Science* 293 (2001): 2105–8.
3 Jeanette Kennett, "Autism, Empathy and Moral Agency," *Philosophical Quarterly* 52 (2002): 340–57.

ANDREW TERJESEN

PART V

CREEPY COGNITION
Talking and Thinking about Serial Killers

CHAPTER 12

THE SERIAL KILLER WAS
(COGNITIVELY) FRAMED

Serial Killers, Real and Imagined

Dexter Morgan: Witnessed the gruesome murder of his mother at a very young age. Subsequently adopted by a Miami police officer. Currently works in forensics for the Miami police as a blood-splatter analyst. Unmarried. Lives alone in an apartment. Has a girlfriend. Handsome. Smart. Glib. Serial killer. Number of murders unknown, but the ones we know about involve dismember-ment of the victim's body done as meticulously as possible. Still active. Fictional character created by author Jeff Lindsay.[1]

John Wayne Gacy, Jr.: Had an abusive, alcoholic father who called him a "sissy." Married twice, both marriages ending in divorce. Lived out-side Chicago and ran a small construction company. Active in local Democratic politics – there is a 1978 photo of him with then-First Lady Rosalynn Carter. Entertained children at parties in the guise of "Pogo the Clown." Serial killer. Believed to have killed 33 male ado-lescents and young men, at least 27 of whom he buried in the crawl space of his home. Convicted of rape and murder for these crimes. A real person, the "Killer Clown" was executed by lethal injection in Illinois on May 10, 1994.[2]

Two serial killers, one real, the other fictional. Both seem to fit our commonsense image of the serial killer as one who appears "normal" on the surface, who holds a job and has community engagements, but who harbors darker, murderous urges that apparently cannot be controlled.

The distinction between real and imagined serial killers is immaterial to questions of how we popularly, in American culture, view serial killers. In fact, it might be argued that fictional serial killers frame our perspective on those who commit serial murder more than the real killers themselves. Fans of Dexter are privy to his internal world because in both the Dexter novels and television series, Dexter narrates the details of his life. In the case of Gacy, however, we have little access to his private thoughts and our understanding of him is based solely on what we know of his crimes, bits and pieces of his biography, and the subsequent denials he often made as to his responsibility. As a result of these different perspectives on the inner worlds of serial killers, Dexter seems, at least partly, sympathetic. We know why he kills who he kills because he tells us about the horrific early childhood experiences that led to his behavior. Gacy, on the other hand, may be just as sympathetic from the perspective of a horribly abusive childhood, but our knowledge of it is fragmentary, so we tend to focus on what we do know: his killing of male adolescents for perverted sexual pleasure. With this aspect of the Gacy story as our focus, it is hard to be sympathetic to the conditions that determined his homicidal acts.

The Dexter and Gacy narratives raise interesting questions about the moral standing of serial killers. On the face of it, serial killers are ethically unproblematic: they are immoral. On more careful reflection, and taking into account philosophical debates over concepts like *free will*, *moral agency*, and *determinism*, the surety of our moral judgment begins to teeter. It turns out that the matter of moral responsibility is complicated by issues of whether we freely choose all our actions, and whether there are people who might be excused from moral responsibility because of some extenuating circumstance beyond their control.

This, we will see, is precisely the issue when it comes to serial killers: Are they, or are they not, in control of their actions? If the various ways that the idea of a serial killer persuasively impacts our image of such murderers, then how we, by extension, view their moral agency will also be implicated in this popular view. The examples of Dexter Morgan and John Wayne Gacy, Jr. provide us with an entry point into the debates over free will and moral agency. We'll start with Dexter.

Dexter

The first Dexter novel, *Darkly Dreaming Dexter*, opens with the protagonist stalking his next kill. The target: a Catholic priest who teaches music to young children at an orphanage. The priest is himself a serial killer, sexually molesting and murdering young children – boys? girls? we are not told – who are in his charge. Dexter is outraged by such behavior and, typically for Dexter, believes that he has a responsibility to right this wrong. His resolution is to dispatch the priest at the same location where the priest has buried seven of his victims. Dexter knows this location because he has been observing the priest for some time. And over this time, Dexter's urge to kill the priest grows stronger and stronger to the point where it can't be ignored. He must avenge the children.

Dexter, we learn, is a serial killer with a conscience – he displays a sense of justice, a sense of right and wrong – warped as it may appear to us. But if Dexter kills those who deserve it, he does so as a serially killing vigilante. Ironically, he also works for the police department as a blood-splatter specialist. Both his day job and his nocturnal killing are directed to similar ends – seeking justice, legally in one instance and illegally in the other.

What sets Dexter apart from "normal" people is his peculiar sense of self, really two selves. He narrates his actions in an oddly dispassionate, disconnected way. It is as if he inhabits a body that acts sometimes under his control and sometimes under the control of the murderous force he calls the "Dark Passenger." On the one hand, Dexter fits the stereotype of the serial killer as mentally ill, untethered from reality as others experience it. On the other hand, Dexter has values. He makes it clear that he reviles the priest for targeting children. As Dexter says to the priest he is about to dismember, "But children? ... I could never do this to children.... Not like you, Father. Never kids. I have to find people like you."[3] The way Dexter talks about himself suggests that he is not fully in control of his impulses. He attributes these impulses not to some failing in himself, but to the demands of the Dark Passenger.

Gacy

Our second example, John Wayne Gacy, Jr., was convicted on multiple charges of rape and murder. There was evidence from the physical remains of the bodies unearthed in his home that Gacy also engaged in sexual torture of his victims. Gacy would, over the years after his arrest, proclaim his innocence, despite having confessed to the murders at the time of his arrest and despite the 27 bodies found buried in the crawl space of his home. Gacy claimed, instead, that he had been framed by others who had snuck into his home and buried the bodies without his knowledge. In 1994, shortly before his execution, Alec Wilkinson, a writer for the *New Yorker* magazine, interviewed Gacy in prison a number of times. While we cannot know with any precision the internal world of another, Wilkinson's interview provides us with reasons to question Gacy's sanity.

It is clear from Wilkinson's description of Gacy's demeanor and presentation of self that Gacy is either outright lying about his responsibility for the killings, or that he truly believes he is innocent, or that he is otherwise deluded about his past actions. As Wilkinson puts it, "When Gacy says that he knows nothing about the murders, it's impossible to tell if he really has no memory of them or is just saying that he doesn't. He says that twelve people ... had keys to his house and could have buried bodies in the crawl space while he was traveling on business."[4] This seems like such an improbable way for the bodies to end up in his house that it points to a Gacy deluded or otherwise out of touch with reality.

As part of his original confession, Gacy told police about his sexual encounters with boys and how they sometimes turned into murders by stabbing or strangulation. As Wilkinson recounts it, "A few times Gacy killed two boys in one night. Sometimes he kept a boy's corpse in his closet for a day before burying him. He poured acid on some of the corpses and lime on others, then buried them in graves about a foot deep."[5] Though these kinds of descriptions are likely troubling to most of us, to Gacy they were, in the end, something to be denied. This denial was possible, it seems, because of Gacy's inability to feel empathy or any kind of meaningful connection to other human beings. Wilkinson says that during his interviews with Gacy,

> I often had the feeling that he was like an actor who had created a role and polished it so carefully that he had become the role and the role had become him. What personality he may once have had collapsed long ago and had been replaced by a catalog of gestures and attitudes and portrayals of sanity. In support of his innocence, he often says things that are deranged in their logic, but he says them so calmly that he appears to be rational and reasonable. He has concealed the complexity of this character so assiduously that a person is left to imagine the part of him that carried out the murders.[6]

After exploring Wilkinson's account of Gacy's words and behaviors, we are left with no doubt that not only is Pogo the Clown none other than the Killer Clown, but that this is a clown crazily off-kilter.

Dexter and Gacy: two images of the serial killer. Both may be psychopaths. And both appear to be deluded, though perhaps in different ways. Dexter has a delusion that he is on the side of right and that his mission is to permanently dispatch those he decides are the scum of the earth, like those who rape and murder children. But even here, Dexter tells us that it is the Dark Passenger who is calling the serial killing shots. Dexter is just the vehicle in which the Dark Passenger rides, and Dexter can do nothing but obey his commands. Dexter seems to be claiming that he is not the responsible party in the murders he is commanded to commit for the Dark Passenger. Gacy, on the other hand, is either in deep denial of his actions or he really thinks he did not commit the crimes for which he was sentenced to death. Gacy's delusion is located in his repeated protests that he didn't do it, somebody else did. As a result, he claims that he is not responsible. If both Dexter and Gacy are delusional, can they be held morally responsible for their actions?

Are Serial Killers Morally Responsible?

So, what would it take for us to say that Dexter and Gacy are morally responsible? What is involved in being responsible? First, we must be moral agents, that is, we must be able to intentionally choose our actions and, as part of that, control our urges. Part of choosing our actions is knowing right from wrong. Second, we must have free will.

Choice, intentions, and moral agency

We are morally responsible only when we choose our actions. We often think of ourselves as having choices that other animals do not. We think of dogs, cats, and horses as acting from biological instinct, as driven by a brain hardwired in a particular way. Even if we imagine that a dog can choose to eat or not eat a certain kind of food, we probably do not think of the dog as consciously choosing, but rather as responding to innate preferences. We don't think the dog is a good dog for preferring beef over chicken, or a bad dog for wanting canned food more than dry food. Human choices seem to be more complicated and more influenced by cultural experience and personal thoughts.

Moral agents are morally responsible for their actions. Moral agents are not merely behaving according to instinct or hardwired brain-based responses. They consider their options, and possible consequences of their actions, and have clear intentions to achieve some things and avoid others. While moral agency is generally understood as a human trait, not all human beings have moral agency: people who are severely brain damaged and people of very low intelligence do not understand the world well enough to make meaningful, well considered choices. Likewise, very young children are not usually treated as morally responsible for a temper tantrum. Similarly, an animal that attacks another animal or a person is usually not considered a moral agent; nor we do assume that a killer tornado has homicidal intentions with a grudge against trailer parks.

We consider ourselves to be responsible for our actions if they are intentional and deliberate, and not responsible for the consequences of our actions that are accidents. Accidentally hitting and killing a pedestrian while driving – say because the pedestrian suddenly ran into the street – is considered morally neutral relative to killing the pedestrian because one is driving drunk. This is another reason why we don't blame the tornado – we don't think it decided to do anything. Being able to freely choose, to act intentionally and deliberately, and to discern the difference between good and evil – these are the ingredients necessary for being morally responsible. But can we assign moral responsibility to someone who seems to have no mental mechanism to shut out murderous thoughts and actions? It is one thing to have inappropriate thoughts, but another to act on them uncontrollably. So we have an important issue to deal with: What is *free will*?

Free will and determinism

Freedom to make choices implies at least two choices to select from and that some choices can be judged to be ethically better than others. It also implies that one is not being coerced or otherwise forced to act in a certain way. For example, if someone holds a gun to your head and threatens to kill you unless you stick a pin through the palm of an innocent child, you will probably do it rather than allow yourself to be killed. You could have refused and lost your life, but under less dire circumstances you would never have chosen to hurt the child – your free, unthreatened choice was probably to buy her ice cream. Threats, biological urges, and natural laws remove or lessen moral responsibility. We do not extend moral responsibility to rabid dogs or killer tornados because we do not believe they make choices or that they are able to do differently that which their natures determine they will do. And this introduces the concept of *determinism*.

Determinism says that the actions we take and the choices we make in the present are the result of past causes and conditions. In short, we do not choose at all; how we behave is completely predetermined by events that occurred in the past. We might believe we are making conscious, rational choices, but these beliefs themselves are just caused by past events.

If you are scratching your head in puzzlement because the concept of determinism seems counterintuitive, you are not alone. Surely, you say, my decision to have soup for lunch was not pre-decided by past conditions that are controlling me behind the scenes! But if you have ever believed that something occurred because it was fated or because God preordained it, then you are thinking like a determinist. A *theodicy* – an explanation for why things happen the way they do in the world, especially bad things – is typically deterministic. Thus, if we say that my child died after being hit by a bus because God has a larger plan for her, then we appear to be saying that our child had no choice but to run in front of the bus. Presumably, the child did not make this decision after rational reflection.

Stated differently, determinism is the idea that each and every event that occurs in the world is inevitable and unavoidable because all events are the result of past conditions that give rise to what occurs in the present and, in turn, what will occur in the future. Determinism, on this view, is an inviolable law of nature. If determinism is true, it means that all my actions and decisions as a human being are out of my direct control. My actions may seem to have required a choice on my part, but, in reality, I was only acting in response to environmental cues or other stimuli.

We can only hold someone morally responsible if her or his actions and decisions are not entirely determined ahead of time. After all, if we did not act with free will, but rather were manipulated by a deity or acted solely on the basis of some biological response, we did not deliberately choose our actions, intend the consequences, or differentiate between good and evil.

If determinism is true, then our belief in free will is false – it is not possible to be held morally responsible for any action because no choices or decisions were ever available to the actor. In this case, serial killers are not responsible for any of their actions because they have no control over them; they are fated to kill. If our belief in free will is true and determinism is false, then we, and serial killers with adequate IQs and control over their drives, are morally responsible. But there is a third option: *compatibilism*.

The compatibilist view holds that even if determinism is true, we can still be responsible for our actions because moral responsibility is compatible with determinism. But, you rightly ask, how can this be so? If all things are predetermined then how can we be free to make choices? The philosopher Daniel Dennett has recently argued for one version of compatibilism using an evolutionary perspective. In *Freedom Evolves* (2003) he lays out a claim that even though human actions and decisions are predetermined by the laws of nature, it is nevertheless possible for us to act according to free will because we have evolved the capacity to do so. Returning to our example of the dog, we might assume that Rover has not evolved to anticipate different possible consequences for an action, nor to choose based on his best guess regarding those consequences. We humans, on the other hand, have come to a point in our evolutionary development whereby we can make decisions based on the outcomes we seek. So, for example, I might be determined by my genetic makeup to have high cholesterol. This is pre-programmed, as it were, and I cannot change it. But, from Dennett's compatibilist perspective, my brain has evolved to allow me to make choices to eat certain kinds of low cholesterol foods, to exercise, and to do other things to mitigate what is already determined.

If compatibilism is true, then serial killers might be completely responsible for their actions. Even if they have biologically based urges, they may still have the ability to compensate for them. I choose low cholesterol foods. They might choose forms of violence that do not involve murder. But if their brains are very different from normal human brains, they might not be able to make these choices.

Moral Responsibility: Emotions and Cognitive Frames

So, are serial killers morally responsible or not? As this discussion has suggested, whether you hold serial killers morally responsible or not will largely depend on your view of free will and determinism. And we have no way of proving or disproving any of those views. Even if we conclude that human beings generally have enough free will to be held morally responsible, do serial killers fall into a different category – like babies and dogs – that precludes them from moral agency because they are deemed to be psychologically or mentally deficient or abnormal?

Looking at the cases of Dexter and Gacy, it is apparent that, among other things, their moral compasses point in odd directions, they exhibit a selective lack of empathy, they display emotional estrangement from other human beings, and guilt and shame are conspicuously absent. They fail to develop deeply significant human relationships; rather, their relationships seem to be a shell or a sham or a veneer meant to feign normalcy. And if they are so disconnected from their own actions, feelings, and normal human responses, how can they evaluate the consequences of their actions in a way that would let them choose? That is, if their interpretation of the world is so different from ours, can we really say that their choices are intentional and deliberate, or that they know right from wrong? Moral responsibility, after all this discussion, is still a very problematic notion!

A challenge to how we view moral responsibility in general, and the responsibility of serial murderers in particular, comes from a new approach to philosophy and ethics that is called *experimental philosophy*.[7] Experimental philosophers want philosophers to stop sitting around thinking about how people conceptualize the world, create categories, and make ethical judgments. Instead, they run empirical experiments meant to find out how human psychology actually functions.

Rather than arguing about abstract concepts like free will and determinism, trying to define each concept in order to come to some definitive resolution to the philosophical problem of free will, we should find out how much emotional reactions affect the moral judgments of "normal" people. Rather than analyzing free will in terms of other concepts like determinism, which only leads to myriad conceptual problems, we should observe how people make moral choices. Experimental philosophers like Joshua Knobe and Shaun Nichols seek an understanding of how human cognitive processes operate.

Research by Knobe and Nichols strongly suggests that people's emotional, affective responses to a particular ethical scenario will impact whether one sides with the compatibilist or incompatibilist perspective. Thus, we seem to intuit an understanding of moral responsibility depending on our affective reaction to the particular details of the case under evaluation. In discussing our reaction to an account of a gruesome murder, we might be repelled by the bloody details and aghast at the inhumanity. But we might also feel empathy for the perpetrator if, for instance, we learn that the murderer was subject to horrendous abuse as a child. Knobe and Nichols argue that when reading the kind of narrative that induces strong mixed emotions, it is extremely difficult – and unlikely – to assign moral responsibility in a dispassionate manner:

Any normal reader will have a rich array of reactions, including not only abstract theorizing but also feelings of horror and disgust. A reader's intuitions ... might be swayed by her emotions, leaving her with a conclusion that contravened her more abstract, theoretical beliefs about the nature of moral responsibility.[8]

It is precisely in our affective responses to the details about the lives and crimes of serial killers like Dexter and Gacy that we are most likely to locate our judgment of moral responsibility.

But if emotions play such a significant role in our moral judgments it is because our feelings are experienced within specific frames of experience. *Frames*, a cognitive science concept, are the way we mentally represent particular categories of our experience. So, for instance, when you go to a restaurant, you seamlessly and without any cognitive difficulty invoke the restaurant frame whereby you know to wait to be seated, to order from the menu, to ask for the check, and to pay your bill. If I say that after dinner at the restaurant we went to the movies, you just assume that I paid my bill before leaving, even if I don't tell you that I did. This is because we share the cultural knowledge of how the restaurant frame operates.

In the case of serial killers, and, in particular, Dexter and Gacy, we seem to have two possible frames operating that determine our emotional response to their stories. The first frame is the abused child frame; the second is the murderous psychopath frame. If we focus on the child frame, we are much more apt to have a sympathetic response to the serial killer. We will still be repelled at the actions taken by the serial killer, but we feel we have some sort of psychological insight into why this person acted as he did, and, further, we might wonder if this person is fully responsible for his actions given the life experiences he's had to endure. This seems to be one popular response to the Dexter character. Gacy, however, is the poster child for the murderous psychopath frame. Because we have so little concrete data on Gacy's childhood, and because his story focuses mostly on his murders and denials, our emotional response is unsympathetic. How could he do what he did? We are not provided much material that might make us sympathetic. As a result of the frame through which we view Gacy, and our negative feelings toward him, we are much more apt to find him morally responsible for his actions, even if his actions are no more heinous than those of Dexter.

If frames impact our moral judgments so dramatically, then we see how fiction writers change our view of their characters by framing them

👤 WILLIAM E. DEAL

in certain contexts and giving us some facts and not others. Similarly, the media might frame a candidate or an issue in a sympathetic or unsympathetic way.

So, in the end, our judgments of moral responsibility are not just a matter of rational thought, but of how the frames through which we view the world impact our emotional responses. But emotion is important not just in understanding our moral judgments, it may also explain why Dexter envisions himself as directed by the Dark Passenger and Gacy seems so unable to accept responsibility for his actions. Gacy fails to frame his deeds in a way that causes him to feel remorse, because he does not feel empathy for his victims. But without this frame he will not have the emotional responses necessary for him to think of himself as a moral agent. After all, if nothing bad was done, then there are no responsible parties. And if Dexter frames himself as saving the world from evil, then he is a good person who does bad things.

NOTES

1   Jeff Lindsay's Dexter novels include *Darkly Dreaming Dexter* (2004), *Dearly Devoted Dexter* (2005), *Dexter in the Dark* (2007), and *Dexter by Design* (2009). These novels are the basis for *Dexter*, a Showtime Networks television series.
2   For a concise biography of Gacy see Eric W. Hickey, *Serial Murderers and Their Victims*, 4th edn. (Belmont: Thomson Wadsworth, 2006), pp. 185–6; and Michael Newton, *The Encyclopedia of Serial Killers*, 2nd edn. (New York: Facts On File, 2006), pp. 85–7.
3   Jeff Lindsay, *Darkly Dreaming Dexter* (New York: Vantage Books, 2004), p. 11.
4   Alec Wilkinson, "Conversations With a Killer," *The New Yorker*, April 18, 1994; reprinted in Alec Wilkinson, *Mr. Apology and Other Essays* (Boston: Houghton Mifflin, 2003), p. 245.
5   Ibid., p. 246.
6   Ibid., p. 248.
7   For an overview of the emerging field of experimental philosophy, see Joshua Knobe and Shaun Nichols (eds.) *Experimental Philosophy* (Oxford: Oxford University Press, 2008).
8   Joshua Knobe and Shaun Nichols, "Moral Responsibility and Determinism: The Cognitive Science of Folk Intuitions," *Noûs* 41, 4 (2007): 664–5.

CHAPTER 13

WOLVES AND WIDOWS

Naming, Metaphor, and the Language of Serial Murder

Two Killers in Montana

Watching from 60 yards away, he studied the two young sisters as they meandered comfortably together through the meadow. It was early evening in the fall of 1919, less than a year after the Great War had at last drawn to a close, and they soon would be heading down the hill, back toward the ranch house in the foothills of Montana's Little Belt Mountains. He had come to the area a few years earlier and managed to eke out a living at various farms and ranches here and in the neighboring Highwoods. A loner all his life, he liked it here. He liked not being noticed by most folks despite the fact that his arrival happened to coincide with a rash of horrific murders that left some residents frightened, some angry. Law enforcement officials seemed at a loss to bring a halt to what local residents referred to as the "reign of terror" of a prolific killer whose predation in and around several small central Montana towns ultimately spanned 15 years.

The older of the two sisters, hearing the authoritative voice of the rancher below, edged ahead of her more carefree sibling, who stopped to tug at the soft blue grama grass, reluctant to retire just yet. It is unlikely that she saw or heard her attacker before he descended on her, grabbing her by the throat and thrusting her to the ground. His method of attack had been less well defined when the spree began; once clumsy and unsure, now he performed his impassioned, bloody routine with efficiency, purpose, something that approached finesse. Once he immobilized his victims, the six-foot, white-haired serial killer systematically eviscerated them, likely even as they sustained a weak pulse. Disgusted locals eventually dubbed him the "White Wolf."

During the very same period, another suite of murders took place here in Montana and in neighboring Idaho. Beginning in 1915, one by one, five of Lydia Trueblood's six husbands succumbed to a fate akin to what is, in the animal world, called *sexual cannibalism*. Black widow spiders are so called for the occasional inclination of the females – which are black rather than brown, like the males – to kill and devour their mates during or immediately following copulation. It is entirely fitting and unsurprising that contemporaries referred to Trueblood as the "Black Widow," a nickname given freely and often to such toxic, murderous women. Indeed, the term describes an entire category of serial killers, women whose deeds liken them to a cold, creepy, highly venomous spider with a penchant for widowhood and a moral code that assaults our own.

How do we account for our habit of affixing tags like "White Wolf"? Why do we prefer to refer to Lydia Trueblood as the "Black Widow," rather than by her formal moniker? Obviously, one's name is an incredibly intimate facet of our identity. Still, there's something generic about a proper name. My surname, "Zirngibl," existed long before I arrived on this earth, and even my given name is one that my parents assigned to me having no inkling as to who or what I would become in life. In this sense a proper name is fairly detached from the person it describes. Although I am fairly confident that no one other than myself is named "Wendy Zirngibl," despite its exclusivity, this moniker is less evocative of my personality, my interests, my history, my physical presence than, say, my CB handle, "Red." And especially now, in the cybernetic twenty-first century, each of us tends to generate a host of electronic identities, from individuated and often quite descriptive email addresses to blogger profiles.

There is something about these deeply personal identifiers that appeals to us. We use them as a way of asserting who we are or showing what we like about ourselves. So in labeling someone "Black Widow" we assert who she is – who and what we deem her to be, and what it is about her that matters most to us. Nicknames suggest familiarity and give us a sense of having a handle on the bearers of those tags. For some reason it pleases us to refer to "Shoeless" Joe Jackson, whose nickname serves as a signpost to remind us of this old-time Chicago White Sox slugger's rather endearing, very personal habit of playing baseball barefoot. There have been many, many

"Joe Jacksons" but only one "Shoeless Joe." Here, the nickname lends a nice sense of familiarity, but also, importantly, instantaneous clarity.

A metaphor has the same sort of value. This figure of speech that draws a comparison between two seemingly disparate subjects for the purpose of illuminating something about one or both of them performs a function similar to the kind of work that a nickname does. When Lydia Trueblood faced exposure as a serial killer her critics growled "that woman is a black widow!" and the metaphor ultimately evolved into a nickname. The way we feel or think about others informs the way we discuss them; the language that we use can be incredibly telling, but what exactly is it telling us? Philosophically speaking, what is behind the metaphor and our convention of name-calling?

What's in a Name? The Wolf and the Widow

We look to the philosophy of language to consider our use of names and the ways in which we refer to specific individuals. A few terms should simplify our analysis. A *speech act* is a linguistic device that does one of several types of work for us as, perhaps, a warning: "Drop the knife, or else!"; or a request: "I would like you to hand me that knife"; or a description: "Have you ever seen such a sharp knife?" *Dubbing* a serial killer "Black Widow," for example, and subsequently using this title to discuss her, constitutes a descriptive type of speech act. But the description in this case does much more than simply identify a trait or two of the subject. Since the nickname communicates a host of information (and just the right kind of information) about Trueblood, the identity of the Black Widow – indeed, the span of her history beginning with the first deed that earned her this descriptor – is encapsulated in a single term.

The relationship, therefore, among the killer, her proper name – the spoken, written, or imagined words, "Lydia Trueblood" – and her designated title, "Black Widow" – is extremely important. The term *reference* describes this relationship; both "Lydia Trueblood," a primary identifier, and "Black Widow," a secondary identifier, refer to the person, Lydia Trueblood, whom we know as the *referent* of the names. Likewise, the famously barefoot ball player from Chicago is the referent of the secondary identifier "Shoeless Joe," as well as the referent of his primary identifier, "Joe Jackson." Typically, a person's proper or legal name serves as a

WENDY M. ZIRNGIBL

primary identifier, while a nickname, which came later and is far more subjective, tends to be a *secondary identifier*.

Finally, while her notoriously earned title indicates Trueblood the individual, in an act of *denotation*, she herself *exemplifies* the inauspicious moniker. This last term is nicely descriptive for our purposes; as we have considered, the killer, through her vile acts of serial murder by way of sexual cannibalism, does indeed exemplify the term "Black Widow."

The names "White Wolf" and "Black Widow" triggered an emotional response in the individuals who knew of these two allegedly loathsome beings; each name was heavily invested with meaning. For the Black Widow, this investment was twofold: by summoning the literal referent – the spider – the nickname instantly conjured fear and disgust. But more importantly, this consummately descriptive term reminded people why they were aware of this otherwise-stranger; to be sure, they likely knew nothing at all about her except for her notorious propensity for domestic brutality. In hearing the appellation "Black Widow," a contemporary resident of Idaho or Montana instantly understood it as a reference to Trueblood, making for a linguistic simplification that avoided the need to re-explain repeatedly who was being discussed and in which context she was being discussed. Its descriptiveness made communication more efficient. Furthermore, uttering this name allowed the speaker to indulge in a sort of judgment of this woman, by effectively reducing her to the sum of the decidedly pejorative label.

Naming: Putting Practice into Theory

Clearly, unlike proper names – birth names, usually – a nickname often is based on particular outward traits or qualitative properties of the referent. The proper name "Lydia" far less powerfully denotes our serial killer than does "Black Widow." But can a philosophical theory usually reserved for proper names nonetheless further our analysis?

The *descriptivist theory of names*, associated predominantly with Gottlob Frege (1848–1925) and Bertrand Russell (1872–1970), posits that a proper name is, in fact, synonymous with the *descriptors* – accumulated through a lifetime – of the person who holds the name. Descriptors are simply facts about the person being described. We use a series of descriptors to distinguish one person from another, and those distinguishing facts, according to description theory, become the meaning of the name. According to this Fregean theory, the *moniker* "Lydia Trueblood" (as distinct from the *person*) then shares its meaning with the following specifications: (a) the woman from Pocatello, Idaho who married Robert C. Dooley; (b) the person who murdered five husbands, a brother-in-law, and her daughter; (c) the serial killer known as the "Black Widow." Regarding (a), there is little that should interest us, except as it relates to (b) and (c). To be sure, without (b) and (c) the first descriptor loses much of its meaning. Nevertheless, the *person* Lydia Trueblood embodies all of these descriptors, even though the relevance of such descriptors, taken individually, is highly subjective.

Consider: the surname of her third-grade school teacher, for instance, while possibly important in some sense in the context of her life history, is utterly inconsequential to her later identity as the Black Widow, and is therefore not embedded in this title. (It is also, therefore, of minimal interest to us as a society.) On the other hand, if the name of her third-grade school teacher were Dooley, then we could assign some relevance to this fact with respect to the name of her first husband, Robert C. Dooley. My point is that although we could produce a wealth of descriptors for any given person to match with the proper name of that person, these descriptors often can prove utterly banal and ultimately useless in helping us to understand that person.

The name "Black Widow" derives its meaning from two discrete sources: Trueblood herself, by her repeated acts of villainy, and the public, who judge her actions to be horrific, extraordinary, warranting a second designation over and above her proper name. By merit of her criminal deeds, Lydia Trueblood underwent a second *baptism*, as it were, whereby she assumed the name "Black Widow." Suppose that we apply the same type of Fregean analysis to this society-appointed title as we used above for her proper name, generating a list of descriptors that "Black Widow" then would represent. Such an exercise produces quite different results, because a nickname is a societal designation meant to describe only a few crucial aspects of its bearer. "Shoeless Joe" reminds us of the bearer's freedom from footwear, but does not call to mind his birthday, relatives, or favorite food. While seldom does a proper name provide any true description of its bearer, the identifier "Joe Jackson" can be used to formally seek facts about the man because we attach full histories to proper names. "Trueblood," the word, corresponds to the woman's beginning, her end, and everything between; "Black Widow," the appellation, begins only with the first drop of poison.

To consider from this new starting point, the surname of the serial killer's third-grade teacher, unless it is "Dooley" or some other name directly related to her life as a married (and widowed) woman, has absolutely no business showing up in any descriptor of the person, Black Widow. Because this nickname describes only the serial killer Lydia Trueblood, the details of Trueblood's life, taken as a whole, do not equal the details of the Black Widow's life. The latter has a much shorter – albeit a good deal more consequential – list of descriptors.

So how does this slightly modified appropriation of the descriptivist theory of reference help us to understand the names we often assign to exceptional figures such as serial killers? By illustrating one way in which a name functions – as a label affixed to the exemplifier of a set of specific descriptors – this theory has allowed us to discern, in a gently technical sense, between two names with the same referent. Whereas we can sense on an emotional level how the name "Lydia Trueblood" differs from the name "Black Widow," Frege provides a logical structure for parsing this difference.

In the end, the new label, along with the assortment of specific, memorable features and facts that informed the woman's second baptism, replaces her proper name as a primary identifier; this process effectively submerges the real person to allow the emergence of a distilled being, stripped of much of her life's context. Lydia Trueblood disappears and the Black Widow, undiluted and all evil, materializes in her place. Do we, then, prefer "Black Widow" to "Lydia Trueblood" because of the ability of the former to offer us a pared-down, simplified, one-dimensional version of the killer that is easy for us to digest, dissect, and discuss?

At other times, it seems, the proper names of serial killers such as Jeffrey Dahmer and Ted Bundy *become* their deeds, and cease to indicate the ordinary human beings they were at birth. In the very same process as occurs in the re-dubbing with nicknames, the surnames "Dahmer" and "Bundy" are shorn of any pre-murder baggage as they undergo rebirth as heavily laden labels attached to sick, wicked behavior. We hear Jeffrey Dahmer's name and automatically conjure in our minds a range of hideous crimes against humanity; the word "Dahmer" is now shorthand for unimaginably perverse, cannibalistic serial murder. At this point, no rational person wants to bear the name "Dahmer."

Metaphor: Wolf in Sheep's Clothing

In effect, Jeffrey Dahmer, perhaps the ultimate serial killer due to the grotesque nature of his notorious crimes, has come to symbolize human depravity. Similarly, history indicates that the wolf owns this type of distinction in nature. Long regarded as an enemy of both humans and other animals, the wolf is a demonized creature that Theodore Roosevelt once famously described as the "beast of waste and desolation." Prior to its resurrection, brought about by environmentalist sentiment in the second half of the twentieth century, federal and state government officials as well as private landowners in the US destroyed this powerful predator almost to the point of extinction. Wolves had been eliminated from most of their haunts in the Old World and even vanished from much of Asia amid a frenzy of human-led annihilation. People for centuries have hated and feared wolves, and many still regard the canids as relentless, cruel, amoral killers.

We are indoctrinated quite young with the notion that a wolf exemplifies the villain. The fearsome and devious foe so many of our fairy-tale heroes must face is some variation of the Big Bad Wolf. In one fable, the cunning and underhanded predator assumes a deceptive facade, donning a sheep costume in order to get closer to its prey without detection. One is reminded again of Ted Bundy, whose suave demeanor and handsome appearance enabled him to capture and slaughter his own prey. While Bundy certainly registers as the most sinister "wolf in sheep's clothing" one can imagine, the fable cliché remains popular as a highly derogatory metaphor indicating something harmful wearing a benign disguise.

We use anecdotes and language to express our anxieties about the wolf – just as we do the serial killer – to such a high degree that our negative tales and pejorative use of the wolf's name end up reinforcing those anxieties. Indeed, like "Dahmer," even the word "wolf" has become more than the term literally implies, value-laden and saturated with meaning. There exist no common wolf metaphors that make positive connections: the unadorned term refers to a lecherous man who is a menace to the many women he lustily pursues. Similarly, "wolfing down" food suggests a greedy and vulgar manner of devouring a meal, reminiscent of the way in which large predators tend to eat. In short, any comparison that involves "wolf" is bound to be unflattering.

The stigma attached to this animal has stayed with us: so powerful are our centuries-old associations that even though many of us harbor quite positive feelings about the flesh-and-blood wolf and its place in the world, the old, mythological wolf still resides somewhere in our consciousness. It is this wolf of the imagination that supplies the perfect metaphor for the serial killer.

Metaphor: White Wolf Revisited

So what about the White Wolf, who terrorized those central Montana communities in the 1920s? The end of his story reads thusly: at long last, a posse of two men, exasperated and unwilling to give up another victim to this monster, set out with two tracking dogs in the spring of 1930, bent on resurrecting the old vigilante ways made famous in the years before Montana's entry into statehood four decades earlier. Finally, the dogs found him, and one of the men wasted no time before firing a bullet into the left cheek of the killer. His "reign of terror" ended abruptly in that moment. Six feet long, including the tail, the striking blond wolf became legend in Montana; his stuffed remains currently occupy a place of distinction at the Basin Trading Post in the town of Stanford.

Here, I must apologize for cheating just a bit. In fact, "White Wolf" was just that – a white wolf. Like "Black Widow," the moniker "White Wolf" carried a descriptive quality, although in the latter case the name was quite literal. Still, contemporaries regarded the animal – a serial killer of a different variety – with a similar brand of contempt; the economic losses suffered by cattle ranchers ranged in the thousands of dollars. In 1920s rural Montana such a financial strain, equivalent to ten times that amount in today's economy, was devastating to most stock growers.

Nevertheless, the name "White Wolf" as a serial killer's nickname is utterly believable because we are so accustomed to adopting the beleaguered predator as a metaphor for all manner of villainy. Consider again the black widow spider. Here, we choose a creepy, loathsome creature to serve as a stand-in for our serial killer. Is Lydia Trueblood a spider? Of course not, but identifying her as a spider, and this specific type of spider, teaches us some important things about her and prompts us to think about her in a certain way. The value of a metaphor lies not in its literal truth but in this ability to instruct or to trigger a mode of thinking. Herein is another example of the power of language to reflect and reinforce our emotional responses to our environment – alas, an environment where wolves, black widows, and serial killers all dwell.

What kind of work does a metaphor do for us? The *substitution (comparison) theory* holds that a metaphor offers two subjects that we compare in order to distinguish their overlapping qualities. We could say, for instance, that a serial killer is a wolf; we intuitively understand this speech act to indicate that the serial killer shares some characteristics of the wolf or reminds us of its fellow predator. In this case, thinking about the serial killer relative to the wolf (our traditional, negative view of the wolf, anyway) would yield a list of commonalities that might include fierceness, amorality, lack of empathy, monstrous or bestial nature, cunning, and blood lust, to name a few. Once we understand the point of the metaphor, according to the substitution theory, we discard the original metaphorical term, "wolf," and retain only its meaning. In the serial-killer-as-wolf case, then, we come away with the message that a serial killer possesses more than its share of odious traits. The task of the metaphor has been to illustrate the person committing the murders in such a way that the listener instantly and easily comprehends which characteristics the killer possesses and that the killer, like a wolf, deserves our reproach.

But perhaps a metaphor is more than an expendable comparison between two contextualized entities and is rather a process of explanation and learning that ultimately enlightens our understanding of both terms. Analytic philosopher Max Black (1909–88) offered an *interactionist theory* in response to the traditional substitution theory. By Black's reckoning, rather than illuminate only the serial-killer half of the comparison, the metaphor affects the meaning of both the serial killer and the wolf via a process of *mutual enhancement*. But at the same time that certain aspects of each are accentuated, other characteristics undergo suppression for the sake of refining the subjects of the metaphor. As we saw in the course of dubbing with nicknames, a distillation of meaning occurs, which renders two *narrowed* (simplified) but more easily understood subjects.

Through this process of interaction, we again learn to harbor only feelings of reproach for the individual so vile as to be most closely related to none other than the wretched wolf. But the metaphor simultaneously reinforces our contempt for the wolf, conflating it now with the worst possible specimen from our own species. In a sense they turn into each other, or at least become mutual proxies, basically inextricable. Perhaps the werewolf, represented in folk mythology as the greatest possible human abomination, is in fact an embodied metaphor.

I Am Become Wolf: Anthropomorphism and Zoomorphism

Finally, let's consider two important aspects of the metaphorical link between serial killers and creatures of the non-human realm such as wolves and black widows. Our examination of the White Wolf and the Black

Widow allows us to bring to bear two phenomena known as *anthropomorphism* and *zoomorphism*. The former expression refers to the convention of contemplating, perceiving, and describing (other) animals in human terms. Often, the question of anthropomorphism arises in philosophical discussions of religion: while Judeo-Christian tradition, for one, suggests that God fashioned human beings in his own image, one might conclude instead that we humans cast a supreme deity in our own image.

When Friedrich Nietzsche (1844–1900) tackled the matter of anthropomorphism, his analysis extended far beyond the realm of religion: the philosopher observed the pervasiveness of anthropomorphic thinking in our every association, including our engagement with the natural environment. Nietzsche believed that *humanizing* nature facilitates our mastery of it – and central to mastering nature is not only appropriating its elements for our own use, but simply understanding it.

When we anthropomorphize we tend to hold other beings to human standards of conduct and sensibility. And as the wolf's long, unfortunate history alongside humans demonstrates, this animal unreasonably bears a great many anthropomorphically appointed attributes of the worst kind. By a strange circular logic, only by humanizing the wolf via the imposition of decidedly un-wolflike moral codes and sentiments such as empathy can we fully assert the villainy of this predator, and at length appropriate it to then demonize our wolfish serial killers. In effect, this process reassigns those misplaced human traits from wolves back upon humans; but having been filtered through the "beasts of waste and desolation," the traits prove all the more damnable.

Returning to the black widow, it is clear that spiders do not marry in the human sense of the word, and widowhood is a status reserved for human women who have lost their husbands to death. But referring to members of the infamous genus of spider (*Latrodectus*) as *widows* performs a few tasks for us. First, it is simply descriptive and enables a familiarity with the spider by assigning it a human label. Second, it narrows the identity of this creature to its occasional performance of one striking deed and casts the practice of sexual cannibalism in a way that subjects arachnids, of all things, to the same moral accountability that people impose on themselves. In both cases, the name "widow" simplifies the spider so that we may understand it and thereby master it in a Nietzschean sense. Third, of course, the black widow has proved quite useful as a metaphor for the female serial killer of the Trueblood type, as we again borrow from nature and thereby assert our mastery of it.

The flip-side of anthropomorphism is zoomorphism, or the attribution of animalistic properties to people. When we describe serial killers as black widows and wolves (which, by the way, we do, the false example of the White Wolf notwithstanding), we actually dehumanize them. Recasting murderers like Lydia Trueblood as non-human creatures by way of zoomorphism performs the opposite function that anthropomorphism performs, but to the same effect: these metaphorical nicknames do violence to both the creature of comparison, whether wolf or widow, and the serial killer.

Strange Bedfellows

Humans achieve a strange sort of intimacy with other animals in the context of serial murder. First, killers borrow not only a range of attributes from maligned creatures such as wolves and black widows, but at times adopt, or find themselves labeled with, their names – those deeply personal identifiers that distinguish them among similar unfortunate beings. Second, their shared experience as subjects of the same metaphor can result in a tightly entwined super-identity that amplifies the treachery of each, whether cannibalistic spider, demon-wolf, or mass murderer. Third, casting humans as black widows through zoomorphism and wolves as humans through anthropomorphism renders a fluid exchange of attributes among these wolves, widows, and serial killers. Although the intimacy is merely semantic, it is indeed language that largely informs our understanding of these creatures, for better or for worse.

For Further Contemplation

A list of a few creature-inspired serial killer nicknames is provided for those who wish to practice their anthropomorphism and zoomorphism, contemplate the nature of metaphor, and consider how our use of labels changes our understanding of the world and the human and non-human animals residing in it:

- Leslie "Catweasel" Bailey
- Joseph "Alligator Man" Ball
- Albert "The Werewolf of Wisteria" Fish

- Leroy "The Werewolf" Francis
- Vasili "The Moscow Wolfe" Komaroff
- Major Ray "Rattlesnake Lisemba" Lisemba
- Michael "The Wolf" Lupo
- Archie "Mad Dog" McCafferty
- Donald "Black Panther" Neilson
- Earle Leonard "Gorilla Murderer" Nelson
- Heinrich "Beast of the Black Forest" Pommerenke
- Melvin David "The Sex Beast" Rees
- Sergi "Hippopotamus" Ryakhovsky
- Charles Gumurkh "The Serpent" Sobhraj
- Lucian "The Red Spider" Staniak
- Alan Michael "Buzzard" Stephens
- Jean-Baptiste "Human Tiger" Troppmann
- Lydia "Black Widow" Trueblood

CHAPTER 14

AN ARRESTING CONVERSATION

Police Philosophize about the Armed and Dangerous

Police are on the front lines in pursuit of serial killers, and their words can give us a perspective on murder that is rich with real-life experience. Aristotle (384–322 BCE) advocated a method for learning about the world called *natural philosophy*, in which our philosophical theories emerge directly from our observations in day-to-day life. The Los Angeles Police Department (LAPD) has seen several infamous serial murderers pass through its jurisdiction, from "Southland Strangler" John Floyd Thomas, Jr., to the still-at-large, unidentified, "Grim Sleeper."

I was lucky to find two retired California police officers willing to talk to me about what their years on the force taught them about murder, murderers, and life. Diane Amarillas, former Deputy Sheriff for Marin County, and Karen Kos, former Sergeant with the LAPD, share their tales of murder cases, serial killers, and the public misperception of these dangerous perpetrators. This interview scene is re-created from both online and face-to-face interviews with these two exciting and knowledgeable professionals. Thank you, ladies, for your information and insight!

The Interview

S. Waller (SW): Welcome! Thanks for coming here today, and for being a part of this volume on serial killers and philosophy. I'm interviewing both of you to give our readers a professional law enforcement perspective on serial killers. I hope to bring some philosophy to our discussion, as well as portray your experiences with murderers and serial killers. First, what were your positions with law enforcement, and when and how long did you serve in that role?

Diane Amarillas (DA): I was a Deputy Sheriff for Marin County, California for 15 years, from 1990 to 2005. I was assigned to court floor security as a bailiff for most of my career. I saw many interesting court cases over the years, a few of them were for murder, but I wasn't assigned to any serial killer cases. Fortunately, those are rare.

Karen Kos (KK): I was a Sergeant with the Los Angeles Police Department. I worked there officially for 13 years, from 1988 to 2002, and I continued to consult with them for several years after that.

SW: Tell me about some of the experiences you have had as law enforcement officials with murderers – serial or otherwise.

DA: I met many murderers as a bailiff. Trials usually last for months, so I could be with a defendant every court day for the duration. I got to know many very well. Of course, they couldn't be entirely themselves, as I was a person who could be called to testify if they made any spontaneous statements about the case.

SW: Give us some of the highlights.

DA: I remember one case with a woman who was really disconnected from reality. She chopped up another woman and then stabbed herself repeatedly in the throat. She said she'd heard voices, demons in her head. Most cases weren't like that one; most were over money or something like that.

For example, in one case, a young man killed his father because he wouldn't give him money. So much for family values! Money often overrides what we might think of as love ... in another case, a man killed one of his girlfriends with the help of another guy, to get her money. These are really common ... I remember in another case, a woman and her boyfriend hired a man to kill her husband. It was just like the movie *Double Indemnity*. Money is a common motive. In another case, an au pair and her boyfriend killed her employers over money. They also shot the dog, but left the baby unharmed.

SW: Maybe she was attached to the baby she was taking care of? That doesn't really explain the dog, though ... anyway, what about other cases, and other motives?

DA: Sure, there are also plenty of drug related murders – that's no shock. I remember a drug related case where a man killed his brother over money and their business. In another drug related case, two men killed another over meth, after being "up" for three days. I can only imagine that the lack of sleep alone would impair your judgment and likely make you more volatile.

SW: What else? Any other cases that come to mind?

DA: In another case, a young man killed his ex-girlfriend with a lamp cord because he didn't want her to be with anyone else. This one stuck with me because he told me that the biggest problem in society is testosterone gone wild. I think this showed a certain presence of mind.

SW: Wow, yes. He seemed to understand his own drives or imbalances. That self-reflective quality isn't terribly uncommon among serial killers. They usually aren't psychotic, like the first woman you mentioned – the one who stabbed herself in the throat – was. They're generally pretty socially savvy and quite manipulative, which means that they understand quite a bit about how other people tick, and can play on their – our – desires and fears.

DA: Speaking of manipulators, I remember a very interesting case … a "family" with a man and four "wives" was brought into custody because they had neglected a child to the point of death. The story just got weirder as it unfolded. It turns out they had 16 children between them, all very bright with different levels of growth challenges from malnutrition.

SW: Some philosophers might take that example to indicate a different kind of killing altogether – killing through neglect is a form of *letting die,* while actively ending a life is *killing.* The motives, the psychologies behind them could be very different, and philosophers debate about the morality of each. Some argue that letting die is not as immoral as killing, though in this case, the fact that they were the parents of the children would probably make many ethicists think their lack of action on behalf of their children is quite evil.

DA: I only met one person in 15 years that I would consider "evil." He didn't have a conscience and he wasn't a murderer…. He was a rapist.

SW: There's plenty of philosophy in that comment as well. First, we can ask whether feeling remorse over an action that harms someone makes you a better person or not. Am I allowed to keep hurting people as long as I feel bad about it? Second, we could argue that rape is more evil than murder precisely because the victim does go on living, and in a very violent case, that victim could be very psychologically damaged, fearful, and disempowered. If the victim suffers a fate worse than death, we can ask whether the deed is morally worse than the act of killing.

KK: But when someone is dead, that person never gets the opportunity to recover!

SW: Yes, that's also a philosophical position – the opposing position. People who still have their lives can work toward recovery, while people who are murder victims never have that chance. But no matter which position we take, we're judging the evilness of the action by looking at how much the victim was impacted by the attack. This is using a *principle of harm* to make a moral judgment – harm is evil, more harm is more evil, and preventing harm is part of doing good. It's not the only way to make a moral judgment, but it's a very popular and quite sensible method. In fact, it's probably one of the principles that the criminal justice system is based on – those who do harm to others in society need to be removed from society to protect everyone else ... but I'm getting us way off topic here, and we were working with some interesting stuff that I'd like to get back to ... clearly you've experienced lots of different killers with lots of different behaviors and motives. So, drawing from these experiences, would you say that there are different types of serial killers or murderers? How would you classify them?

DA: There are both different kinds of victims and different kinds of perpetrators. Perpetrators can be classified according to the reasons that they commit the crimes, or by the different methods they use to kill their victims. For example, some killers kill strangers, while some kill people they know. Some are very orderly and systematic, while others leave a very chaotic crime scene. If you're talking about psychological terms to describe a perp [perpetrator], like *psychopath*, I would classify all of them as psychopaths – otherwise I wouldn't say there are types.

KK: I disagree ... there are definitely different types, but the categories are going to depend on who you talk to. Diane is right that for police purposes it doesn't matter what psychological type they are – just what their behavior is – because that's relevant to how we capture them. And we know some behaviors very well. We know that killers tend to stay within their same socioeconomic status and their own race. Blacks kill blacks and whites kill whites. Middle-class killers kill middle-class victims – killers seek victims that are in the same social class, or sometimes go down a class. We know that killers and child molesters, most often (though this is really changing) are still middle-class white males that range in age from 23 to 43. However, it appears that it's becoming more equal opportunity in the last 15 years.

SW: Wow, this distinction between the psychological profiles and the behaviors of serial killers reminds me of a philosophical school of thought called *verificationism*, which would emphasize catching criminals by knowing their behaviors and not their psychological profiles. For the early twentieth-century verificationist philosophers, all of science, and really any meaningful human activity, was measured by its observable results. They thought humans should avoid speculation that leads nowhere and stop theorizing about things that could not be observed or measured by scientific instruments. In other words, theories about what goes on in the minds of others are useless, meaningless, and foolish unless they lead directly to observable results. Verificationists wouldn't care what psychological type a serial killer has, but they'd catalogue their behaviors in order to catch them more efficiently. Karen, can you tell us a little more about your three kinds of serial killers and I'll try to imagine how a verificationist might react to your classifications ...

KK: Great. I tend to think that there are three main personality categories for serial killers: the *thrill-seeker*, the ones that are *on a mission*, and the *power rapists*. Of course, there are subcategories with each one.

SW: Okay, give details ...

KK: Thrill-seekers kill for the thrill of it – the thrill of controlling someone, the thrill of outwitting the police, the thrill of doing something risky and dangerous. They enjoy the "rush" of the action just as shoplifters or pyromaniacs do. And just like shoplifters and pyromaniacs, the rush dies down once they've succeeded, at which point they need another "fix." They aren't satisfied with life without that rush.

Serial killers that are on a mission think they are removing the unworthy from the planet. Dexter might fall in this category, even though he is fictional, as well as the two old women in *Arsenic and Old Lace*, who think they're helping people by removing them from this life.

The *sexual sadists* or power rapists do not kill for sexual gratification; they kill for the power. They're driven to torture and kill others in order to feel dominant and powerful.

Some people add another category, the *comfort killers*. They kill family members, presenting themselves as comforting, friendly forces in the lives of their romantic partners, brothers and sisters, and others with close emotional ties before murdering them before receiving insurance monies and inheritances. I wouldn't consider these people serial killers because their motives do not really center around the act of killing. *Black widows* – or *widowers* – kill for the insurance money and not because they have a drive to kill. They'll stop when the potential for inheritance is gone and they don't particularly enjoy killing. They just want the profit that comes with it.

There is another group of people who believe that child molesters very easily become killers – that they are selfish and predisposed to protect themselves at all costs, so they'll continue to molest victim after victim until they kill, because they are finally in a situation where they're afraid someone's going to reveal them or get them arrested – and they don't want to get caught, so they kill. This is a very controversial theory, not everyone agrees with it by a long shot. If it's right, it would make child molesters a specific kind of serial killer – one that kills for self-protection or kills to protect their ability to keep on molesting.

SW: According to the verificationist doctrine, these psychological types are only meaningful if they result in different behaviors. It seems like someone could kill a relative or romantic partner for sexual gratification and end up being classified as a comfort killer because they played that role in the life of the victim. Likewise, a serial killer "on a mission" could kill prostitutes, but so could a "power rapist" or "thrill-seeker." Even a child molester could be killing because there is a threat of being caught, or for a sexual thrill, or for the power. If we look at behavior alone, it's pretty hard to tell which psychological profile fits each killer. That's important to think about – these psychological types get assigned to people based on behaviors, but the behaviors are not so clear, not so distinct from one another, that we can be sure of the psychological type we're assigning.

This uncertainty really doesn't stop us, though. Philosophers who still wanted to know what made people tick got very impatient with the verificationists. Recently, philosophers have gone back to doing "philosophy of mind" because we don't stop wondering about other people's thoughts and emotions just because we can't see them firsthand. We watch people's behaviors carefully because we do want to know what is going on in their minds. Or, as Eminem once said, he was just fascinated with "serial killers and their psyche and their mind states."[1]

DA: You like Eminem?

SW: Maybe. I suspect there's a little Slim Shady in all of us … we all want to know what makes killers tick, what goes on in their minds.

KK: Well, if we really want to get into other people's minds, we should talk about my grandfather, because he was a multiple murderer, with some serial killer behaviors!

SW: Wow! Yes, please talk about him! But … what's the difference between multiple murderers and serial killers? How could he be both, or have the attributes of both?

KK: There's controversy about making the distinction between serial killers and mass or multiple murderers. Mass murder happens all the time – these are the cases where someone pulls out a gun and shoots everyone in a McDonald's or in a high school. Multiple murderers kill many people, often in a series, but they do it for the money, or the mafia, and they will stop doing it if they don't get paid. They don't have an interest in the killing by itself – they just have an ... unfortunate employment situation. Sometimes, multiple murderers kill a bunch of people simply because they're committing other crimes and they have to get rid of the witnesses or there is some incident and they have to kill in order to escape. These "incidental" murders are opportunistic and not particularly organized or well thought out, and their perpetrators are not as conniving as the typical serial killer.

Serial killers will keep killing and killing forever, because they're driven to do it. True sociopaths kill for fun – they need to do it – it's a compulsion; it's an end in itself. Often, serial killers take trophies or kill in a specific "signature" way. Hit men and other multiple murderers aren't interested in the victims or the acts, so they don't do those things. While hit men and serial killers often know their victims, hit men stalk people because their jobs, financial circumstances, or bosses demand it, while serial killers stalk people because they're driven to kill.

Both multiple murderers and serial killers are difficult to catch because the victims are relatively random and so hard to link back to the killer. These killers don't form bonds with many people and probably travel a lot and so they kill in different areas. It's very hard to link crime to crime across states, over time, given a variety of victims.

SW: So, was your grandfather a hit man?

KK: No, my grandfather was a multiple murderer but not for hire – that I know of. He didn't have some of the cold, calculating features that are often thought of as the hallmark of serial killers. He killed impulsively and emotionally. He stalked his victims and killed people he was angry with or those he disagreed with. He was twice convicted and twice acquitted in Texas, where he killed Hispanics. The racism in Texas allowed for the acquittal. My grandfather was pretty smart about who he got angry with and who he killed – immigrants were below the legal radar at that time. Also, Grandpa was a truck driver – he was all over the place and so he was hard to track, hard to find. That mobility gave him great freedom to blow up at whomever, wherever. He killed a person because he didn't like the breed of dog he owned, or what truck the guy was driving ... he would start a verbal confrontation, track the guy down, stalk him for a while, and kill him.

SW: Several of the essays in this volume discuss the ability of serial killers to think ahead (Winters, Schechter and Schechter, Terjesen, Gray).

Do you think he was thinking ahead when he'd get angry and fall into a murderous rage?

KK: He did think of the consequences in that he didn't want to get caught. In that way he was typical – serial killers are so scary, in part, because they tend to pick on the weak, or the elderly, or children, or the disabled, or women. They pick on the powerless and exploit it – like immigrants, prostitutes, runaways, etc. … people who won't be reported missing right away, people who won't have someone looking for them … this is part of being a bit smarter, more calculating and more reflective. Serial killers can plan ahead in self-interested ways. But there are stories my parents tell that reveal that my grandfather wasn't as thoughtful as he could have been about protecting himself from legal repercussions. The big one, the "big murder" that he did – he brought the whole family. There was a bartender who told my grandfather that he was too drunk, and he cut him off – he wouldn't serve him any more liquor. He brought the family in the car and made them pretend to be sleeping, but the whole family actually watched while he killed the guy. My grandfather always used knives – he killed him with a knife, which is very up close and personal.

SW: Were you frightened of him? Did you interact with him a lot as a kid? What else can you tell us about him?

KK: He adored his grandkids. His children despised him, but he treated his grandchildren very well – we never saw that side of his personality. So, I liked him, though I only knew him when I was quite young. The stories I told you come from stories my parents told me. I don't have an adult view of him or who he was … I knew another killer when I was a bit older, a friend of the family. He was 16 years old and one day went to a neighbor's house and brutally raped and murdered an 11-year-old girl. Is he a serial killer? From what we know about people who commit these sorts of crimes so early, we can be pretty sure that he'd probably continue. The disturbing thing for me is that, well, he seemed like a normal teenager to me.

SW: Serial killer Denis Nilsen once said, "A mind can be evil without being abnormal." That is really disturbing. So, how do you go about catching these guys?

DA: Well, it's not always a "he," although murder is more common for males. You learn pretty fast that what Karen said is right on – they all look like everyone else – no one just looks like a killer, or seems like a killer, and some are very charming and bright. Fortunately, everyone makes mistakes, and that's how investigations work.

SW: I'm reminded of something Eminem said in a *New York Times* interview – I have it here – May 21, 2009 – he said, "You listen to these people talk, or you see them, they look so regular. What does a serial killer look like? He don't look like anything. He looks like you. You could be living next door to one. If I lived next door to you, you could be."[2] So, that has to make the investigation hard work!

KK: I can't believe you like Eminem. Anyway, investigating any crime is a long process. The elements of investigation of a murder scene are: securing the scene, collecting evidence, talking to witnesses, and building the case.

Securing the scene is the most important, because you don't want the scene, evidence, or witnesses to be corrupted by other elements/people. That's why the first few hours/days after a crime are critical – there's always a trail left behind, and the more immediate the investigation, the cleaner and clearer the evidence. Once you know that no one has tampered with or spoiled the scene, you can gather all the things you need to make the case.

I was involved in securing the scenes for evidence collection and would go out and look for subjects that had been identified by profilers. When a murder occurs, they start a book – not a board like you see on the cop shows on TV – if they actually used a board, they'd run out of wall space really fast! All the evidence, plus a diagram of the crime scene, details about the furniture position and location, and lots of details about the body condition and position, plus details about the blood – where, how much, how it projected, all of that evidence gets compiled, and more. Addresses, makes and models of cars on the street, and their license plates, plus many photographs of the scene – everything is included. Access is very limited at these crime scenes – even other officers don't walk through. The techs collect the blood, the bullets, the fingerprints, all that stuff. The initial statements are taken and then everyone is reinterviewed within a couple of days. People remember things once they start thinking about what happened and all these little details come out. The investigating interviewers canvass the area, going from house to house, asking questions. Over several days or even weeks they establish a timeline of what occurred and when. It takes a long time to put all the pieces of the puzzle together.

SW: Anything to add, Karen?

KK: No, that's a good summary.

SW: Can you give us a take-home message about murderers?

DA: The most memorable thing about these experiences for me – the take-home message – is that there's always a circumstance that drives

S. WALLER, DIANE AMARILLAS, AND KAREN KOS

people over the edge. The rapist I mentioned earlier – something made him snap. If we could isolate the stress-tolerance threshold for each individual in society and notice when he, or she, is getting close to the edge, the world would be a much safer place. There are usually signs that someone is becoming dangerous or violent. We just need to pay attention.

KK: The take-home message for me is about this ridiculous culture where people get obsessed with serial killers. They have a fantasy about them and it's so distorted that they're not even frightened by the reality. I think that people don't really believe in serial killers – the whole thing gets so fictionalized by the media – we cheer for Dexter, and are fascinated by, if not friendly toward, "Mickey and Mallory" of *Natural Born Killers*. We enjoy Hannibal Lecter's macabre sense of justice, and Dr. Phibes – Dr. Phibes is an almost sympathetic character – he only wants to punish those he thinks murdered his wife. We're charmed by him because he misses his wife. Heck, people are still writing fan letters to Charlie Manson! But real serial killers are real people running around killing ten, twenty, a hundred people and never getting caught.

And we don't all have alarms! Think about it!

Serial killers are charming and they blend in very well, like Ted Bundy. A common trick is to use a ploy to get trust … they need help with something, they get you to walk over, to pull over, or to stop in the parking lot next to their van …

SW: Thanks for talking about all of these things, and for letting us do philosophy about your experiences of murderers and serial killers.

NOTES

1 Jon Pareles, "Get Clean, Come Back: Eminem's Return," *New York Times, Music Section* (May 21, 2009): AR1.
2 Ibid.

PART VI

PSYCHO-OLOGY

Killer Mindsets and Meditations on Murder

CHAPTER 15

PSYCHOPATHY AND WILL TO POWER

Ted Bundy and Dennis Rader

 We all expect monsters. We hear about serial murders, we find the crimes monstrous and incomprehensible, but we turn on the TV and find relatively normal folk; quiet people, mostly. They are people with families and jobs; people who fit in and go unnoticed. Dennis Rader, the BTK killer, was a code enforcement officer, a Cub Scout leader, and president of his church. He chose the name "BTK" to signal his intention – B(ind them), T(orture them), K(ill them). John Wayne Gacy was a building contractor who did side jobs as a clown; his family had no idea that he was seducing and killing young men. Ted Bundy was bright, good looking, and personable. People were drawn to his good looks and confident manner. He was an up and comer in the ranks of the Young Republicans. So, what gives?

Monstrous acts do not necessarily proceed from monsters. When we perceive the acts from outside and rightly experience horror, we naturally project the horror of our perceptions onto the person committing the acts. When those acts are unthinkable, like serial sexual murder, we expect that the person who committed the acts to be as horrible as the acts themselves. But ultimately we find the evildoer pedestrian, his life outside of the crime and its contexts relatively unremarkable. It is Hanna Arendt's vision of the *banality of evil*.

But the notion of a perfectly ordinary serial killer is baffling. The enormity of these acts demands that the people who commit them *must* be monsters. We are given to believe we should be able to identify the monsters – much like Dorian Gray's portrait or Baron Harkonnen from *Dune*, we expect monsters to wear their evil plainly, on their faces and in their flesh. We want to think of them as insane, or possessed, or something dark and different, but we come to understand that the monsters appear as we do and walk among us with the appearance of respectable citizens.

Our first impulse is that these evildoers must be crazy, wanton criminals or something else. More often than not, serial killers are *psychopaths* – superficially charming people with little or no capacity for empathy, remorse, or compassion. They are rational, but not moral, in many ways like Nietzsche's *superman*. They know their deeds are unacceptable to the world at large, but they are compelled, by a curiosity or a fantasy, to kill. Where we would be held back from these explorations by compassion or a learned fear of punishment, they go about their projects with as little feeling as a bug collector who, without hesitation, kills a moth in ether so he can pin it to a piece of cardboard. They pursue Nietzsche's *will to power*.

Psychopaths versus Psychotics

Psychopathy is the diagnostic term for people we call psychopaths. They are not crazy. They are in many ways sane, practical, and able to function in the world. Crucially, however, they live without conscience, compassion, or remorse. As a result, they are unable to learn the kinds of felt associations that create a sense of right and wrong, the moral restraints that prevent us from living out our own fantasies and perversions. As psychologists sought to describe the problem, they labeled such people *morally insane*: possessed of rationality, but incapable of the moral distinctions that the rest of us take for granted. Hervey Cleckley, the first scientist to frame our current understanding of the problem, described them as affected by a *semantic dementia* – the inability to make emotional and moral distinctions in language.

Psychopaths are not *psychotic*. In the context of serial murder, the confusion between *psychosis* and psychopathy stems from the commonsense assumption that the people who act as they do cannot be sane. The linguistic confusion also arises because until the middle of the twentieth century the word *psychopathy* was often used generically to describe any form of mental illness. Starting in the 1930s, the word came more and more to represent the specific problem of the person without conscience or the

♠ RICHARD M. GRAY

possibility of empathy. By the 1940s it was more completely associated with psychopathy as we now understand it, and today it is a technical term.[1]

Psychopaths are differentiated from psychotics in that they have been diagnosed with a personality disorder, a systematic pattern of behavior that is lifelong and pervasive but that does not disorder their capacity to function in the world. Non-violent psychopaths might be characterized as suffering from a character flaw.

Psychotics see things that are not there and often have auditory hallucinations; they cannot differentiate between truth and delusion. Their lives are often unmanageable and severely disordered. Psychotics are often driven by their delusions. The "Son of Sam," David Berkowitz, was told by the neighbor's dog to take the gun and kill the children. Charlie Manson was convinced that the Beatles had told him that he was the herald of the new age and the reincarnation of Jesus Christ.

Psychopaths are often curious about how things look or might feel. They may be seeking sensations or new ways to encounter their missing humanity, but they know what they are doing, they know it is wrong and harmful; they are simply untouched by the enormity of their crimes. If they *seem* to be moved emotionally, it is often part of an intellectual game, or just a fear of being caught. Dennis Rader became incensed when he thought that the police lied to him about the safety of communicating by computer disk. To that point he had bested them at every turn, but then they lied to him. The police cheated. Similarly, in their statements and allocutions, the psychopathic killers are coldly rational. They know precisely what they did and how they did it. They can even tell you on some level why they did it. Not so with psychotics.

Finally, psychopathy seems to be determined by genetics more than socialization. Recent studies have shown that although the anti-social behavior that often accompanies psychopathy has a strong relationship to social class, intelligence, and upbringing, psychopathy itself – the callous, conscience-free, remorseless personality – is the fruit of genetics, not socialization. True psychopathy is inborn.[2]

The Psychopath

We can begin to obtain a deeper level of understanding of psychopathy by considering several of its root characteristics. The psychopath is characterized by:

superficial charm, the absence of delusions and psychoneurotic manifesta-
tions, unreliability, insincerity, lack of remorse or shame, inadequately
motivated antisocial behavior, failure to learn from experience ...[3]

Superficial charm describes the psychopath's capacity to say the right
things, to draw you into his or her frame of reference. Ted Bundy exuded
it. He was alternately confident and childlike and able to win the confidence of almost anyone. It is said that he was a natural salesman. Dennis
Rader was not quite so smooth, but was known as an upright citizen. The
people in his church knew that they could depend on Dennis. No one
suspected what these men did or were capable of doing.[4]

This trait, superficial charm, may relate to the way a psychopath learns.
Scientific analysis reveals that psychopaths most readily learn what
pleases. They learn to discriminate between things that are associated
with reward much better than they learn most other things. Superficial
charm may simply be an expression of the fact that beyond all of their
deficits, psychopaths can learn what works in interpersonal situations.
They have a marked incapacity to anticipate danger or dislike. Although
they can learn to mimic normal emotions in the appropriate situations,
they often have no idea what they actually mean. As a result they become
chameleon-like and learn to blend in. They learn the right words but
there is no substance behind them.[5]

It is now a truism that the diagnosis of anti-social personality disorder
(ASPD) includes many psychopaths, but not all psychopaths are anti-
social. What is the difference between ASPD and psychopathy? ASPD is
characterized by a history of remorseless criminality – conning, lying,
and criminal activity. In addition to serial killers and serial rapists, a large
component of non-criminal psychopaths participate in the highly social
venues of religion, entertainment, and corporate business.[6] In his ground-
breaking book *Snakes in Suits*, Robert Hare, the modern guru of psychopathy, discusses the many psychopaths that walk our streets without
revealing themselves through anti-social behavior. He believes that up to
1 percent of corporate CEOs may be "snakes in suits."[7]

When they are violent, their violence is purposeful. It is not a response
to insult or injury, it is a relatively casual, impulsive act; someone or
something got in his way and it needed to be removed. In the opening
credits of the Showtime series *Dexter*, the psychopathic protagonist is
seen lying in his bed as a mosquito lands on his arm and begins to draw
blood. Dexter's eye focuses on the creature and without a glimmer of
thought, he swats it into oblivion. Psychopathic violence is like that: cold,

objective, sometimes necessary, sometimes not. Common criminals and individuals with ASPD, by contrast, use *reactive violence*. They respond emotionally and spontaneously. Neurophysiologists and psychologists have shown that reactive violence – automatic violence in response to threat or emotion – is less common among psychopaths than among individuals diagnosed as anti-social, although members of both groups are more reactively violent than non-members.

It seems that all psychopaths are simultaneously emotionally cold or indifferent to the suffering of others, impulsive, and relatively irresponsible. Robert Hare and many other researchers report that on a deep biological level the disorder does seem to divide into two factors.[8] The first factor accounts for their lack of empathy, remorselessness, and callous indifference to human suffering, and is shaped largely by genetics. Up to 60 percent of this trait is inherited. The second factor, which is associated with their irresponsibility, impulsivity, and anti-social behavior, has a strong environmental component. Although there is some genetic influence on the second factor, the particular way the individual psychopath is impulsive and irresponsible is determined to a large extent by upbringing, environment, and experience. Indeed, the level to which a psychopath engages in violence is directly related to his intelligence and socioeconomic status: rich smart psychopaths are less violent than poor uneducated psychopaths.[9]

Again, consider the fictional psychopath Dexter. Early in life, Dexter discovers he has a penchant for bloodletting. Caught in the act, his adoptive father teaches him a relatively acceptable way of managing this urge: kill the bad guys. In the real world, real-life Dexters are likely to be taught the ways of big finance, stardom, and big-tent ministry rather than safe ways to kill. Those less fortunate learn the law of the street and often become violent criminals. In many ways the non-violent psychopath is the perfect twenty-first century CEO: cold, rational, and willing to do anything for a profit.[10]

Psychopaths are unreliable. It's interesting to note that in early theories psychopaths were identified as suffering from a semantic disability, as their words never seemed to match their actions. But the real deficit probably lies in a failure to consider future consequences. They know how to say the right thing, and because they generally do not have the ability to anticipate how others might react when they don't follow through on their words, they often prove to be unreliable (though sometimes reliability has been learned as a useful means for attaining some short-term outcome). There may also be a problem with attention.

When psychologists evaluate children for psychopathic potential, attention deficits often combine with a callous indifference to others as predictive factors for adult psychopathy.

Other research tells us that in psychopaths the *amygdala*, the brain's center of emotion, is damaged. This means that they are not only indifferent to the feelings of others but the normal processes of learning, including conditioned fear and conditioned pleasure, are defective. In the normal person, our sense of responsibility is balanced between our fear of consequences and our desire for reward. Although their reward systems work on an adequate level, the fear of punishment, disapproval, and consequences more generally are not present to keep them on track. They lose attention or find other things more interesting.

Learning disabilities are common in psychopaths. They do not learn to fear or anticipate the hurt that others will experience as a result of their actions. Although they learn to respond to reward better than they learn fear-based responses, they are still not great learners. In fact, psychopaths learn best by discriminating between two stimuli. They can tell what works as opposed to what doesn't. This means that they can learn to choose between two options – but they don't choose based on punishment, they choose based on effectiveness.[11]

Language and the Emotional Brain

Insincerity is the mark of a person who is facile with language but either lacks or is unconcerned with any sense of the true meaning of the words. Psychopaths are often not particularly good with language. Studies show that while psychopaths do not differentiate between emotional and non-emotional words, *normals* do differentiate, responding to the emotional words more quickly and also experiencing an increase in skin conductance. For psychopaths, all kinds of words are the same; they just string them together to meet their needs. Because they respond best to what works, they can say all of the right things and mean none of them. Because they have no fear of being caught, they are free to say what they must to accomplish their ends.

Other researchers have shown that the content of the verbal narratives created by psychopaths is often unconvincing, but psychopaths often present a facade of confidence that makes them seem more believable. Because they have no fear of being wrong – they lack *amygdalar connections* that would produce that fear – they speak with unbowing surety. Even when caught in a lie, a psychopath presses on, unfazed and unconcerned with the revelation of their dishonesty. Recent research confirms that humans tend to believe confident narratives over coherent narratives.[12] In conversation, psychopaths are superb manipulators; normal people perceive them as confident and persuasive.

Curiously, their written language often reveals underlying difficulties that may not appear in their speech. Listening to Ted Bundy or Dennis Rader speak produces a very different response from reading their writing. Bundy failed the grammar portion of the bar exam and Rader's first note to the police was so badly crafted that police thought he was foreign-born. This divergence in speaking and writing skill may reveal one way in which psychopaths are impacted by their inability to learn on an emotional level. In the context of a conversation, there are enough cues from the other person to guide the psychopath's use of language so that it is relatively more fluid. When subject to formal questioning, psychopaths are often unconvincing; however, in conversation, they do well. Writing is generally solitary, so when they write they may not be provided with enough cues or feedback to guide their verbal responses toward manipulation.[13]

A wonderful interview between Ted Bundy and Dr. James Dobson was originally aired in 1989, shortly after Bundy's execution. At the time of the interview, Dobson, a preacher, was an anti-pornography crusader and Bundy a psychopath who used pornography to stimulate his fantasy life. Throughout the interview, you can watch Bundy as he feeds back to Dobson the exact words that he wants to hear. Sitting with his head slightly turned down and away from Dobson, Bundy, with a near smirk, created his last moments of TV glory by "gaming" the preacher. Bundy's words were cynical and chosen with some precision. Bundy reflected the preacher's language back to him, and any language he uses which might betray emotion is canned, repetitious, and meaningless. A significant fact not noted in the preface to the interview is that Bundy and his lawyers had hoped for a stay of execution based upon his cooperation. (Repentance, jailhouse conversions, and offender cooperation are common last-minute ploys of the condemned.)

On the fourth page of the interview transcript, Bundy makes the following statement:

I was a normal person. I had good friends. I led a normal life, except for this one, small but very potent and destructive segment that I kept very secret and close to myself. Those of us who have been so influenced by violence in the media, particularly pornographic violence, are not some kind of inherent monsters. We are your sons and husbands. We grew up in regular families. Pornography can reach in and snatch a kid out of any house today. It snatched me out of my home 20 or 30 years ago. As diligent as my parents were, and they were diligent in protecting their children, and as good a Christian home as we had, there is no protection against the kinds of influences that are loose in a society that tolerates ...[14]

But all of the evidence and Bundy's own statements suggest that by the time he was a pre-teen he was already alienated from family and friends and devoid emotionally. Bundy played to the crowd as he always did. He was providing the answers that would inevitably gain Dobson's approval. These answers are suggested in Dobson's introduction to the piece. With tears in his eyes, Bundy described the monster that took possession of him when he had been drinking and exacerbated his craze to kill: violent pornography.[15]

It is almost impossible to appreciate the pure cynicism of Bundy's statements without watching the video. Although Dobson indicates that Bundy wanted to warn the world about the evils of pornography, it is apparent that all Bundy really wanted was a chance to stand before the cameras again and to project an image of his own choosing. Since the interview, researchers have shown with considerable reliability that pornography does not foster violence *except* with psychopathic personalities.[16]

Empathy, Lack of Shame, Insincerity

Remorselessness and lack of shame arise in people who either have not developed the capacity to relate to others' suffering or have become hardened. In either case it is impossible for them to relate to the pain that they have caused or to feel shame for the things they have done. Both of these capacities require the ability to relate to the suffering of others or to feel the reality of deserved consequences. Psychopaths can do neither. For most people, emotional words and scenes lead to heightened activity in the amygdala as the emotional sense of the situation overcomes them, often shutting down higher functions. For psychopaths, the amygdala responds less powerfully to the same items and when it does respond it does so in step with higher cortical activity. The cortex is the brain area associated with rational thought and interpretive functions. So, psychopaths presented with an emotional stimulus have to think about its meaning and rationally make sense of it in order to parse their response. They do not feel the effects of others' fear, sadness, or pain, so they have to work to interpret their environment.

This characteristic appears clearly in the allocution of Dennis Rader, the BTK Killer. Standing in court before the judge, the victims' families, and the assembled press, Rader listened as the judge read out the details of his offenses. Without blinking an eye, Rader stopped the judge at several junctures to correct some minor detail. Unmoved by the enormity of his crimes or the responses of the people gathered there, Rader makes almost casual responses to the facts in the case; at one point making mouth noises as he sought a precise fact. This is a man who cannot even begin to appreciate the impact he had on others.

In the same court scene, Rader appeared monstrously insincere as he cried, hoping that God would receive him after this ordeal was over. He portrayed himself as saddened by the prospect of divine punishment, but as willingly putting his trust in God. In a context calling for compassion, the expression of remorse and deep shame, Rader is only concerned for himself. Perhaps he believed he was doing the right thing, or perhaps he simply felt threatened; in either case his concern appeared to be for his own eternal comfort. Nothing else mattered.

It is tempting to view this type of behavior as *dissociation*, the clinical term for the way an individual distances himself from ideas that are too painful or too upsetting to allow feeling. But Rader's behavior is different. The psychopath is not distancing himself; the response is not protective. His words and actions are cold and heartless because *he lacks the capacity to feel*. It is exactly that incapacity, his innate ability to dissociate, that makes serial murder possible.

Fantasies

Fantasies, in general, create patterns of actions, scripts for action that people can follow. For non-psychopathic fantasies it may be the perfect job interview or the perfect date. For the psychopathic serial murderer, it may be the idealized sequence of hunting, capturing, torturing, killing, and disposing of the victim.

There is a significant body of evidence to suggest that psychopathic serial killers' criminal activities are guided and shaped by fantasy. Fantasies arise in all children and adolescents as a means of dealing with issues of inadequacy and inferiority. In the psychopathic individual, for whom the normal attachment and maturational changes of adolescence may be particularly difficult, fantasy may become a significant means of dealing with developmental stressors. As with all children, the themes of such fantasies focus on domination, sexuality, and the overcoming of existential stress. There are, however, several differences between the fantasies of normal adolescents and those generated by psychopaths.[17]

However aberrant the fantasies of normal people may be, they are almost always constrained to the realm of fantasy by *moral sensitivities* learned in the course of development. We don't act out our fantasies because we possess a conditioned fear of the emotional responses of others, and we anticipate the probable consequences of doing so. The roots of our moral sensitivities, then, are fear and foresight. Psychopaths have neither fear nor foresight. They do not learn conditioned fear reactions or genuine empathetic responses that might guide them; and without such guidance they do not differentiate between appropriate and inappropriate fantasies. Interestingly, they function in the world because they learn not to talk about their fantasies and conquests to others; they learn from seeing others' prior bad reactions. They learn to avoid fights because they can experience direct fear in an immediately physically threatening circumstance. But they fail to anticipate future fear or pain based on abstract environmental cues. A gun in the hand of a present adversary is frightening and a cue to leave, but a police car down the block is easily ignored. These mental limitations can lead them to believe that a violent resolution may be as fully acceptable as a more moderate response is to a normal person. While they may know intellectually that certain actions are "wrong," that wrongness is an intellectual construct. Rather than fearing the abstract punishment and actively avoiding it, they may view it either as an unwanted complexity (it would be inconvenient, or annoying, to be arrested) or as something that makes the activity more exciting (the thrill of potentially being caught).

Witness Dexter in season one. In the course of his inner monologues he reflects on how no one may know what he does or how he feels about it. He knows that murder is wrong and that others find the behaviors abhorrent. During the first season he encounters his biological brother, who invites him to murder his adoptive sister. He is seriously tempted because he would finally have someone he could talk to. Dexter does not experience fear, though anyone else in that situation might fear the murderous drives of the brother or the potential legal consequences of joining

RICHARD M. GRAY

a brotherly killing team. He's not really worried about the future, either, even though his sister just might have been awake and might have seen him pause to consider his options.

Dennis Rader was convinced that he was smarter than the police and that he would not be caught. To satisfy his fantasies he would dress in his victims' clothes, tie himself up, and lay in shallow graves. However, confronted with direct fear, he was not immune to the real fear of being caught. Once he became aware of the possibility of apprehension in pursuing this "project," he became fearful and fled.

Ted Bundy had fantasies of domination and possession. He declared that there was no greater power over a person than feeling their last breath escaping from their body. Yet, he too experienced the direct fear of apprehension. This was not the conditioned fear that might prevent living out the fantasy, but the fear engendered by the real presence of a dead body in his house or car and the possibility that someone might find it.

Part of the psychopathic fantasy may be type of victim chosen. A recent series of serial killings in Milwaukee, Wisconsin focused on prostitutes. Ted Bundy preferred fairly standard middle-class women of college age. Dennis Rader had a certain look and type in mind. Women were designated as appropriate or inappropriate for his idea of a "project."

For some killers, specific patterns of language, actions, and ways of binding, torturing, or killing are preferred. Holmes and Holmes describe patterns requiring specific scripted language patterns. Dennis Rader used a characteristic kind of cord and type of knot to bind his victims. It is not uncommon to find that the victims have had specific kinds of piercings, patterns of injuries, and locations of injuries. All of these represent attempts to replicate the offender's fantasy scheme that ultimately guides his offense behavior.[18]

There is another difference between the fantasy life of psychopaths and normals. Normal individuals are often distracted from fantasy by the competing calls of other interests and desires. Even amid fantasy, normals experience distraction and move on to other interests and desires. In contrast, psychopaths are often single-minded and highly focused. Psychological tests have found them to be very difficult to distract from a task once they have begun. Emotional distractions in particular have little capacity to move them, probably due to their emotional response deficits and the fact that their fantasies are not weakened by the usual moral constraints that hamper their expression in normals. There is also evidence that excitement may be a more salient aspect of experience than any other for the psychopath. Because fantasy is different, because it is exciting, because it represents an intense experience in what is normally an emotionally flat life experience, the psychopathic serial offender may respond preferentially to acting out his fantasy – something most of us rarely get to do.[19]

Fantasy builds predispositions to action. Through the mechanisms of internal practice, self-reinforcement (usually through masturbation), and the reinforcement provided by the altered state of consciousness itself, the fantasies of psychopathic serial offenders can become powerful motivators of behavior.

The Serial Killer and Nietzsche

The psychopathic serial killer stands before us as a person who, on a very real level, has an alien perspective on good and evil: moral and immoral. He knows the words, but the attitude of conventional morality has often been replaced by the cold discipline of exclusion and an incapacity for normal human affection. As a result, his highest good becomes the *will to power* over others.

These observations immediately bring to mind Friedrich Wilhelm Nietzsche and his 1886 work, *Beyond Good and Evil*.[20] Nietzsche proposes the possibility that there is not simply a single moral sense, but an attitude of morality whose expression differs from context to context, class to class, and culture to culture. He argues that at root, all of life and all psychology is driven by the will to power and that every manifestation of culture is ultimately rooted in the single urge of an organism to express dominion over its environment, its fellows, and in humanity itself. He suggests that when we transcend the entrenched notions of good and bad, when we begin to see that good and bad only have meaning with regard to a social hierarchy and milieu, we will see that true morality is about disciplined action determined by the value of the outcome.

The psychopathic serial killer is typically a man (Aileen Wuornos is one of the few documented female serial killers) who is incapable of many natural responses. He is by nature Nietzsche's man with a heart of brass. But he has not risen above good and evil by virtue of vision, rank, or discipline, as would Nietzsche's *übermensch*; he has never comprehended the difference between good and evil except as semantic categories. Lacking the capacity for most of the categories of emotion that are

♠ RICHARD M. GRAY

natural to humans, he is a person who, exercised by the need to hide his deepest nature, builds his life in terms of outcomes and disciplines which he creates from his own world of fantasy.

Nietzsche suggests that morality is about discipline. It is the application of one's self to the task of meeting the multiple requirements of an art, a science, or a theology; it is the disciplined self-molding – often as intentional deception and misrepresentation – that sharpens the mind to the point of superiority and the possibility of bold action. It is a self-molding that occurs in a social context and an emotional context, an attitude of morality. Whereas, in the superior man envisioned by the philosopher, this may give rise to exceptional leadership (he cites Napoleon, Julius Caesar and Leonardo da Vinci as examples), the psychopath is subjected to discipline out of necessity. In order to survive in the world, he must learn to emulate, dissimulate, and build masks of sanity. As a result, the psychopath often becomes the facile liar, the artful bully, or the insistent con-man who knows how to go through the motions to get his way. Where the Nietzschean superman awakens to destiny, the minor intellect of the psychopath is only strengthened in deceit and self-delusion, all the better to follow his ultimately petty, narrow, and selfish fantasies.

Beyond Good and Evil indicates that life is by nature cruel; indeed, at the heart of many of our customs, cruelty and exploitation lurk as integral elements in the flow of life. The predator is not regarded as evil or low, but merely as the expression of the basic characteristic of all living things, the will to power. The lion, the conqueror, the artist – all move toward an end that is life-affirming, for their own enrichment and that of the world in which they dwell. They bring order into the world, fulfilling the natural order of life through their actions. In this same context, however, although we may see the serial offender as a predator, he is an unnatural predator. His will to power is perverse, as it serves no end but his own fantasy. Even though he deludes himself with narcissistic fantasies, he remains an aberration, trapped by the narrow constraints of his own perversity, seeking to prove his superiority, but always inevitably falling short. Ultimately, according to Nietzsche, there are failed evolutions, men who aspire to greatness but lack the moral discipline to achieve it. In the case of the psychopathic serial killer, the inadequacy is not a failure of vision, but a simple incapacity: he is incapable of creating a vision larger than himself and incapable of the perseverance under discipline (due to his many deficits in learning and attention) that marks the superior man.

NOTES

1 Theodor Millon et al., "Historical Conceptions of Psychopathy in the United States and Europe," in Theodor Millon et al. (eds.) *Psychopathy: Antisocial, Criminal, and Violent Behavior* (New York: Guilford Press, 1998), pp. 3–31.

2 Henrik Larsson et al., "A Genetic Factor Explains Most of the Variation in the Psychopathic Personality," *Journal of Abnormal Psychology* 115, 2 (2006): 9.

3 Daz Bishopp and Robert D. Hare, "A Multidimensional Scaling Analysis of the Hare Pcl-R: Unfolding the Structure of Psychopathy," *Psychology, Crime and Law* 14, 2 (2008): 117–32.

4 Unless otherwise noted, references to Ted Bundy's statements and attitudes are taken from Stephen G. Michaud and Hugh Aynesworth, *The Only Living Witness: The True Story of Serial Sex Killer Ted Bundy* (Irving: Authorlink, 1999). Likewise, unless otherwise noted, Rader's statements are derived from the Wichita Eagle Archive at www.kansas.com/btk/ (accessed September 25, 2009).

5 James Blair et al., *The Psychopath: Emotion and the Brain* (Oxford: Blackwell, 2005).

6 Scott O. Lilienfeld and Hal Arkowitz, "What 'Psychopath' Means: It Is Not Quite What You May Think," *Scientific American Mind* (2007); available online at www.sciam.com/article.cfm?id=what-psychopath-means.

7 Paul Babiak and Robert D. Hare, *Snakes in Suits: When Psychopaths Go to Work* (New York: Collins Business, 2007).

8 There is evidence for two, three, and four factor models; however, the genetic differences reference the same factor in all of the models.

9 Robert D. Hare, *Without Conscience: The Disturbing World of the Psychopaths Among Us* (New York: Guilford Press, 1998).

10 R. J. R. Blair et al., "The Development of Psychopathy," *Journal of Child Psychology and Psychiatry* 47, 3–4 (2006): 13.

11 Ibid.

12 Craig R. M. McKenzie et al., "Overconfidence in Interval Estimates: What Does Expertise Buy You?" *Organizational Behavior and Human Decision Processes* 107 (2008): 179–82.

13 Jeremy Quayle, "Interviewing a Psychopathic Suspect," *Journal of Investigative Psychology and Offender Profiling* 5, 1–2 (2008): 79–91.

14 James Dobson, "Fatal Attraction: Ted Bundy's Final Interview," available online at www.pureintimacy.org/piArticles/A000000433.cfm (accessed September 25, 2009).

15 Ibid.

16 Kevin M. Williams et al., "Inferring Sexually Deviant Behavior from Corresponding Fantasies: The Role of Personality and Pornography Consumption," *Criminal Justice and Behavior* 36, 2 (2009): 198–222.

17 Dion G. Gee et al., "The Content of Sexual Fantasies for Sexual Offenders," *Sexual Abuse: A Journal of Research and Treatment* 16, 4 (2004): 315–31; Bruce A. Arrigo and Catherine E. Purcell, "Explaining Paraphilias and Lust Murder: Toward an Integrated Model," *International Journal of Offender Therapy and Comparative Criminology* 45, 1 (2001): 6–31; Ronald M. Holmes and Stephen T. Holmes, *Profiling Violent Crimes: An Investigative Tool* (Thousand Oaks: Sage, 2002).

18 Holmes and Holmes, *Profiling Violent Crimes.*

19 Blair et al., "The Development of Psychopathy."

20 Friedrich Wilhelm Nietzsche, *Beyond Good and Evil*, trans. Helen Zimmern (Raleigh: Hayes Barton Press, 1997).

CHAPTER 16

THE THREAD OF DEATH, OR THE COMPULSION TO KILL

The Epistemology of Murder

What do we really know about serial killers? First of all, let us acknowledge that virtually anything we think we know about serial killers comes from movies and television shows. We may have grown up with tales of Jack the Ripper, but do we truly fathom the depths of his psychic darkness? When I was growing up I watched a movie on television that delved into Jack's misogyny. "I loathe you all!" he uttered with vehemence and spittle to a hapless woman. This doesn't seem entirely unlikely; a person who preys upon women, murders them, slices out their uteruses and nails them to walls seems pretty consumed by hate-filled issues over women, sexuality, and birth. But again, what do we really know?

Other images of serial killers may be far more unrealistic. Hannibal Lecter is probably one of the first fictional serial killers to come to mind. But is the image of a profoundly sophisticated, genteel, educated, esthete-murderer realistic? It doesn't have to be in order to grip our imaginations. But alas, we may be intrigued by a cold murderer who is simultaneously an intellectual genius, who has incisive insight into the human soul, who listens to classical music with rapture, and who can take sinister satisfaction in getting someone to rip his own face off. We may be entranced by a charming psychopath who can bite the faces of his own victims, who can escape police custody by wearing a face he has just peeled off his victim like the skin of a kiwi, and who finally takes a vacation in the tropics, where he'll have his own psychiatrist for lunch.

One might certainly ask why we find the image of such a ruthless murderer so appealing. After all, many viewers admire him, not least because of his wry sense of humor and intelligence. One may also find the idea of a genius who exacts vengeance on morons kind of satisfying. But that reads *us*, and that is my point. These tend to be our own fantasies and we really don't know all that much about cold-blooded killers, or people who fly planes into buildings in the name of God.

What is a terrorist? The simple definition is a person who takes violent actions against unarmed civilians in order to make them afraid for political purposes. But as just mentioned, that is simple and inadequate. There are different kinds of "terrorists," and one can find so many different definitions that one starts to realize that the word itself may be inadequate. It lumps all sorts of people into one category, from those who do try to terrify a populace for political purposes, to those defending themselves against perceived oppressors, to those who have an explicitly religious purpose, to those who hate their governments, to those who strike back at invading empires. There are over a hundred definitions online. The only one I never found was the definition of a terrorist as the leader of a country (and his bespectacled sinister lackey) who invents all sorts of lies about disastrous weapons in the hands of evil enemies, so that his own population will be scared into supporting an illegal war that will terrify and murder hundreds of thousands of people.

To continue: one may actually arrive at a cogent definition of "terrorist," but my point here is that the word itself is incredibly loaded. First principle: when you don't really know what you are talking about, you have to stop pretending you know something. Epistemology is the study of knowledge. Thus the great Scottish philosopher David Hume (1711–76) could investigate religion, for example, and ask what we really could say in the absence of evidence. What do we really know? Our "knowledge" is often a fantasy and it often ain't worth haggis.

Our prejudices and biases really do mangle and predetermine what we *believe* we see in the world. In psychology this is called "proactive interference." Our perceptual schemas funnel whatever we "see" into preexisting patterns and categories, like cookie dough going though that mutilation machine that makes them into stars and moons. So we believe we see, but we react to our own fantasies and then believe that's the way things really *are*. Yes, we may be very tempted to see a person of another culture or ethnicity and wonder if he is dangerous, listen to Republicans and wonder if they have been breastfed, or watch Harry Potter fans and believe instantaneously that they must be fruitcakes, but are they really the confections we make them into?

The philosopher who probably taught us most about prejudice was Nietzsche (1844–1900). He believed each person's philosophy was a confession and that we continually distort and mutilate our perceptions of the world because we are too terrified to cope with it. Truth kills! We invent all sorts of fictions, though we take them to be reality. According to Nietzsche, we are so attached to these fantasies that only a monumental act of self-vivisection can rip through our illusions. We have to be Jack the Ripper to our own emotions. Otherwise, we will just project our own fantasies onto others. The conviction that one is right proves nothing. Nor do faith, certainty, or the belief that one has "evidence." As Nietzsche says, *convictions are prisons*. Thus, the crucial philosophical conundrum was how to ever understand oneself, given our false but certain feeling that we really "know." One can be absolutely and utterly convinced that clipping one's toenails can cause a tidal wave, as people did in medieval Japan, or that sacrificing a virgin and wearing her clammy skin will make the crops grow, as did the Aztecs, or that every Muslim is an insane fanatic bent upon our total destruction. History is a record of bizarre prejudices, figments, and deliria.

Worse, our conceptions are often horribly biased to the point of actually harming people. When we call someone a terrorist, we are already deciding before we know anything that he is an "evildoer," as one recent intellect has stated. We believe *a priori* (prior to any real knowledge) that he is an insane, frothing lunatic who hates our freedom. Now there *are* people who seek to harm America, but who are they? I think the film *Harold and Kumar Escape from Guantanamo Bay* is a fine example of the way we fantasize (make fantastic, or distort) our enemies. When a horny, pot-smoking American kid gets on a plane, the old woman sitting nearby is so paralyzed with fear that she transforms his handsome, Indian face into the menacing countenance of bin Laden, the image of the wicked terrorist laughing from within the tresses of his long black beard because he is about to cause mayhem and destruction.

Actually, this kind of reaction, though immensely funny in a film, is an appropriate social commentary. We have all been misinformed by TV fiction and the media (for the present I distinguish these), and we have all inherited some of the prejudices of our parents, communities, and time periods. And we have our own limitations, idiosyncrasies, and neuroses. Some of these are severe enough to make us more violent, prejudiced, and paranoid. However, Harold and Kumar teach us an important lesson about fear. We cannot underestimate (or "misunderestimate," as G. W. Bush once said) how much terror actually makes us crazy. This isn't just about freaking out and buying duct tape to seal up our windows against anthrax attacks. Studies have shown that things that trigger the fear of death actually cause us to become more violent to those considered different from ourselves, and that we become far more defensive and hostile about our worldviews. I advise readers to go online and do a search on "Terror Management Theory." Hundreds of studies worldwide have shown that we can be unconsciously stimulated into becoming more prejudiced, xenophobic, and nationalistic. One of the more recent studies demonstrated that ordinary, democratically minded people ordinarily opposed to the military policies of the government could be stimulated to support those very same policies.

Yes, we are that susceptible to fear. (Here one may recall my previous reference to a government raising the terror level in order to panic its own people into supporting an illegal war.) No wonder that the woman on the plane transformed Kumar into bin Laden. After 9/11, people looked around for enemies to destroy. In New York, taxi drivers were attacked. I was called in to counsel people who had escaped from the World Trade Center, and in one session I had to comfort a woman who had just fled the towers as they were falling. Having barely escaped with her life, she came home an emotional wreck. Then one of her neighbors spotted her, thought that she must be a Muslim (she was a Latina), and sicked his dog on her.

So before we even attend to what a "terrorist" is we have to realize that he isn't necessarily what we imagine. Our own prejudices and fantasies are at issue and when we map all those biases onto people we don't know, all we have is some ridiculous picture that insults someone, makes fun of them, ignores their grievances, and enables us to believe that our country can do anything to anyone without recrimination. (By the way, I'm not blaming America here. Far from it!) I'm just saying that we tend to call all sorts of people names that de-legitimate them before we know anything, and perpetuate a kind of blissful ignorance that justifies our own harming of civilians with equally ridiculous excuses.

So, with Hume, one asks, what do we really know? Let us begin by momentarily putting aside what we think we know about terrorist violence, serial killers, and murder. Are terrorists and serial killers different? Of course they are! In crucial ways! The serial killer is usually a lone wolf driven by his own particular history and psychopathology to torture, murder, and even take trophies. Though he may have strong convictions and purposes that serve as rationales for seeking out his victims, the serial killer is rarely driven by ideology, political cause, or theological commitment. The person conventionally defined as a terrorist often operates under the auspices of political or religious ideology, defines himself as a member of a particular group or social cause, and as such justifies his acts as subservient to a sanctimonious act of reprisal, destruction of the infidel, or eradication of an enemy who has wronged his people.

But perhaps we may learn something if we set aside what we think we know; in other words, the prejudices and fantasies we have been considering for the past few pages. The study of serial killers and terrorists challenges and interrogates our assumptions about the causes of violence.

Violence and Human Nature

What makes a person kill? If you live in New York, you might think a disrespectful look is all it takes. One of my (former) friends kicked in a taxi driver's window, yanked him out of the cab, and stepped on his neck, just because the driver had honked at him. Yes, we know New Yorkers are barbarians, but that is also what they said about the Yale students who participated in the Milgram studies. Here the experimental test subjects were asked to push a button that they thought would provide electric shocks to people. Approximately two thirds of the students continued to administer electric shocks to their victims (actually actors) no matter how excruciating the feigned screams were. The cheap and obvious jab at Yalies and New Yorkers notwithstanding, the studies suggested that given permission to be violent, most people would be.

Apropos of New York, this gives us the impression that life resembles *Lord of the Flies*. In William Golding's novel, a bunch of children are stranded on an island and before you know it they start murdering each other. A horde of malicious, homicidal kids run around the forest hunting a pig, screaming "drink his blood!" Soon after, they start killing other children, beginning with the pudgy nerd with glasses. Readers of *Lord of the Flies* often take this to mean that people would kill if the ordinary rules and punishments were taken away. Were the veneer of civilization peeled back, we would see the primal violence that lurks beneath. This is enormously important, philosophically and politically. It asks us to fathom human nature and the causes of our misery.

There has long been a debate in philosophy between those who see human beings as innately violent and self-serving and those who see people as a *tabula rasa*, or blank slate, until corrupted. Both of these images have influenced the way we envision violence and their cadences have trickled down into contemporary literature and popular culture. In *The Lord of the Rings*, for instance, the evil orcs were once noble elves until corrupted by the dark lords. In *X-Men*, the nefarious Magneto was an innocent boy until the Holocaust made him bitter. And the notion that people become violent when harmed is not without merit. But the view of people as selfish and sinister also seems to resonate with us, and so we imagine *The Children of the Corn*, the fantasy that deep down kids are cold-blooded killers. And we resonate with *Lord of the Flies* because we fear that childhood innocence conceals uncontrollable violence. Once you stop looking, their true evil will emerge like some kind of horrible alien that murders everything in its path.

Actually, a more attentive reading of *Lord of the Flies* shows us that the marooned children aren't violent at all until some of the kids decide to put on adult uniforms and establish law. Until then, they loll around on the beach eating fruit, and only after they don uniforms do they start to order each other around, bully one another, force others into submission, and punish the wicked. Only then does violence emerge, as a destruction of evil, as ritual execution.

So what can this teach us? It teaches us that as selfish and depraved as people might be, murder is not just an instinct or some sinister lurking force waiting to erupt. It reflects the need for control in the wake of helplessness and vulnerability. What we have are terrified children suddenly separated from their parents, who start to impose rules and regulations, see punishment as necessary for society, start to ritualize murder, envision hungry predators out in the darkness, and then finally break into tears at the realization of how illusory the whole thing is when they are finally rescued by real adults. We too may learn a certain lesson about how our own fear and imagination inspire us to envision wicked enemies out to get us, and how our own terror compels us to coerce, punish, or even murder others.

The Gestation of Terrorists and Serial Killers

Paranoid imagination of evil may indeed emerge from terror, as I mentioned earlier. But let us take a moment to dwell upon the idea that the coerciveness and punitiveness that arise from that fear displace and inflict it on others. That displaced fear not only leads to scapegoating and violence toward those deemed "outsiders," but persecutes and damages the individuals within a society. Sometimes this scapegoating is obvious, as in racial or ethnic violence, and sometimes people are sadistic to their own children. As Stephen Diamond writes, "Scapegoating is indeed a sort of demonization: we project our deepest fears, darkest impulses, least acceptable qualities, and most despicable, malicious motivations onto another person."[1] My point here is that the fear of evil is inflicted on our *own* society and its *own* children.

Psychological studies continually show that violence is often the result of protracted shaming, coercion, neglect, and abuse of children. Thus Diamond asserts that "Traumatic childhood abuse creates a pathological generation comprised of the 'walking wounded': psychologically crippled adults."[2] The violence we see in "ordinary" kids who have been shamed and beaten is a kernel of the more extreme process of what psychologist Lonnie Athens describes as *violentization*, which has several stages in the gestation and acclimation of violence. The process begins with brutalization, subjugation, and coercion, the systematic humiliation, ridicule, and exposure to an environment where violence is glorified and the kid is goaded into believing that belligerency is the only way to prevent others from brutalizing him.[3]

The cognitive process is fascinating as well. While many people are shamed and humiliated, few are subjected to an environment that enables them to overcome their guilt and anxiety about killing others, or nurtures the expression of their rage. This process is germane to how we understand both human nature as well as diverse forms of violence. It demonstrates (1) how frightening it is to kill others unless systematically goaded into it, (2) how much violence relates to excruciating feelings of shame and vulnerability, (3) how much that violence is the expression of rage and a *protest against* that shameful vulnerability, and (4) perhaps most importantly, how much murderers displace all that humiliation and resentment onto their victims, avenging old wounds and lashing out against others who become substitutes for the real people who formerly inflicted the violence.

We are a long way from the notion that ordinary children are monsters or that people are lasciviously brutal by nature. Does this have any relation to serial killers or terrorists? Once again, if we put our assumptions aside, we may find that this early wounding and brutalizing process is the catalyst for each of these compulsions to murder.

As indicated, there are virtually countless definitions of terrorism. There are also countless theories propounded by experts on terrorism. For the moment, let us restrict the analysis to the object of America's most recent paranoid anxiety, violent Muslim extremists. CIA analyst Jerrold Post wrote of the *psycho-logic* of terrorists, describing how violent ideologies were seductive to certain people because they could channel their own personal anger issues and thus find a socially accepted or even noble outlet for their violent desires.[4]

More recently, numerous psychologists who have worked with violent offenders also found that their conscious ideology masked a life history of profound shaming and abuse, and that again the perpetrators of violence were avenging their own helplessness and humiliation on surrogates for their abusers. Scott Atran, one of the most prominent contemporary experts on terrorism, has also tracked down and interviewed active *jihadi* terrorists. (Why they don't kill him outright is a curiosity for many of us.) Atran has discovered that jihadis often form groups based on social networks. They meet at soccer games and are introduced by other friends and relatives. They form groups that allow them to express their grievances and voice wishes to redress injustices. Atran concludes that the formation of jihadi groups strongly resembles the formation of gangs. Perhaps these forms of violence are not entirely dissimilar.

A number of psychologically oriented researchers of terrorism also write about the way the radical ideology of terrorism is a mask that legitimates deep-seated pain, wounds, humiliation, and rage. While terrorists may cite religious scripture, or claim their impetus comes from religion, one must always ask why the vast majority of faithful Muslims never commit murder. Islam is not the cause, as much as there may be certain violent messages in the Qur'an (certainly fewer than there are in the Bible). But the book isn't making the whole Muslim world murderous. Rather, some groups use scripture to sanctify their own agenda, and thus some scholars have asked what murdering civilians in the name of God does for certain people. I think Walter Davis elucidates the process with profound insight, claiming that those who inflict terroristic violence use their sacred doctrine as a way of transforming excruciating feelings of pain and abjection into sacred triumph. Displaced rage becomes an apotheosis when mythologized as the desire of God. They become proud heroes who vanquish injustice, depredation, and misery by ascending to paradise as agents of heaven. No longer pathetic nobodies, they are the most esteemed, proud warriors, who will go from poverty and victimization to eternal paradise and victory as they inflict death on their evil victims.[5]

The differences between the gangs and groups subject to violentization (described above) and terrorism are crucial, and yet there may be a consanguine process of transforming profound, very personal feelings of shame, rage, and woundedness into vengeance. Let me introduce something else that may be pertinent. In *Beyond the Pleasure Principle*, Freud describes a game that he observes his grandchild playing. The child takes a spool of thread and throws it away, babbling what Freud interprets as "Fort!" (gone!), and then yanks the spool back, shouting "Da!" (there!). The child repeats this game over and over with obvious pleasure. Freud begins to notice that this game seems to be tied to the frustration the child experiences when his mother leaves the house, and discerns that beyond pleasure, there is also a kind of anger in the throwing, in the yanking back, and in the control. The game seems to symbolize the child's anger at his mother and his need to control and avenge himself, symbolized by the object he throws and yanks back with so much fervor. Freud then uses this vignette to introduce the idea of the *repetition compulsion*, in which games and many other activities symbolize pain and trauma while trying to overcome them.

The intensity and aggression of the compulsive scenario reflect the pervasiveness of the inner wounds and conflicts, the way shame, humiliation, and feelings of self-loathing still grip the self and clamor for retaliation. For many of us, childhood embarrassments or losses may compel us to pursue ambitions that overcome feelings of ineptitude and make us loveable or superior. In more pitiable cases, we may seek impossible resolutions to those ancient losses by trying to manipulate others into being substitutes, and recreate the very rejections, hostilities, and losses that drove us to find those substitutes. Or we may act out our need to blame others for our problems, get into destructive relationships, or get revenge on those who harmed us, as suggested. In virulent cases, we may become Captain Ahabs, bursting forth all our past misery and rage from our heart's hot shell, pursuing our victims round perdition's flames, persecuting and harming others with the feeling of being the victim, not the victimizer. As Michael Eigen tells us, killers often believe or dream of themselves as victims, and this image of the self-deceived predator compelled to murder the ghosts of his past and avenge old wounds by pursuing unfathomed surrogates is one picture of the terrorist I would like to suggest here.[6]

The serial killer, too, repeats his own traumatic mortification and *terrorizes* his victim into a state of abject helplessness before murdering him. Christopher Bollas suggests an additional sinister element: that the person murdered is not just a surrogate for the victimizing parent or other, but for himself.[7]

Unlike other killers indoctrinated into an environment of violence, many serial killers seem coldly rational, charming, or shy. But the rage is still there, ever seeking redress for soul murder, and the serial killer may behave in a kindly, gentle, helping way to create feelings of trust that may be betrayed and violated.

Studies in sexuality and violence also indicate that innumerable erotic scenarios replay past traumas in order to vanquish pain and humiliation. The spectrum, intensity, compulsivity, and rage of such erotic scenarios vary immensely, and with serial killers we often discover a profoundly injured psyche inflicting his rage onto victims in sexual scenarios that involve a mixture of intimacy, pleasure, and death. "They are searching for an apocalyptic sexual orgasm that will compensate – by giving them a sense of power, importance, and superiority – for all the abuse they have suffered."[8] Some serial killers, like Dahmer, actually rip open their victims, have sexual intercourse with their intestines, and ejaculate into their exposed viscera. The killer recreates, implants, and transcends past wounds and psychic death through sexual and psychological merger with the victim.

Sometimes the corpses are cherished as surrogates of the murdered self. The killer revisits the wound, disturbed and fascinated by the death he witnessed outside himself when he was once killed emotionally. He seems to experience fascination and panic with the moment of death, and recreates it to inflict and overcome it. Like those deemed terrorists, serial killers repeat their catastrophic woundedness by inflicting it on others. This is the thread that runs through their massacres. Alas, the differences are so glaring! But perhaps we can pause for a moment to reflect. As much as it would make some "experts" crazy to suggest that some terrorists also sexualize death, I'd like to suggest that there is a crucial element of sexual conflict in religious terrorism.

Clearly, terrorists are not having sex with their immolated victims. The hatred of wanton sexuality, sexual freedom, promiscuity, and the female body that does run through the writings of numerous Muslim terrorists suggests considerable sexual rage that permeates the very moral and religious justification of their acts. (By the way, one can actually find such statements;

they haven't just been made up by right-wing propagandists.) There is a curious admixture of misogyny, contempt for sexual pleasure, moral outrage against sexual decadence, and the moral demand for masculine, invulnerable warrior discipline that disdains temptation. Women are disgusting, dirty, and inferior, whereas they are pure and virginal in paradise when divested of their gruesome, predatory, visceral qualities. They are so sexually disturbing that they can only be loved when divested of what makes them actual women, and the perfect woman is a purified, ethereal virgin who does not actually exist. Real women are so contaminated that 9/11 hijacker Muhammad Atta said he didn't want a woman near his charred corpse.

What I would suggest, psychologically, and most outrageously to those who just do not believe this kind of nonsense, is that hyper-masculine warrior aggression that deems effeminacy contemptible is a serious psychological defense against desiring sexuality and needing love. The emotional pain is so strong that one may actually look to God for permission to kill those who are decadent, weak, and sexual. My suggestion, then, is that while there are numerous complicated motives for terrorism, one recurring, pervasive, compulsive drive is the need to inflict one's own suffering on others, to murder sexual desire and weakness in a virtuous, "pious" way. One can mask one's sexual problems and rage by pretending God really hates others for being evil. It is a vastly different strategy from the lone serial killer, yet it seeks to obliterate other souls with its own rage, while transcending its own pain, helplessness, humiliation, and terror of death. Despite the pious disguise, he may be a serial killer in sheik's clothing.

Conclusions

The experts in various fields don't always agree (I wonder if they ever do). Let us not forget that there is a diversity of terrorists and serial killers, and an incredible complexity of human motivation. One surefire way to remain a complete ignoramus is to lump people into rigid, cumbersome, ridiculously simplistic categories, stereotypes, or psychiatric diagnoses. Doing so may provide a nice feeling of certainty and understanding, it may make you feel smart, and it may make you less afraid, but it is actually a method that makes a virtue out of refusing to think. Let's not forget how variegated behaviors can be funneled into ready-made categories that predetermine how we see and judge people. So we shall not stereotype all of our murderers. Some terrorists are religious fundamentalists and others are not.

Not all of them fear contamination by women and write a last will demanding that after their death no woman come near their charred corpse. And not all serial killers nail uteruses to the walls or hear dogs talking to them. Not all were abused as children, and some of them may be genetic psychopaths. So we need not have one grand unification theory of slaughter.

And yet if indeed we forget what we think we know, and use the information gleaned from the study of actual murderers, might we learn anything? And indeed, what can we learn of human nature, if we have one? We may certainly learn something of the complex causes of murder and that very pitiable human wounds beget spectra of violence. We may learn that the thread that runs through these disparate murders is our very normal, human vulnerability to the cruelty, terror, and malice people may inflict in repeating cycles, and on further generations of children. It is not just anomalous lunatics that murder. As Fred Alford says, "When we are faced with intolerable, uncontainable dread, the natural tendency is to identify with the persecutor, becoming the agent of doom, as the only way to control it."[9] The sinister implication here is our *own* vulnerability and the ease with which we can inflict cruelty on others, or even slip into slaughter. As distant as we are from psychopathic killers, our own dread and the manipulation of our psychotic anxieties have enabled us to become agents of death. We not only defend it, we castigate those who question our vengeance with hate and spittle.

NOTES

1 Stephen A. Diamond, *Anger, Madness, and the Daimonic* (Albany: State University of New York Press, 1996), p. 51.
2 Ibid., p. 6.
3 Lonnie H. Athens, *The Creation of Dangerous Violent Criminals* (Urbana: University of Illinois Press, 1992).
4 Jerrold Post, "Terrorist Psycho-logic," in Walter Reich (ed.) *Origins of Terrorism: Psychologies, Ideologies, Theologies, States of Mind* (Baltimore: Johns Hopkins University Press, 1990), pp. 25–40.
5 Walter Davis, *Death's Dream Kingdom: The American Psyche Since 9/11* (London: Pluto Press, 2006).
6 Michael Eigen, *The Electrified Tightrope*, ed. Adam Phillips (Northvale: Jason Aronson, 1993) p. 193.
7 Christopher Bollas, *Cracking Up* (London: Routledge, 1995).
8 Carl Goldberg, *Speaking with the Devil* (New York: Penguin, 1997) p. 32.
9 C. Fred Alford, *What Evil Means to Us* (Ithaca: Cornell University Press, 1997) p. 58.

A SOLEMN AFTERWORD

A Message from the Victim's Network

Missing

On Thanksgiving Eve, 1974, Vonnie Stuth disappeared from her Burien home outside of Seattle, Washington. An unfinished Thanksgiving meal was left on the table and Vonnie and her coat were gone. Todd Stuth, Vonnie's husband, began to make calls. After discussions with family and friends, the only hint of Vonnie's disappearance was her earlier mention of a phone conversation, in which she had said that a man from the neighborhood had come to the door offering a dog. Time passed, the holiday dinner was cleared, and there was no word from Vonnie. Finally, Todd reported her missing. While Todd was frantically searching, Vonnie's mother Lola Linstad was caring for Linda Barker's children after school. When Linda arrived at Lola's home to pick up her kids, Lola said, "I am sorry my house is a mess but my daughter is missing." When someone has vanished, we can barely take care of ourselves and we find it difficult to maintain the energy to care for others.

This disappearance was one among many in 1974; a horrible time for the State of Washington. Since the beginning of the year, co-eds from University Campus in Western Washington had been slipping out of sight – one by one, they were reported missing. In July of the same year, two young women went into a crowded state park and vanished. Witnesses were able to describe a young man with an arm in a sling. Some of the witnesses overheard him ask one of the missing young women to help him lift a boat onto his car; the witnesses also heard him introduce himself as "Ted." This "Ted" was later identified as Ted Bundy. For too long, no one in the missing girls' families knew-where they were and whether they had been abducted by the terrifying Bundy.

Organization

In the wake of the 1974 disappearances, Lola Linstad and Linda Barker made a move of community solidarity. With the help of a *Seattle Post-Intelligencer* reporter, they contacted the families of the missing; on February 25, 1975 the first meeting of Families and Friends of Missing Persons and Violent Crime Victims (FNFVCV) was held. Twenty-five local family members attended. We all shared our frustrations about the criminal justice system; everyone agreed that suspects' rights were given more importance than the rights of the victim in all too many cases. The group found strength in each other and we found a venue for improving our situation both emotionally and legally.

We developed an extensive emotional support system for ourselves. We started support groups for families and friends of homicide survivors and sponsored the writing of "Grief by Homicide," the first publication to address the emotional impact homicide has on the survivors. The author, Richard Cress, has also published *The Value of a Smile*, a book chronicling the disappearance and loss of his 13-year-old son and how the family coped when the son's body was recovered and homicide was confirmed.

On the legal front, we began to fight for victims' rights. FNFVCV proceeded to examine the criminal justice system and acted to make changes that would improve the lives of victims. At first, we held public talks in which members of the criminal justice system spoke about their methods, rules, and procedures for investigation. This information exchange benefitted all involved, and provided the foundation for what would eventually become national legislation for the rights of victims.

Success! Victims' Rights

In 1975, although rights for the accused in the United States were guaranteed under the Sixth Amendment of the Constitution, a similar guarantee for victims' rights did not exist. During that horrible year in Washington State, victims had no rights and were often excluded from criminal proceedings after testifying. Victims were not notified when offenders were released. As a result of the efforts of many victim support groups like FNFVCV across the country, the first victims' rights legislation was passed through Congress in 1982. Today, victims (and witnesses) have a right to:

- Protection from intimidation and harm
- Be informed concerning the criminal justice process
- Reparations
- Preservation of property and employment
- Due process in criminal court proceedings
- Be treated with dignity and compassion
- Counsel

We are making progress and we asked President Obama to do even more. You can always visit our website to learn more about our current projects in victim's advocacy: www.fnfvcv.org.[1]

In the end, Bundy was not responsible for all of the disappearances of 1975. But he was not the only perpetrator of homicide in the area. Vonnie Stuth's killer was a sex offender from Michigan named Gary Addison Taylor, who was responsible for several murders in Michigan and Texas. He plead guilty to Vonnie's murder after questions were raised regarding possible police misconduct in Texas.

Control and Empowerment

We all are horrified by murder, but if your loved one is missing it is even more devastating. Waiting, and not knowing, is draining, difficult, and scarring, as is learning that homicide was the cause of death. We find that we have little control over when, if ever, we will learn the truth, and that we are unable to save them if we cannot find them.

The loss of control persists after the loved one is found. When the remains of a friend, or a sister, or a son, are found, the survivors find themselves completely at the mercy of forensic identification professionals. Once the process of determining the identity of your loved one is not something you can control, it is very easy to raise the question: What if they made a mistake? What if my husband, daughter, brother, or friend is still out there somewhere?

Closure is also not easily found at a funeral. An open coffin funeral is impossible because the deceased is either physically unviewable or still missing. If the victim is never found, we survivors can't help but entertain the hope, however tiny, that something else might have happened and one day our loved one will walk through the door, or contact us.

Groups like FNFVCV can help you take control of your experiences and can give you a way to help others through legislation, support, and victim advocacy. Contact us, grieve with us, and empower yourself and others.

Mary Miller
Director of Special Projects
Families and Friends of Missing Persons and Violent Crime Victims

Mary Miller joined the group having battled the criminal justice system since May 1973, when her daughter Kathy Miller went missing after she answered an ad for a summer job. Kathy's prospective employer, Harvey Louis Carignan, went on to murder several more women in Minnesota and is suspected of many murders.

NOTE

1 Accessed September 25, 2009.

A TIMELINE OF SERIAL KILLERS

Serial killer	Where	When	Victims			Fate
			Number	Type	Fate	
Lui Pengli	China	144–121 BCE	100	indiscriminate	violence	exiled
Locusta	Rome	54–69	unknown	indiscriminate	poisoned	executed
Ethne the Dread	Wales/Ireland	ca. 200–225	unknown	young males	consumed	unknown
Gilles De Rais	France	1435–1440	80+	children	violence	hanged
Peter Stumpp (plus wife and daughter)	Germany	1564–1589	16	various	various	executed
Christman Gniperdoliga	Germany	1568–1581	964	various	various	executed
Gilles Garnier	France	1572–1573	4+		various	executed
Elizabeth Bathory	Hungary	1590–1610	600+			exiled
Giulia Tofana	Rome	?–1633	600		poisoned	executed
Marie-Madeleine-Marguerite d'Aubray, Marquise de Brinvilliers	France	1666–1676	50+		poisoned	executed
Catherine deShayes (La Voison)	France	?–1680	1,000+			
Darya Saltykova	Russia	1756–1762	100+	females	various	life
Micajah and Wiley Harpe	USA	1790s	unknown	indiscriminate	various	Micajah killed; Wiley executed
Anna Zwanziger	Germany	1796–1810	4+	indiscriminate	poisoned	executed

Name	Country	Dates	Victims	Victim type	Method	Outcome
Samuel Green	USA	1817–1822	unknown	indiscriminate	various	executed
William Burke and William Hare	England	1827–1828	17	indiscriminate	various	Burke executed; Hare immunity
Delphine La Laurine	USA	1833–1842	87+	Slaves	various	unknown
Helene Jegado	France	1833–1851	23	indiscriminate	poisoned	executed
Servant Girl Annihilator	USA	1884–1885	7	girls	hacked	unknown
Mary Cotton	England	1851–1873	20	children and husbands	poisoned	executed
Eusebius Pieydagnelle	France	1870s	6+	various	violence	executed
Bender Family	USA	1872–1873	unknown	various	various	unknown
Maria Swanenburg	Netherlands	1880–1883	27–90	indiscriminate	poisoned	life
Dr. Thomas Cream	UK and USA	1881–1892	5	women	various	executed
Jack the Ripper	England	1888	5+	women	mutilated	unknown
H. H. Holmes	USA	1890–1894	8+	various	various	executed
Joseph Vacher	France	1894–1897	11	various	various	executed
Henri Landru	France	1914–1918	11	women and one boy	strangled and stabbed	executed
Carl Panzram	USA, Africa	1915–1929	22+	various	various	executed
Fritz Haarmann	Germany	1919–1924	24	various	various	executed
Raya and Sakina	Egypt	1920–1921	several	women	dismembered	executed
Joe Ball	USA	1936–1938	5–20	various	fed to alligators	suicide
John Christie	England	1943–1953	6+	women and baby	strangled	executed
Dr. Marcel Petiot	France	1944–1946	27+	various	various	executed

| | | | Victims | | | |
Serial killer	Where	When	Number	Type	Fate	Fate
John Haigh	England	1944–1949	6–9	women mainly	various	executed
Ed Gein	USA	1944–1957	2+	women mainly	various	insane
Caroline Grills	Australia	1947–1953	4	family	thallium	life
John Bodkin Adams	England	1949–1956	160+	indiscriminate		life
Henry Lee Lucas	USA	1960–1983	189+	indiscriminate		life
Ian Brady and Myra Hindley	England	1963–1965	5+	children	various	life
Zodiac Killer	USA	1963–1973?	5–37	indiscriminate	various	unknown
Gilbert Jordan	Canada	1965–1988	8–10	women	poisoned	life
Fred and Rose West	England	1967–1987	10+	females	various	Fred suicide; Rose life
Wayne Boden	Canada	1969–1971	3+	women	raped and strangled	life
Dead Corll	USA	1970–1973	27	boys	raped and strangled	killed by accomplice
Arthur Shawcross	USA	1972–1990	14	various	various	life
John Gacy	USA	1972–1978	33+	boys	raped and strangled	executed
Ted Bundy	USA	1973–1978	26+	women	various	executed
Peter Sutcliffe	England	1975–1980	13	women	bludgeoned	life
Harold "Fred" Shipman	England	1975–1998	218+	elderly patients	overdosed	suicide
Jack Unterweger	International	1976–1992	10–11	prostitutes	raped and strangled	life
David Berkowitz (Son of Sam)	USA	1976–1977	6	young couples	shot	life

Name	Country	Years	Victims	Target	Method	Sentence
Kenneth Bianchi and Angelo Buono (Hillside Strangler)	USA	1977–1978	10+	women	strangled	life
Richard Chase	USA	1977–1978	6	women	various	executed (suicide)
Pedro Lopez	Colombia, Ecuador, Peru	1978–1980	300+	Young girls	raped and strangled	life
Andrei Chikatilo	Soviet Union	1978–1990	53	indiscriminate	various	executed
Jeffrey Dahmer	USA	1978–1990	17	males	dismembered	life
Leonard Lake and Charles Ng	USA	1980–1985	12–25	various	various	Lake suicide; Ng executed
Tylenol Killer	USA	1982	7	indiscriminate	poisoned	unknown
Bobby Joe Long	USA	1984	10+	women	various	executed
Richard Ramirez (Night Stalker)	USA	1984–1985	14	various	various	executed
John Glover	Australia	1988–1991	6	elderly women	strangled, bludgeoned	life
Aileen Wuornos	USA	1989–1990	7	men	shot	executed
Ivan Milat	Australia	1989–1994	7	hitchhikers	shot and stabbed	life
Anatoly Onoprienko	Ukraine	1989–1996	59	indiscriminate	various	life
Alexander Pichushkin	Russia	1992–2006	48–63	indiscriminate	various	life
Marc Dutroux	Belgium	1995–1996	4	mostly young girls	various	life
Robert Pickton	Canada	1997–2001	6–52	women	various	life
John Muhammad and Lee Malvo (Washington Sniper)	USA	2002	16	indiscriminate	shot	Muhammad executed; Malvo life

NOTES ON CONTRIBUTORS

MARK ALFANO, MA, MPhil, is writing a dissertation on the ethics of surveillance. He teaches at the City University of New York and is co-owner of an online test prep company. The closest he's come to this book's topic is eating breakfast, begging on the subway, and dreaming that he's Mohammad Ali fighting Joe Frazier (a cereal killer, a serial shiller, and an ethereal chilla, killa, and thrilla in Manila).

SUSAN AMPER is an Associate Professor of English at Bronx Community College of the City University of New York. Her book *How to Write about Edgar Allan Poe* was published in 2007. Professor Amper's published work includes essays on *Lolita*, *Bartleby the Scrivener*, and now *Wise Blood*, soon to appear in a collection of new essays about the novel. Dexter is her hero and she tries to be like him in every way.

MATTHEW BROPHY teaches as a Visiting Professor at Minnesota State University, Mankato. Neighbors would describe him as a pretty nice guy who tends to keep to himself. He lives with his beautiful wife and above-average child in Minneapolis. Matthew, who received his PhD in philosophy from the University of Minnesota, does not condone serial killers in real life, but finds they make for great television.

WILLIAM E. DEAL is Severance Professor of the History of Religion in the Department of Religious Studies and Professor of Cognitive Science in the Department of Cognitive Science at Case Western Reserve University. His teaching and scholarship focus on theory and interpretation in the academic study of religion, religion and cognitive science, comparative religious ethics, and Japanese religious and ethical traditions. He is co-author of *Theory for Religious Studies* (2004) and author of *Handbook to Life in Medieval and Early Modern Japan* (2007). He never ever thought he would write an essay on serial killers.

ERIC DIETRICH, PhD, is Professor of Philosophy at Binghamton University. Before studying philosophy he was a concert pianist and mountain climber. He is the author of numerous papers, most recently on paraconsistent logic and true contradictions. He co-authored, with Valerie Hardcastle, *Sisyphus's Boulder: Consciousness and the Limits of the Knowable*, a book on consciousness's resistance to scientific explanation. He is also the editor of the *Journal of Experimental and Theoretical Artificial Intelligence*. He is married to Tara (see below to understand how brave he is).

JOHN M. DORIS, PhD, teaches in the Philosophy-Neuroscience-Psychology Program and Philosophy Department, Washington University in St. Louis. He works at the intersection of psychology, cognitive science, and philosophical ethics, and has authored or co-authored numerous papers in this region for many journals. His book *Lack of Character* (2002) argues that experimental social psychology problematizes familiar conceptions of moral personality. Doris has been awarded fellowships from Michigan's Institute for the Humanities, Princeton's University Center for Human Values, the National Humanities Center, the American Council of Learned Societies, and (three times) the National Endowment for the Humanities. In 2007 he was awarded the Society for Philosophy and Psychology's Stanton Prize for interdisciplinary research in philosophy and psychology.

RICHARD M. GRAY, PhD, is Assistant Professor in the School of Criminal Justice and Legal Studies, Fairleigh Dickinson University, Teaneck, NJ. Prior to his appointment at FDU, he served for more than 20 years in the US Probation Department, Brooklyn, NY. His published works include *Archetypal Explorations* (1996), *Transforming Futures* (2008), and *About Addictions: Notes from Psychology, Neuroscience and NLP* (2008). Dr. Gray received his BA in psychology, his MA in sociology, and his PhD in psychology. Besides being attracted to sociopaths, he is interested in addictions, motivation, and altered states of consciousness.

TARA FOX HALL is a safety and health inspector at a metal fabrication shop. She received her bachelor's degree in mathematics and chemistry from Binghamton University. She divides her free time unequally between writing novels and short stories, chainsawing firewood, caring for stray animals, target practice, and contemplating – though not committing – murder for hire.

AMANDA HOWARD is an Australian-based true crime author and undergraduate studying for her Bachelor of Social Science (Criminal Justice) at Charles Sturt University. *Serial Killers and Philosophy* is her seventh book on crime, and her third collaboration. Her book titles include *Innocence Lost: The Crimes that Changed Australia*, *Predators*, *River of Blood: Serial Killers and Their Victims*, *Terror in the Skies*, *Million Dollar Art Theft*, and *The Lottery Kidnapping*. She has spent the past two decades interviewing serial killers and violent criminals from across the globe and has appeared on many international documentaries and news programs, as well as in numerous speaking engagements and radio interviews. She has recently completed her first crime fiction manuscript, as well as a children's book on global warming. Howard spends her time with her husband and two young children (who continue to show her that there is always time for an impromptu karaoke session) – when she is not taking calls from serial killers!

CHRIS KEEGAN, PhD, is Assistant Professor of Philosophy and Africana and Latino Studies at the State University of New York at Oneonta. His research and teaching address the political, moral, and legal consequences and concerns of liberation and protest by democratic means. Incidentally, while he may be occasionally anti-social, he is by no means psychopathic, regardless of his actions at department meetings.

MARY MILLER is Director of Special Projects at Families and Friends of Missing Persons and Violent Crime Victims, and her family has experienced the attack of a serial killer firsthand. She hopes this volume will further our understanding of serial killers and help us to learn how these tragedies can be prevented. She'd like to say something funny, but she will settle for the wisdom of silence.

J. S. PIVEN, PhD, teaches in the Department of Philosophy at Case Western Reserve University, where his courses focus on philosophy of religion, existentialism, psychoanalysis, and metaphysics. He has earned interdisciplinary graduate degrees in the fields of psychology, religion, philosophy, and literature, and has studied at the National Psychological

Association for Psychoanalysis training institute. The central focus of Dr. Piven's research is on the psychology and philosophy of religion, exploring the nature of belief systems, the dynamics of dogma, faith, violence, and apocalyptic eschatologies. He is the editor of *The Psychology of Death in Fantasy and History* (2004) and *Terrorism, Jihad, and Sacred Vengeance* (2004), and author of several books, including *Death and Delusion: A Freudian Analysis of Mortal Terror* (2004). He has recently completed *Slaughtering Death: On the Psychoanalysis of Terror, Religion, and Violence*. He believes that terrorists and serial killers, like our government, are misunderstood and misunderestimated.

ELIZABETH SCHECHTER recently received her PhD in the philosophy of cognitive science from the University of Maryland, after completing a dissertation on the "split-brain" phenomenon, and will soon begin a postdoctoral fellowship at the University of Oxford. She was prepared for the skepticism of those questioning the wisdom of a career in philosophy after a childhood spent answering the question, "Your dad does *what?*" She has never killed anyone … yet.

HAROLD SCHECHTER, PhD, is a Professor of American literature at Queens College, the City University of New York. His essays have appeared in various newspapers and magazines, including the *New York Times*, the *Los Angeles Times*, and the *International Herald Tribune*. Of his more than two-dozen books, he is best known for his non-fiction books on true crime, including *The Serial Killer Files*. Neighbors have described him as a "very nice, friendly man who wouldn't hurt a fly," though some have wondered why he spends so much time at night digging in his back yard.

DAVID SCHMID is an Associate Professor in the Department of English at the University at Buffalo. The winner of the Milton Plesur and the SUNY Chancellor's Awards for Excellence in Teaching, he teaches courses in British and American fiction, cultural studies, and popular culture. He has published on a variety of subjects, including the non-fiction novel, celebrity, film adaptation, Dracula, and crime fiction. He is also the author of *Natural Born Celebrities: Serial Killers in American Culture* (2005). He is currently working on a book-length project entitled *Murder Culture: Why Americans are Obsessed by Homicide*. Over the years, he has become used to stopping (or even worse, starting) conversations at cocktail parties when he describes his interests.

ANDREW TERJESEN is currently a visiting Assistant Professor of Philosophy at Rhodes College in Memphis, Tennessee. Previously he taught at Washington and Lee University, Austin College and Duke University. Andrew has long been interested in moral psychology and the history of ethics, especially issues surrounding the concept of "empathy," which has been the subject of essays for *The Office and Philosophy* (Wiley-Blackwell, 2008), *Heroes and Philosophy* (Wiley, 2009), and *Twilight and Philosophy* (Wiley, 2009). He's not sure if this makes him a potential serial killer or just a pragmatist, but he has speculated about "non-traditional" means for increasing the number of permanent jobs in philosophy.

MANUEL VARGAS is an Associate Professor of Philosophy at the University of San Francisco. Previously, he was a fellow at the Radcliffe Institute for Advanced Study at Harvard, and has held visiting appointments at Stanford University, the University of California Berkeley, and the California Institute for Technology. His research interests include the free will problem, moral psychology, and Latin American philosophy. He is not a fan of psychopaths or serial killers, but he keeps writing about them anyway.

S. WALLER, PhD, is an Associate Professor of Philosophy at Montana State University, Bozeman. She researches the serial killers of the animal world – bottlenose dolphins, cats, and wolves – in order to better understand the human mind. Her articles have appeared in *Journal of Cognitive Neuroscience* and *Synthese*, among others. She admits to having urges to control others and to hack, slash, and maim, but has successfully channeled them into editing this volume. The contributed essays are her only victims, so far.

ANDREW M. WINTERS, MA, is a graduate student in the Department of Philosophy at the University of Colorado, Boulder, and a philosophy Lecturer at the University of Colorado, Denver. His research interests include metaphysics and epistemology. He has taught courses on logic, language, and horror. Andrew wonders: "Without serial killers there would be enough horrors in the world to keep us on edge, but would it be as interesting a world?"

WENDY M. ZIRNGIBL is a PhD candidate in environmental history at Montana State University, where she examines the cultural and ecological relationships among humans and other animals, principally wolves. A particularly macabre aspect of her research in Yellowstone National Park, where she has worked for the past four years, is the ongoing study, documentation, and contemplation of skulls collected from wolf carcasses in the field. Zirngibl harbors an adoring fascination with serial killers, particularly of the quadrupedal variety.